BRIDGING A GREAT DIVIDE

Bridging a Great Divide
The Battle for the Columbia River Gorge

KATHIE DURBIN

OREGON STATE UNIVERSITY PRESS • CORVALLIS

The paper in this book meets the guidelines for permanence and durability of the Committee on Production Guidelines for Book Longevity of the Council on Library Resources and the minimum requirements of the American National Standard for Permanence of Paper for Printed Library Materials Z39.48-1984.

Library of Congress Cataloging-in-Publication Data

Durbin, Kathie.
Bridging a great divide : the battle for the Columbia River Gorge / Kathie Durbin.
    pages cm
  Includes bibliographical references and index.
  ISBN 978-0-87071-716-1 (alk. paper) – ISBN 978-0-87071-717-8 (ebook)
  1. Columbia River Gorge National Scenic Area (Or. and Wash.)
–History. 2. Nature conservation–Columbia River Gorge (Or. and Wash.)
  3. Columbia River Gorge (Or. and Wash.)–Environmental conditions.
  4. Cultural property–Protection–Columbia River Gorge (Or. and Wash.)
  5. Columbia River Gorge (Or. and Wash.)–Politics and government. I. Title.
  F853.D87 2013
  979.7–dc23
                        2013006155

Oregon State University Press
121 The Valley Library
Corvallis OR 97331-4501
541-737-3166 • fax 541-737-3170
www.osupress.oregonstate.edu

Contents

PART I: THE VISION

PART II: THE LAUNCH

PART III: GREAT DEBATES

PART IV: RESTORING A LEGACY

Foreword

I have just returned from a hike in the Columbia Gorge and it reminded me how much we owe Kathie Durbin for giving us the story of how this magical place was preserved—and how the battle to keep it continues. Wildflower blossoms glistened through raindrops; I didn't know the flowers' names but Kathie would have. Giant moss-covered evergreen trunks towered into the low-hanging clouds and their branches diverted the worst of the rain. Kathie would have reveled in this slosh through the woods.

For Kathie journalism wasn't just a job; it was a passion. She was dogged in pursuit of a story, thorough in gathering facts, accurate in reporting, and fiercely competitive. Her intensity about the things she cared about sometimes turned people away. Others relished her sly sense of humor that skewered the self-important—and sometimes herself. She stepped on some extremely large toes, but even public officials who endured her interrogations respected her integrity. She was more than a top-notch reporter, however; she was a devoted mother to daughters Audrey, Brenda, and Stefanie, an avid hiker, a poet, a cook, a friend, and an excellent companion on the trail or at a party.

After she earned her journalism degree from the University of Oregon in 1975, Kathie stepped into a world where pockets remained of the long-standing prejudice against women reporting general news. She chose to ignore that obstacle and pursue her dream—covering news. She took on every topic she was assigned, always trying to bring readers stories that touched them in some way.

She followed her passion for reporting to the Eugene *Register-Guard,* then to *Willamette Week* in Portland, the Portland *Oregonian* and finally the Vancouver, Washington, *Columbian.* At the *Oregonian* she was assigned to the county courthouse beat and then to education, covering each in turn with enthusiasm. However, it was in her assignment to cover the environment in 1989 that she found her true calling. Jim Britell of the Kalmiopsis

Audubon Society called the six-part *Oregonian* series, "Forests in Distress," that Kathie and Paul Koberstein co-wrote in September 1990 "probably the turning point in the long battle over the fate of our forests."

That battle over logging old-growth forests in the Pacific Northwest—a fight that came to be called the "spotted owl wars"—brought Kathie a national reputation. She even won rare respect from the often insular Washington press corps, whose members tend to disdain reporters from the hinterlands. The forest conflict spilled into Congress and the administration of George H. W. Bush and the Capitol reporters recognized that Kathie's coverage was thorough, accurate, and fair. They read her work to learn where they should look for their next story.

After Kathie left the *Oregonian* in 1994, she and Koberstein co-founded and co-edited *Cascadia Times*. She also chronicled the lengthy forest battle in a fine book, *Tree Huggers: Victory, Defeat and Renewal in the Northwest Ancient Forest Campaign,* published in 1996. That book remains the definitive history of the struggle over management of Northwest forests. She continued writing about environmental issues for *High Country News, National Wildlife, Amicus Journal, Audubon* magazine, *Defenders of Wildlife* and the *Seattle Weekly*. The Tongass National Forest caught her attention and she produced another fine book, *Tongass: Pulp Politics and the Fight for the Alaska Rain Forest,* in 1999. At times Kathie might have found life easier had she been willing to confine her work to less controversial issues. Instead, she continued to find ways to do the work she seemed meant to do.

When the *Columbian* assigned her to cover the Columbia River Gorge she found another subject that engaged her. She reported the removal of the Condit Dam from the White Salmon River and squabbles over land use decisions. As she neared retirement she began to think that the history of the Columbia River Gorge National Scenic Area Act and its effects would make an interesting book. She was right.

Freed from daily journalism in 2011, she sought out the people who had created the act and the people who implemented it and the people who fought against it. As she was completing the interviews and beginning the writing she was diagnosed with advanced pancreatic cancer. It was ironic—as she herself noted ruefully—that now that she had retired and could devote all her time to a project she really cared about she was forced to race the intractable time clock of cancer. She won that race; the book that resulted is truly a triumph of reporting, history, description, and analysis and an excellent read to boot.

Through chemotherapy and radiation she worked on. Even as her strength failed she kept writing. She finished the manuscript working in bed after she was hospitalized. "That's a real deadline," she said with the mischievous smile friends knew so well. The next day she entered hospice care and two and a half weeks later she died.

"This is my legacy," Kathie had told a friend, explaining her determination to finish the book in the face of her devastating illness. It is a fitting legacy from a noteworthy reporter who cared about the world she lived in.

Roberta Ulrich
May 2013

Acknowledgments

This book was born quietly and obscurely, on one of the many reporting trips I made through the Columbia River Gorge between 1999 and 2013. I didn't jot down the specific date when I committed to writing the book. It happened at one of those moments when everything—the great impounded river itself, the majestic mists of its rapids, the hidden waterfalls at its west end, and the bold basalt cliffs to the east—shifted into sharp focus. For the umpteenth time, I realized how privileged I was to be working ground where history and prehistory had left such vivid markers. I was getting paid to chronicle the contemporary history of this far corner. The least I could do was write a book.

The list of those who contributed to the slice of Pacific Northwest history I attempted to capture in these pages is long. It begins, I suppose, with Larry Peterson, my former editor at the *Columbian*, who casually added the Columbia River Gorge to my list of beat assignments when I arrived at the Vancouver, Wash., newspaper in the summer of 1999.

History was being made that summer as the Washington courts debated the limits of authority of the 1986 Columbia River Gorge National Scenic Area Act. Specifically, the courts were debating whether the Bea house, a house built in outright defiance of the act, could remain on its site, or whether it must be moved. The Washington Supreme Court ultimately ruled in favor of the Bea house and Skamania County and against the power of the Columbia River Gorge Commission to order the structure relocated from a highly visible bluff in the heart of the gorge. The Bea house ruling was one in a string of momentous political and judicial tests to which the landmark Scenic Area Act was subjected in its first twenty-five years. Regardless of the specifics of these cases, in every one the law survived constitutional challenge.

In the course of reporting *Bridging a Great Divide*, I had the opportunity to interview each of the six executive directors of the Gorge Commission and many of the commissioners named to the panel by the governors of the two states and the six gorge counties. These extensive interviews put in context the slow evolution of political attitudes toward protection of the 86-mile-long National Scenic Area, which spans the crest of the Cascade Mountains.

I am particularly grateful to Chuck Williams, founder of the Columbia Gorge Coalition, a true visionary who called early for federal protection of irreplaceable gorge landscapes; Don Clark, who as chief executive of populous Multnomah County reached out to Oregon civic leaders, including U.S. Sen. Mark Hatfield, to lay the groundwork for a regional gorge campaign; Jeff Breckel, who worked behind the scenes with gorge supporters on both sides of the river to craft a politically viable bill; and Jurgen Hess, a Forest Service landscape architect who grasped early the unique challenges the new Scenic Area Act would pose for an agency long accustomed to carrying water for the Northwest timber industry. In the new National Scenic Area, the Forest Service would have direction from Congress to place protection of scenic, natural, recreational, and cultural values above all others.

I am grateful to Bowen Blair, the young attorney who served as the first executive director of Friends of the Columbia Gorge, for spending most of four years in Washington, D.C., recording the arduous legislative path the act followed in its improbable journey from draft legislation to passage by Congress. It was Senator Hatfield who ultimately persuaded President Ronald Reagan to sign the bill, even though it violated the president's deep and fundamental support for private property rights. It was U.S. Sen. Bob Packwood, Oregon's other powerful Republican senator, who rescued the bill from a disastrous plan by the two governors to water it down and render it meaningless. But it was Blair who gave us the colorful backstory, jotted down in caucus meetings and Capitol Hill hallways and midnight committee hearings that otherwise would have gone unreported.

No book attempting the subject of the Columbia River Gorge would be worthy of the effort without a sampling of photographs that capture its diverse landscapes and the quality of its constantly shifting light. I shall be eternally grateful to the amazing nature photographer Darryl Lloyd of Hood River, who offered me the unrestricted use of twenty-five of his gorge photographs, each custom converted from stunning color to sublime black and white. In addition, Troy Wayrynen, the photo editor at the *Columbian*, offered me the use of two dozen stunning news photographs at a generous price. Many of these photos accompanied my own stories, published in the *Columbian* between 1999 and my retirement from the newspaper in December 2011. The staff of the Columbia River Gorge Commission provided a digital map of the National Scenic Area.

Finally, the editors at Oregon State University Press showed great patience and flexibility throughout the ten months it took me to complete and revise the manuscript after I was diagnosed with cancer in April 2012. I am grateful for their faith in this project and their willingness to forge ahead despite many uncertainties. Thanks, Tom, Mary and Jo. Thanks to Adair Law, the book's copy editor, who at one point made a special trip to my Portland hospital room to pick up the thumb drive containing the finished manuscript. Finally, thanks to my dear longtime friend and colleague Roberta Ulrich, who offered to produce the book's index. I quite literally could not have made it to the finish line without the help you all provided!

Kathie Durbin
February 25, 2013

The Columbia Gorge, Crown Point and Vista House. Photo by Darryl Lloyd.

Introduction
The Gift in Our Back Yard

The Columbia River Gorge National Scenic Area begins where Portland's eastern suburbs end. It's a gift bestowed by nature and protected by far-sighted, public-spirited people beginning in the early years of the twentieth century.

I moved to Portland in the 1970s, a decade before Congress established the gorge as the nation's first national scenic area. Even then it beckoned, a mystical realm that drew me deeper in with every season. In a photograph tacked to the wall above my desk, my mother smiles at me, her face lit by a sunbeam filtered through fir branches on the Multnomah-Wahkeena Falls Trail. Nearby is a framed print of the iconic photograph of Indians fishing from platforms above Celilo Falls, back when the Columbia River still plunged over the great falls in a torrent, wild, churning, undammed. On rainy winter Sundays I leashed my golden retriever and headed east up the gorge to the muddy Oneonta Gorge Trail, where I let the spray and the rain wash away the ennui bred by too many winter hours spent indoors in the city. Later, when I got to know the gorge better, I made regular winter pilgrimages to the dry bluffs and golden meadows at its eastern end, in search of sun. Almost always, somewhere between Hood River and The Dalles, the clouds lifted and shards of sunlight penetrated the gloom.

In 1999, the gorge became a professional as well as a personal passion when I was assigned to report on gorge politics, economics, and environmental issues for the *Columbian*, the daily newspaper in Vancouver, Washington. I threw myself into learning about a region steeped in Pacific Northwest history that was weathering a tough economic transition and deep divisions over its future.

Much of the recent history of the Gorge National Scenic Area Act recounted here is adapted from stories I wrote for the *Columbian* between 1999 and 2011 as the newspaper's Columbia River Gorge beat reporter.

One Long Day

The best way to understand what's been saved and what's been lost in the Columbia River Gorge is to go there. It's possible to drive the entire length of the Scenic Area, both sides, in one long day. The gorge is wonderfully accessible. Almost anytime, except when winter ice turns its roads treacherous, you can get in your car and head east, past the outlet malls, gas stations, and industrial parks of Troutdale. On the far side of the freeway bridge over the Sandy River, suburban sprawl stops. A natural world of water and rock and forest stakes its claim. A tasteful sign announces the abrupt transition: Entering the Columbia River Gorge National Scenic Area.

Off to the north is the Sandy River Delta, Oregon's western gateway to the gorge. For decades, it was the site of an aluminum smelter. During those years, cattle grazed the fields and destroyed hundreds of acres of wetlands. The Forest Service owns the land now, and after years of effort it is making headway in eradicating invasive blackberry thickets and restoring wetlands. On summer weekends, dogs and their owners swarm over the low-lying delta, taking advantage of its off-leash sites.

On the Washington side of the river, narrow Gibbons Creek marks the western boundary of the Scenic Area and the eastern boundary of the Port of Camas-Washougal. The highway skirts the waterfowl world of Steigerwald Lake National Wildlife Refuge. This restored wetland, once destined to become an industrial park or a site for storing spent nuclear fuel, was saved by Congress and local conservationists and is now accessible by a popular trail. Beyond the refuge, a haven for ducks and Canada geese, stands of rare white oak climb toward Cape Horn, the premier viewpoint on the Washington side of the gorge.

Back on the Oregon side, Interstate 84 will speed you into the waterfall area, though to truly experience its misty forests and carved-basalt bridges and railings, you must turn off at Troutdale, follow the Sandy River to Corbett on the Historic Columbia River Highway, and climb switchbacks to the premier vantage at Crown Point, with its recently restored art deco Vista House.

Spectacular waterfalls cascade down the walls of the gorge and pool at bridges along the old highway. Most of this property was donated for public use by Portland philanthropists early in the twentieth century. Wildflower species found nowhere else bloom here. The old highway allows you to experience the falls at a leisurely pace, stopping at each waterfall along the route, getting out of your car and soaking in the sights and sounds of water spilling from the steep mossy walls of the gorge. Bridal Veil, Latourelle, Horsetail, Oneonta, Wahkeena, Multnomah, and more—each waterfall has its own majesty. Eventually the old highway plunks you back onto the interstate just west of Bonneville Dam and you are face to face with the industrial infrastructure that harnessed the Columbia River in the 1930s to generate power and build the Northwest economy.

Near the crest of the Cascades, the south wall of the gorge reaches skyward. Astonishing basalt cliffs, domes, slopes and outcroppings rise toward the north face of Mount Hood, with its talus slopes and alpine lakes. Most of this rugged land, including Mount Defiance, elevation 4,900 feet, is now protected within the Mark O. Hatfield Wilderness, established by Congress in 1984.

Cascade Locks, Hood River, Mosier, The Dalles—each gorge town on the Oregon side has its charms. At Cascade Locks' marine park, you can walk above the old lock that once provided safe passage for boats and barges around treacherous rapids. At Hood River, world-famous among windsurfers, gentrification has planted its flag and the new upscale face of the gorge is on display—restaurants and brewpubs and windsurfing shops and a park where visitors can watch intrepid sailboarders launch and ride gorge gusts back and forth across the Columbia River, like colorful dragonflies.

Mosier, a village sixteen miles west of The Dalles, is a politically progressive outpost with its own windsurfing beach, an ice cream parlor, and back-road access to some of the most dramatic landscapes in the mid-gorge.

The Dalles is an old city with a long history—farming, ranching, aluminum smelting—and an emerging identity, thanks in part to the megasearch engine Google, which arrived in 2006 and built a computing center the size of two football fields. Here, pioneers on the Oregon Trail came face to face with the treacherous rapids of the Columbia River.

The Dalles Dam looms at the east end of town. A few miles east, just inside the Scenic Area, is Celilo Village, for millennia the most important Indian fishing site and gathering place in the Northwest. The Dalles Dam drowned Celilo Falls in 1957. At the rebuilt village of Celilo, and at a well-equipped fish launch and fish processing site on the river below, tribal fishermen and their descendants still pursue their fishing culture.

Crossing the Columbia River on Highway 97, you'll pass through Dallesport, not really a town but an expanse of bleak treeless land that

Klickitat County boosters once hoped to turn into an industrial magnet. Instead, the county has reaped its fortune from a regional landfill to the east, outside the Scenic Area, and an astonishing wind energy boom that has transformed the county's eastern half.

East of Dallesport you'll pass Columbia Hills State Park, where fragments of Indian rock art are on display, and Dalles Mountain Ranch, an old cattle ranch that's now a state park, with stunning views of the eastern gorge, displays of vintage farm equipment, and an annual festival to show off its early-spring wildflower spectacle. At the extreme east end of the Scenic Area is Wishram, an old railroad outpost separated from the river by railroad tracks.

Headed back west on Washington Highway 14, you'll pass through Lyle, a charming old railroad and sheep-ranching center, and cross the Klickitat River, where an old rail line has been converted to a hiking trail that climbs the river canyon. Klickitat County, settled by ranchers and loggers, now promotes tours of farms and wineries.

Between Lyle and Bingen, Highway 14 tunnels through basalt cliffs, passing backwater lakes cut off from the Columbia by railroad trestles. Bingen is a mill town that is holding on despite a decades-long downturn in the timber industry. White Salmon, a separate residential town on a bluff above Bingen, enjoys some of the most breathtaking close-up views of the gorge. Below, along the river, the highway passes by the buildings of the old Broughton Mill complex and a popular windsurfing beach near a federal fish hatchery.

The White Salmon River enters the Columbia at Underwood, near a tribal fishing site. In October 2011, a Portland utility breached a ninety-eight-year-old dam three miles upriver that had blocked salmon and steelhead runs for nearly a century. The explosion, viewed by people all over the world via live video feeds, was both spectacular and symbolic. Condit Dam became the highest dam in the nation ever to be breached by explosion. It gave hope to conservationists, tribal fishermen, and others who hope one day to see other Columbia River Basin dams dismantled.

Continuing west on Highway 14, you arrive at Stevenson, the county seat of Skamania County, historically one of Washington's most timber-dependent counties. About 90 percent of the county is federal or state forest land. Just 40 miles from the Portland-Vancouver suburbs, Stevenson is now a bedroom for commuters who work in the metro area, the site of an upscale convention center, and a colorful day-trip destination, with a summer bluegrass festival, a smattering of restaurants and shops, and a scenic waterfront with a pier that extends toward Cascade Locks across the river.

Presiding over a bluff just west of town is Skamania Lodge, a hotel and convention center with an eighteen-hole golf course that is responsible for Stevenson's relative prosperity. Built in part with Scenic Area Act money, the lodge is one of the economic success stories in the gorge and the largest private employer in the county.

West of Stevenson, Bonneville Dam comes into view again, with its transmission lines and fish ladders and the dam's second power station. At a window deep inside the dam complex, visitors can watch salmon pass by on their ancient, mysterious journey to upstream spawning grounds. Just to the west is the neat, modern town of North Bonneville, built from scratch on traditional Indian fishing grounds after the original town was razed to make room for the second powerhouse.

Further on is Beacon Rock, an 848-foot-high volcanic plug visible for miles in both directions, named by members of the Lewis and Clark expedition. Along this stretch are Sams Walker and St. Cloud Day Use Areas and Doetsch Ranch, now part of Beacon Rock State Park. Trails wind through meadows offering expansive views of the Columbia River and the waterfalls and cliffs across the river. Artifacts from Indian settlements have been discovered at many sites along the lower river.

Three national wildlife refuges now grace the western Gorge: Franz Lake, Pierce Lake and Steigerwald Lake. The U.S. Army Corps of Engineers purchased these properties as mitigation for wetlands destroyed by the construction of the second Bonneville Dam powerhouse.

On to the tiny hamlet of Skamania, where a few subdivisions were built before the Scenic Area was established and many more were on the drawing boards.

At Cape Horn, a turnout on Highway 14 looks out on a green quilt of meadows and forests that extends all the way to Beacon Rock and beyond. Many battles over development were waged here. On the bluff above, a subdivision was platted but never happened. Today, it is the site of an overlook dedicated to gorge benefactor Nancy Russell. The simple basalt amphitheater was dedicated in August 2011 to mark the twenty-fifth anniversary of the National Scenic Area.

From Cape Horn it's a short drive west into Clark County, where a sliver of wooded land east and north of Washougal within the National Scenic Area includes rare stands of Oregon white oak along the highway. Descending into the flats, the road passes the wetlands of the Steigerwald National Wildlife Refuge, now a protected stopping-off place for waterfowl on the Pacific Flyway.

Just beyond its entrance is the western boundary of the National Scenic Area. On the far side of Gibbons Creek, civilization asserts itself. The road skirts the Port of Camas-Washougal, a sewage treatment plant, gas stations and fast-food outlets in Washougal and the paper mill in Camas.

Vancouver's eastern suburbs reach to the edge of Camas. There's a huge gravel quarry and then comes the Interstate 205 or Glenn Jackson Bridge, which opened in 1982, triggering alarm about the potential reach of suburban sprawl between Washougal and Stevenson. Cross the bridge and you're back in heavily urbanized Northeast Portland.

In a day and 200 miles, give or take, you've passed through westside woodlands and waterfalls and crossed over the spine of the Cascade Mountains, traveling from rainforests to oak-studded grasslands and back.

You've passed through geological epochs too: The great basalt flows that formed the Columbia River Basin, the cleft in the Earth carved by Ice Age floods, the millennia when Native Americans lived in harmony with this landscape, harvesting its bounty of salmon and game and wild plants.

You've followed a portion of the route taken by the Corps of Discovery at the beginning of the nineteenth century. The discoveries of Lewis and Clark led to the great western migration on the Oregon Trail. Here logs, sheep, and grain were loaded onto rail cars, rich gravel deposits were mined, apple orchards planted, salmon harvested using huge fish wheels that depleted the great salmon runs. Many of the small towns and farms and orchards established by settlers along this route remain.

Bonneville Dam and The Dalles Dam dominate the river today. Freeways and highways and railroads parallel the river as it flows through the gorge, cutting off easy access to the Columbia's shores.

You've traversed history and arrived in the twenty-first century, with wind turbines and server farms and brewpubs and towns wired for Wi-Fi. An era of restoration has arrived. Dams on many small tributary streams have been dismantled. Old logging roads have been eradicated. Land damaged by logging and mining and livestock grazing has been healed. There are new trails and parks and inns and wineries. Two abandoned sections of the historic highway have been restored and are now popular hiking and cycling trails.

Wealthy and influential Portlanders and a handful of grassroots activists pushed for protection of the gorge. Rural property owners had to adapt. It wasn't easy, and the battles over what is appropriate development continue to this day.

The Forest Service used appropriations from Congress to acquire thousands of acres of private land and restore them for public use. Land trusts stepped up to buy other pristine properties to protect them from development.

The law did not close the door on development in the gorge. But it did limit industrial development to existing towns and cities. A quarter century later, the gorge sustains a robust economy based on tourism, outdoor recreation and technology. Two gorge legacy industries, agriculture and timber, survive in a region where those industries have mostly been left behind. Not every gorge community yet shares in the economic transformation. But in its first quarter century, the act has shown the path to a more deliberate and considered pattern of development in the Pacific Northwest.

The old path is still in evidence. Suburban housing has replaced the strawberry fields and farms that once covered Oregon's rural east Multnomah County. Sprawl has fragmented the forests of Washington's eastern Clark County. At the other end of the gorge, beyond Oregon's Deschutes River and along the crest of Washington's Columbia Hills, a virtual forest of ghostly 400-foot-high wind turbines on both sides of the river rises.

The gorge itself is hardly pristine. Heavily used rail lines and highways border both shores. Clearcuts scar forested mountainsides. Transmission towers march over the mountain ranges. The river is and will remain an essential part of the nation's industrial and transportation infrastructure.

But the National Scenic Area Act put an end to industrial development in the rural gorge. It imposed strict limits on residential development outside thirteen urban areas, especially development that would be visible from towns, highways and the Columbia River itself.

It's possible to overstate the clout of the 1986 law. In the quarter century since its passage, several projects proposed for the gorge have been thwarted, delayed, or abandoned. But many of those decisions reflect changing economic realities and evolving attitudes about the value of natural landscapes. Those changing attitudes have proven as effective at protecting the gorge as the law itself.

Gradually, since 1986, a public consensus has formed about what kind of development is appropriate for the Columbia River Gorge.

Following a fiery fourteen-year political debate, the Confederated Tribes of Warm Springs in 2012 postponed indefinitely a proposed tribal casino in Cascade Locks, Oregon, in the heart of the gorge. Intense lobbying by casino opponents was a factor. But what drove the final nail in the project's coffin was the 2010 re-election of former Oregon governor John Kitzhaber, an adamant opponent of off-reservation casinos.

A proposed large destination resort on the site of the historic Broughton Lumber Company mill complex is in limbo. The timber company that hoped to develop the windsurfing resort spent years winning an amendment to the Scenic Area Management Plan that could allow such a project. But the 2008 economic recession put Broughton Landing on ice.

A wind farm proposed for industrial forest land immediately north of the National Scenic Area boundary won approval from Washington Gov. Chris Gregoire in early 2012. But the governor agreed with critics who insisted that the project be scaled back to reduce its visual impact from inside the Scenic Area, in effect requiring a visual buffer. The decision to downsize the project, coupled with doubts about the availability of clean energy tax credits and future markets for wind power, has left the Whistling Ridge project in limbo for now.

Since 1986, tens of thousands of acres in the gorge previously in private ownership and available for development have been acquired by the Forest Service, the Trust for Public Land, the Nature Conservancy and the Friends of the Gorge Land Trust. With appropriations from Congress, the Forest Service has purchased and restored old rock quarries, grazed-over pastures, a historic ranch and rare oak forests.

These land acquisitions have provided both opportunities and new challenges. Recreation use in the gorge has intensified and diversified. Hikers have more trails to choose from, yet trails are more crowded than ever. Windsurfers, who discovered the gorge in the 1980s, share their favorite launch sites with tribal fishermen and kite-boarders, not always amicably. Mountain bikers flock to Coyote Wall, a dramatic syncline in the east end of the gorge that offers thrills on a makeshift system of steep trails but lacks parking and designated trails.

The Forest Service has more land to manage than it did in 1986, but it lacks funding to establish, improve and mark trails, so much of this new public land remains undeveloped and inaccessible.

Still, the gift that is the Columbia River Gorge National Scenic Area keeps on giving. It is there for all to enjoy, and its delights continue to multiply as private land purchased for public use is restored. A bald eagle overlook near the mouth of the Klickitat River was an unsightly garbage pit not long ago. The Sandy River Delta, once infested with blackberries and other invasive plants, is coming back to woodlands.

As you head out from Troutdale or Washougal, as the distractions of civilization fall away and the basalt walls of the gorge enclose you and you feel the natural world reassert its presence, you too might feel moved to give thanks for this gift.

Part I

THE VISION

The Columbia Gorge viewed from Beacon Rock. Photo by Darryl Lloyd.

Chapter 1
Hardly Wilderness

Imagine no dams, no train whistles, no freeway traffic roar—only the roar of a free-flowing river, as loud as one hundred freight trains, booming and crashing through the basalt chasm of the Columbia River Gorge. Imagine a young Indian sitting on a ledge above the river through seven sunrises and seven sunsets, singing and chanting and running up and down the cliffs, waiting for a vision from the spirits to guide his life.

The cliffs along the north rim of the gorge, near the present site of The Dalles Dam, tell a story of human habitation dating back at least 11,000 years. The basalt walls are etched with mysterious white concentric circles. A cluster of barn owls gazes out from a flat rock. Two black stick figures topped by halo-like rayed arcs adorn another basalt surface. Many figures are punctuated by red and white tally marks, possibly recording the days passed during such vision quests. Figures of elk and mountain sheep nearby date to as early as 5000 BC. Over the centuries these images have been exposed to blazing sun and hard frosts, soaring hawks, and denning rattlesnakes. Some have fallen victim to defacement by humans, in violation of federal law. Nearby, Tsagaglalal, the petroglyph popularly known as "She Who Watches," stares impassively from a slab of basalt. This particular image of Tsagaglalal is but a few hundred years old. Many archaeologists believe the image to be a transplanted death cult figure, representing the Plateau Indians' response to the European diseases that decimated their villages between 1700 and 1840.

Near Horsethief Butte, the indigenous rock art is the most extensive in the Northwest. Until the end of the nineteenth century, these dry bluffs were the heart of a heavily populated trading hub. Indians from throughout the Columbia Basin and beyond—from coastal British Columbia, the Modoc country of northern California and the Rocky Mountains—converged on Celilo Falls and the surrounding area to fish for salmon and exchange trade goods, from seashells to the horns of mountain goats and bighorn sheep.

"There were dozens of villages," said Forest Service Archaeologist James D. Keyser, an expert on the Indian rock art of the Columbia Plateau, on a tour of the painted cliffs at Columbia Hills State Park, east of Dallesport, Washington. "You were probably never out of sight of houses in the 20 miles between The Dalles and Biggs Junction." Clambering over these cliffs with Keyser as guide, it's possible to imagine what life was like for these first inhabitants near the end of the last ice age. Archaeological evidence indicates that humans crossed the Bering land bridge from Asia and dispersed across the Columbia Plateau and the flanks of the Rocky Mountains some 12,000 years ago. In the Columbia Gorge, they found a landscape shaped by the flow of Columbia River basalts and carved by a series of prehistoric floods, triggered when ice dams melted and waters bearing enormous ice floes and tons of debris roared out of Lake Missoula in the Northern Rockies into the Columbia Basin. The floods rocketed across the landscape at 65 miles an hour, stripping away soil, rock, and trees from every landform in their path. They sculpted the basin repeatedly over a period that ended about 15,000 years ago.

At Celilo, the floodwaters plunged over a precipice more than 80 feet high. In the Hood River Valley they deposited sand and silt to a depth of 98 feet. The waters roared past the promontory now known as Crown Point, then entered the broad Willamette Valley at Portland. At present-day Clark County, Washington, they deposited terraces of fertile eastern Washington sediment.

The Columbia River drops 2,650 feet from its source at Columbia Lake in the Canadian Rockies to its mouth at sea level near Astoria, Oregon. Tapping that latent power was key to transforming the vast Northwest wilderness. Stewart Holbrook, the great chronicler of the Columbia River, wrote of the river's carving power:

Gravity, pressure and time took it through the Cascades in the first place, and to get through, the stream had to undermine mountains, crumble them and dig a channel which men have plumbed and found to reach a depth of 300 feet below the surface water, and 215 feet below sea level. In a river this is an extraordinary depth. So is the force that made it.

Humans arrived on the Columbia Plateau, encompassing the watershed of the Columbia River and its major tributaries, about 12,000 years ago, making the region one of the longest-inhabited in the Western Hemisphere. Moving along the flanks of the Rocky Mountains and parallel to the Pacific Coast, these first arrivals "encountered a virgin land filled with herds of mammoth, mastodon, giant bison, ground sloths, and mastodon," Keyser writes. Projectile points left behind by those early hunters have been documented in the gorge and throughout the Columbia Plateau. Early gorge inhabitants found abundant fish, game, roots, and berries. They built a vibrant economy and a sophisticated culture based on the salmon—stupendous runs of husky red-fleshed fish that migrated from spawning grounds as distant as Canada, Idaho, and Montana. They traveled down the major tributaries to the Columbia and on to the Pacific Ocean, where they spent most of their lives foraging for food. Each year salmon and steelhead returned by the millions to their home waters to spawn. Before white settlement and the arrival of fish wheels, fish canneries, and dams, annual runs of Columbia River salmon were estimated at 16 million. Annual runs have now diminished to an estimated one million.

The first gorge inhabitants were river people. They lived in seasonal fishing camps and permanent settlements along the shores of the Columbia and its major tributaries. Their calendars and spiritual traditions revolved around the return of the salmon. They fished with spears and long-handled nets from wooden platforms above the terrifying rapids at Celilo and the Cascades. They left evidence of their culture at island burial sites, on cliffs above the river, at food-gathering areas in the uplands and fishing sites along the shore.

Explorers and fur trappers "discovered" the Columbia River Gorge as they ranged over the Pacific Northwest in the early nineteenth century. Members of the Lewis and Clark Expedition first saw the Columbia on October 16, 1805, when they arrived at its confluence with the Snake River, near today's Pasco, Washington. The Corps of Discovery brought back detailed accounts of the people, plants, animals, and customs its members encountered along the river route. They presented their findings to President Thomas Jefferson. The great western migration was soon in full in full flower. Between 1843 and 1845, thousands of settlers took to the Oregon Trail. Some traveled overland around Mount Hood on the Barlow

Trail. But others braved the rapids of the Columbia River after their arrival by wagon train at Fort Dalles. At Celilo Falls, they let their boats down with lines. At the Great Chute, present-day Cascade Locks, Indians helped them portage their belongings for a price. Most settlers continued west to the promised land of the Willamette Valley, but some stayed on along the river to establish businesses or plant orchards.

The United States was a young nation bent on western expansion. With the arrival of settlers came the development of agriculture, timber, and mining. Small ranches, orchards, and communities began to sprout along the Columbia River shore. The Great River of the West began its transformation to a powerful machine of energy and commerce.

The arrival of white settlers and the U.S. military, sent to protect the newcomers who appropriated tribal lands for forts and homesteads, took a great toll on the Indians of the region. It culminated in the signing of the 1855 treaties between the U.S. government and tribal leaders. Diverse bands and tribes in the Columbia Basin, each with its own language and customs, were forced to come together on reservations far from their villages. Under the 1855 treaties, reservations were set aside for the Confederated Tribes of the Warm Springs, the Confederated Tribes of the Umatilla, the Yakama Nation, and the Nez Perce. The tribes were promised they would retain their right to hunt, fish, and gather wild foods on "usual and customary" lands they had ceded to the U. S. government.

Federal courts in the twentieth century would affirm the rights of treaty tribes to half the salmon that returned annually to the Columbia River and its tributaries. The 1986 Columbia River Gorge National Scenic Area Act recognized the sovereign status of the treaty tribes, stating that land use decisions on tribal lands in the gorge would not be subject to the act's mandates or restrictions. But words in treaties were not always comprehensible to the chiefs of the diverse Columbia Basin tribes. Their vast territories extended from the Wallowa Mountains to central Idaho and included the watershed of the Grand Ronde River, the Mount Adams country, the forested reaches of the Hood River Valley, and the dry grasslands to the east. These were wide-ranging people, tied to the land and the waters of the Columbia Basin by millennia of use.

In the mid-nineteenth century, as the Northwest was poised on the brink of a mass westward migration, a few visionary artists were inspired to begin capturing the beauty of the Columbia River Gorge on film. Their work helped create a mystique surrounding the gorge even before the first roads penetrated the chasm.

Photographer Carleton E. Watkins arrived from San Francisco in the 1860s and traveled by steamship up and down the Columbia. Using a small stereo camera and another camera capable of making glass plate negatives, he made some of the earliest images of the gorge, which are still considered among the greatest landscape photographs ever made. In the early 1900s, photographers Sarah Hull Ladd and Lily White, members of wealthy Portland families, lived aboard a large houseboat in the Columbia and made photographs of gorge landscapes filled with soft light, clouds, and dreamy atmosphere. The women also photographed Indians who lived in the gorge. Their photos, used in travel brochures and magazines, attracted some of the first waves of tourists. Benjamin Gifford, an accomplished photographer, lived in The Dalles in 1897. He took photos of the gorge for railroad murals that were displayed in train stations across the nation.

These and other prominent photographers introduced the world to a romantic vision of the gorge even before most Portland residents had seen firsthand the scenic glories in their own back yard.

Loggers from the Great Lakes region reached the Pacific Northwest in the late nineteenth century. They logged the virgin forests that blanketed the coastal mountains and the lower valleys of the Cascades. They built sawmills and constructed wooden flumes to carry log sections down the steep cliffs of the gorge. By the dawn of the twentieth century, timber was king.

By then, most gorge communities were served by sternwheelers, railroads, or both. Due in part to the steep terrain, logging operations in the gorge were smaller in scale than the vast projects in British Columbia, in the Oregon Coast Range, and on Washington's Olympic Peninsula. Commercial logging for export began in 1848 at Oregon City, the overland terminus of the Oregon Trail.

At Portland's Lewis and Clark Centennial Exposition, in 1905, railroad magnate James J. Hill, whose Great Northern Railroad traversed Washington from Spokane to Seattle, expressed an interest in Oregon. He remarked that he had a good mind to "help with the development of this beautiful state."

For E.H. Harriman, those were fighting words. Harriman controlled the Union Pacific and Southern Pacific railroads, which met in Portland after passing through southern and eastern Oregon. He considered Oregon his domain. The Union Pacific reached Portland by a water-level route along the Columbia's south shore, but there was no railroad between Pasco and Vancouver, Washington in those days. Titanic legal battles ensued between Hill and Harriman. Hill eventually prevailed; the last spike of the Spokane, Portland, and Seattle Railway was driven in 1908.

Construction of a series of locks at the Cascade portage, discussed by Congress as early as 1870, was delayed repeatedly. The Cascade Locks finally were completed in November of 1895. Hundreds of excursionists passed through the 3,000-foot canal and its lifts over the next few years. Their busiest year was 1905, when 1,417 boats passed through. The success of the Cascade Locks spurred a demand for more locks to boost shipping and passenger service between Portland and Idaho. This pleased residents of small communities that had been bypassed by the railroads. In 1915, locks were completed at Celilo, providing passage around the raging Big Eddy Rapids.

Yet passengers and wheat farmers were in no hurry to use the river route. "A fine paved highway was being built up the south side of the Columbia from Portland and almost immediately it became the most talked about piece of road in the Northwest," wrote Stewart Holbrook.

The Columbia River Highway, modeled on the Axenstrasse Tunnel in the Swiss Alps, would offer the first access by paved road to Oregon's gorge waterfall zone and the country beyond. It would launch the campaign to protect Columbia Gorge landscapes from heedless development.

The construction of two enormous federal hydroelectric dams on the Columbia transformed the lower river and ushered in a new era in the gorge. The United States Army Corps of Engineers completed Bonneville Dam in 1938. The Dalles Dam came nineteen years later, in 1957. More dams followed—some public, some private—along the main stem of the Columbia all the way to the Canadian border and beyond. Of the river's 1,200 miles from source to mouth, only 57 river miles remain free-flowing today.

As Bonneville Dam neared completion, the Corps of Engineers made a last-minute effort to photograph and document the many traditional

Bonneville Dam, with cruise ship. Photo by Darryl Lloyd.

fishing sites the Corps had promised to protect or replace in their treaties with the Columbia Basin tribes. These sites were about to be flooded by the impounded waters behind the dam.

The corps had promised to provide replacement or "in lieu" fishing sites for at least two dozen sites destroyed by the dams. It would be seventy years before that promise was fully kept.

For tribal fishermen who depended on the great salmon runs to feed their families and provide goods for trade, the inexcusable delay, and the failure of federal dam-builders to anticipate the dire economic consequences of the new era of dam building, amounted to a slow bureaucratic genocide. The rising waters behind The Dalles Dam inundated Celilo Falls and tens of thousands of petroglyphs and pictographs in a canyon just upstream from Horsethief Lake. In all, The Dalles Dam and John Day and McNary dams to the east, built between 1955 and 1968, drowned at least forty-five archaeological sites. Records of many of these sites survive, thanks to early scientific interest and the foresight of amateur researchers who photographed and made rubbings or tracings of many designs before they were lost.

Shamans carved many of these images, Keyser said. "They had to announce their power. They had to have a greater power than the power that made people sick. These images tell about ancient cultures that can't speak for themselves. This is the patrimony of humankind." Keyser and his team recorded rock art images at more than two dozen sites untouched by the waters that backed up the dams, ranging from a single image to a site containing more than 600 individual examples. But those artifacts remained vulnerable.

"These images have survived for thousands of years," Keyser said on a tour of the cliffs at Horsethief Lake State Park. "One idiot with spray paint could destroy this irreplaceable art." Today, Washington State Park rangers protect the rock art on the cliffs. Public access was closed in 2003 after several incidents of vandalism, and the images may be viewed only on official guided tours. Keyser estimates that 4,000 sites remain within a two-hour drive of Portland, all of them out in the open. Pot-hunters in the gorge looted one of the Northwest's largest prehistoric cemeteries between the 1930s and the 1950s. Yet archaeologists can still draw on a trove of stories and legends from descendants of those who carved their stories into these cliffs. "We have 150 years of Indians across the Columbia Plateau telling us who made them and how they made them," Keyser said. "The ethnography of the Columbia River Plateau is the most extensive in the world."

Forty ancient rock carvings were rescued in the 1950s from the rising waters behind The Dalles Dam. Images of owls, mountain sheep, and mysterious water monsters had been carved into a basalt cliff at nearby Petroglyph Canyon. Well-meaning preservationists blasted the images from the cliffs. "In hindsight it was terrible," Keyser said. "But they didn't know any better then. Unfortunately, they didn't do any formal recording of the rock art." Today, he said, those images would be left in place.

For nearly a half-century the rescued drawings and etchings sat neglected at The Dalles Dam. From 1974 to 2003, they were stored under the dam's fish ladders, in a fenced gravel plot where they acquired a coating of bird droppings. In the fall of 2003, they were moved to a new home at Columbia Hills State Park, just a mile downstream from the cliffs where they had been carved. The Corps of Engineers, the Bonneville Power Administration, and the four treaty tribes worked together to make it happen. Tribal leaders wanted them displayed at a place that would respect their power.

Today a sign posted near these rescued artifacts urges visitors: "Please respect the sacred nature of the images and rights of the First People as they practice their religious ceremonies at this site. Please do not disturb offer-ings left by First People or touch or make rubbings or casts of the images."

By the mid-twentieth century, the gorge was a compromised beauty. Dikes had destroyed wetlands along the river. Dams were turning the mighty Columbia into a series of impounded reservoirs. Railroads and highways lined both shores of the river, limiting access. Clearcuts marred forested slopes; gravel pits pocked the walls of the gorge. The growth of cities to the west and industry to the east had spread a pall of haze. Residential development spilled out of the flatlands of Portland and Vancouver into the west end of the gorge. With the arrival of railroads and freeways, the gorge had become a noisy place. The clamor of traffic invaded its secret canyons and forest trails. The Columbia River Gorge no longer felt wild.

But the gorge remained a scenic jewel. Much of its majesty had survived a century of intensive development. And the belated recognition that new development schemes threatened to destroy that beauty prompted a cam-paign to protect as much as possible of the unspoiled gorge landscape.

Chapter 2
The Watchdogs

Samuel Lancaster, the father of Oregon's highway system, understood that the Columbia River Gorge deserved a highway to match its majesty. "The mind can only wonder at this mighty work of God, done in His own way, on a scale so great that man's best efforts appear but as the work of pygmies," Lancaster famously observed. Eccentric railroad magnate Sam Hill shared Lancaster's vision. He was determined that a modern highway be built to the property he called Maryhill, on a remote promontory above the Washington shore of the Columbia, 103 miles east of Vancouver.

With Hill helping to bankroll the project, Oregon named Lancaster the first state highway commissioner and charged him with overseeing the gorge project. From the beginning, the Northwest's first major paved road was envisioned not as a utilitarian roadway but as a work of art, designed to complement and enhance the scenic grandeur of the gorge. Construction began in 1913, using horses, bulldozers and 2,200 workers. The first 74-mile section was completed in just two years and what a highway it was. The narrow two-lane road twisted, looped, and swirled around hairpin curves and burrowed through lush forests, passing a half-dozen waterfalls that spilled from the walls of the gorge thousands of feet to the Columbia River. "Every curve of the route Lancaster plotted revealed another vista," the Associated Press exulted in a 1988 retrospective. "The mile-wide Columbia, volcanic bluffs rising sharply out of the river plain, lush green forests, spectacular waterfalls and the snowy peaks of the Cascade Range."

Lancaster modeled some sections after highways in the Swiss Alps, incorporating their use of gradual inclines and long stretches of rock wall to stabilize the route. Seven viaducts skirted the edges of cliffs, some supported from beneath by concrete piers. Arched stone parapets marked roadside parks and viewpoints. Two dozen bridges framed their natural settings. The highway passed through four rock tunnels, including the spectacular 390-foot tunnel at Mitchell Point, which featured five arched windows.

The new highway put the Columbia River Gorge on the map, providing motorists with access to the grandeur in their back yard. For the first time, they could drive along the shore, stop to admire the falls and the view from Crown Point, and continue east, crossing from the lush west side to the stark beauty of the arid hinterland beyond the crest of the Cascades.

Oregon's leaders put a high priority on establishing parks in conjunction with state roads. As early as 1913, Gov. Oswald West declared that the state's beaches should be designated as part of the public highway system. Oregon's parks, like the highway system itself, were funded by state gasoline taxes. The development of parks and roadways went hand in hand.

During construction of the highway, many of Oregon's wealthiest and most prominent civic leaders stepped up to help burnish their legacy. Simon Benson, Osman Royal, and George Shepperd gave private lands in the gorge to the city of Portland. These donated lands eventually became Benson State Park, Crown Point State Park, and Shepperd's Dell State Park, all jewels in the crown of the gorge. The Forest Service followed the state's example. In 1915, U.S. Secretary of Agriculture D. F. Houston announced that a 22-mile-long section of what was then Oregon National Forest would be set aside as Columbia Gorge Park. The new park, encompassing the famous waterfall zone, would be set aside for recreation and scenery and would be declared off limits to timber harvesting. Samuel Boardman, widely regarded as the father of the Oregon state park system, served as state parks engineer from 1929 to 1950. He left an enduring mark, dramatically increasing the size of the state park system. Though his best-known acquisitions were on the Oregon Coast, Boardman also took a strong interest in the gorge.

Over time, a series of state and federal waterfall parks and trails protected much of Oregon's western gorge from development. By the 1950s, most of it was in public ownership. But while Oregon civic leaders moved early and decisively to protect the scenic treasures of the gorge, there was no similar commitment from Washington's leaders. The small farms and timber towns east of Vancouver, directly across the river from Crown Point and Multnomah Falls, remained a backwater, largely ignored by political leaders in Olympia and Puget Sound.

Boardman understood the need to protect land on both sides of the river. A case in point was the prominent volcanic monolith the Corps of Discovery had named Beacon Rock. The volcanic plug, 35 miles east of Vancouver, is the most prominent landmark on the Washington side of the gorge. For millennia, it had served as a literal beacon to travelers on the river. In 1915, Henry J. Biddle of Portland bought Beacon Rock to save it from defacement by climbers who left anchors and ropes behind. A descendant of Nicholas Biddle, the first editor of the journals of Lewis and Clark, he had a strong interest in its preservation. Realizing a long-held dream, he built a 4,500-foot-long, four-foot-wide trail to the top, with fifty-two switchbacks. It took two years and $10,000.

In 1931, when the U.S. Army Corps of Engineers began planning for a jetty at the mouth of the Columbia River, engineers set their sights on Beacon Rock as a source of material. Boardman appealed to prominent Portland banker J.C. Ainsworth to intercede with Biddle's heirs to protect Beacon Rock. "Should we not lift our hands to preserve one of the scenic marvels of the Columbia River?" he wrote. "The river is a boundary line but it does not obscure our vision." Biddle's heirs offered to donate the monolith and a nearby waterfall to the state of Washington for a park. But Washington Gov. Roland Hill Hartley refused the gift. In fact, he accused the owners of trying to avoid paying state taxes on the property. In response, Biddle's heirs agreed to deed Beacon Rock and the nearby Pool of the Winds Falls to the state of Oregon for the sum of one dollar, for the purpose of establishing a state park in Washington. "Why should we let the width of a river destroy a scenic asset woven into a recreational garland belonging to both states?" Biddle asked. "How can we stand by and see the death of a relative, though a bit distant?"

This unorthodox gambit had its desired effect. Oregon Highway Commission Chairman H.B. Van Duzer had his doubts about the legality of the arrangement, but he tipped off the *Oregonian*, which wrote a column about the ploy. The response from across the river was immediate. Washington officials criticized Oregon for overstepping its bounds. But in short order Washington had its first state park in the Columbia Gorge.

A staunch conservative, Boardman believed that planning for the gorge should be in the hands of a single administrator, not manipulated by a number of well-meaning organizations that could allow it to be ruined through lack of coordination. But many local officials in Southwest Washington feared the entire gorge might become a massive, glorified park. To them, the orderly development of the region's natural resources was essential. They pointed out that the steep terrain of the gorge already limited the amount of land available for logging, livestock grazing, orchards, and other enterprises.

Surprisingly, it was a federal commission that first recommended setting aside the west end of the gorge for public recreation. It happened in the 1930s, in connection with the construction of Bonneville and Grand Coulee dams. Completion of the two mammoth dams would utterly transform the sparsely populated Columbia Basin. Hydropower from the dams would electrify the rural Northwest, power lumber mills, paper mills, and aluminum smelters, enable the development of the atomic bomb, and begin the transformation of the free-flowing Columbia into a series of long, slack-water reservoirs.

In 1934, the federally sponsored Pacific Northwest Regional Planning Commission, led by John Yeon, the twenty-four-year-old son of prominent Portland lumberman John B. Yeon, undertook a study of recreational values in the gorge. Its 1937 report recommended a network of parks and highways throughout the gorge. Significantly, the panel recommended to President Franklin D. Roosevelt that all industrial development be excluded from the river shore along the 40 miles between Vancouver, Washington and Bonneville Dam. It would be "extremely wasteful" the report said, to encourage industrial growth along that stretch, and "far better to preserve the west end of the gorge for recreation." Such a policy would benefit Vancouver, nearby Camas, and Portland by concentrating industrial development in those urban centers, as the Vancouver *Columbian* noted with approval.

The commission also recommended that the generation and distribution of power from the new dams be handled by a federal authority reporting directly to the president and that a flat rate be charged for power across the region. To offer a cheaper rate at sites closer to the dam, Yeon argued, would create incentives for development of some of the most scenic vistas. Ultimately, his argument would prevail. Congress established the Bonneville Power Administration to market hydropower from federal dams across the Northwest and beyond.

Washington's western gorge did not become a string of state parks. But for the next half-century, it retained its rural character as a mosaic of small farms, meadows and forested slopes, and a string of timber-dependent rural communities. Though the Washington shore could not match Oregon's famed cavalcade of waterfalls, it boasted several locally well-known landmarks. Among them were Cape Horn, a sheer vertical wall topped by a promontory with a sweeping view of the river; Mount Zion, an extinct volcano in the west end of the gorge; Beacon Rock; Wind Mountain and Dog Mountain in the mid-gorge; and a historic hot springs near Carson.

By mid-century, local sentiment for protection of the western gorge was stirring in Washington. In 1953, the Clark County Planning Commission recommended establishing roadside parks along a 12-mile stretch of the Evergreen Highway. A state highway engineer surveyed the beauty spots along the route in preparation for relocation of a section of the existing highway and proposed preserving the wooded parcels, which would soon be bisected by the new highway. The stretch "has long been noted for its scenic beauty, largely because of the magnificent stands of Douglas fir and other natural trees which line the roadway," engineer Fred Gloor said. He noted that the pieces would be too small to build houses on and if not purchased while available, would be "denuded by loggers." But only a few of those forested fragments survived as Vancouver spread eastward toward Camas and Washougal over the next three decades.

In the 1950s, save-the-gorge organizations were established in both states to set limits on logging and development in the gorge and advocate for protection of scenic treasures. Though neither commission had any actual power, both gave voice to the concerns of conservationists and raised awareness of the price the region was paying for unbridled development. Gertrude Blutsch Jensen, a member of the Portland Women's Forum, spearheaded the successful 1953 campaign to get the Oregon Legislature to establish an Oregon Columbia Gorge Commission. Funding came slowly at first, but in 1955 the state Highway Commission set aside $50,000 to acquire park land in the gorge between Wygant State Park and the Sandy River. Parks officials also helped arrange gorge land exchanges involving the Forest Service, the federal Bureau of Land Management and Hood River County. The state itself continued to receive gifts of land from private donors that enabled it to enlarge its gorge holdings.

Where private land was not available for purchase, the commission sought cooperative agreements, zoning ordinances, and other measures to protect scenic views. Multnomah County zoned its portion of the gorge against indiscriminate commercial and industrial development that threatened to spread east from Portland's suburbs.

In Washington, Dorothy Carlson of Vancouver enlisted gorge advocates from Clark, Skamania, and Klickitat counties and asked the legislature to back a Washington Columbia Gorge Commission to save the natural beauty of the gorge. But the gorge remained a distant concern in Olympia, the state's center of political power, and in Puget Sound, where most of the state's population resided. Governor Albert Rosellini, a Democrat, declined to support the proposal, saying the state lacked funding for such an effort. He suggested that pressure be put on the legislature instead. Eventually a Washington Gorge Commission was created and it did serve a watchdog role. In 1960, Carlson formally protested a roadside spray program conducted by state highway crews that killed hundreds of oak and maple trees along Highway 14 from Camas all the way to White Salmon—too late to save those rare deciduous stands. Studies and more studies would be its principal achievement over the next quarter-century. All it could do was serve as a watchdog as development took its toll.

Political geography continued to play a decisive role in the very different attitudes the two states took toward protecting the gorge. In a 1989 essay, longtime Oregon State Parks Director David Talbot wrote, "Trying to get political support to save the Washington side of the Columbia was a losing battle. In Oregon, on the other hand, Portland is the major political base, and (the gorge) is right next door. People are knocking one another over to save the gorge."

The question of what kind of recreation was appropriate in the gorge surfaced soon after Congress passed the 1964 Wilderness Act. The landmark law authorized Congress to establish permanent wilderness areas on federal lands where humans would be visitors and natural landscapes and processes would be undisturbed. At the time, boosters were promoting two tramway projects on the Oregon side of the gorge to move tourists from the shore to viewpoints high on the bluffs above. One would run from Rooster Rock State Park to Crown Point, the iconic promontory along Sam Lancaster's highway. The other would carry tourists from Bonneville Dam up the south wall of the gorge to Munra Point.

J. Herbert Stone, the Forest Service's Northwest regional forester, appointed a committee to look at recreation and wilderness issues in the gorge. Stone attempted to be diplomatic, noting that the tramways "would provide wide views of the Washington as well as the Oregon side of the river." But he said existing plans for national forest lands "do not recognize a place for this development in the Columbia Gorge." Whether the trams would be compatible with the natural and scenic qualities of the gorge he left for others to decide. Stone's focus for recreation was national forest land north of Mount Hood. Washington panelists urged him to consider projects in Washington as well, but the Forest Service had little jurisdiction there, because Southwest Washington's Gifford Pinchot National Forest did not extend south to the gorge.

The Forest Service did, however, voice an interest in protecting forest views on both sides of the river. With the completion of Bonneville Dam, energy transmission had become a contentious issue. The Bonneville Power Administration's transmission towers and power lines marched over the forested mountains and along the ridgelines above the gorge. They were "not generally a thing of beauty," Stone said. The Forest Service was working with the BPA and private utilities to minimize their visual impact, he said, because burying them would be much too expensive.

In 1970, civic leaders from the Washington gorge counties organized a tour of the gorge in an effort to interest the state in more tourist facilities. But it would be nearly two decades until travelers on the Washington side got some of the amenities—picnic tables, parking areas, restrooms, and trails to viewpoints overlooking the river—that Oregon had enjoyed for decades.

In 1973, the Oregon Legislature passed a sweeping land use law. Senate Bill 100 required all the state's cities to establish urban growth boundaries to corral urban sprawl and to write comprehensive land use plans for development within those boundaries. Oregon's economy was still heavily dependent on timber and agriculture. The overriding goals of the law were to conserve Oregon's prime farmland, especially in the fertile Willamette Valley, and to prevent the conversion of the state's most productive forest land to sprawling suburbs. Like all other Oregon cities, Cascade Locks, Hood River, Mosier, and The Dalles in the gorge were required to establish boundaries to contain growth.

Nothing remotely similar was happening in Washington. In fact, it would be seventeen years before the Washington Legislature approved a weak Growth Management Act. The act left most of the authority for land use with counties and cities and exempted rural counties like Skamania and Klickitat from most of its provisions. Though land use regulation was nearly nonexistent in Washington, interest in the natural history of the gorge was growing. In 1973, more than 150 people took part in a "Short Course on the Columbia" sponsored by Clark College and the Washington State University Extension Service. Participants, including elected officials, traveled by boat and bus up the gorge as far as The Dalles. They heard lectures by prominent gorge experts—geologists, botanists, anthropologists, historians—on topics including the great Missoula floods, the cultures of the indigenous people of the Columbia Basin, and the history of early white settlement.

Clarence Irwin, chairman of the Washington Gorge Commission at the time, believed that public awareness of the unique features of the gorge was essential to building support for protection. The tours continued into the mid-1980s and remained popular. Jeff Breckel helped organize some of those tours. In 1978, he became the state Gorge Commissions' first paid staff member. Hired with a $15,000 federal grant, Breckel provided support to both state gorge commissions and became a pivotal player in planning for the future of the gorge after federal legislation was proposed.

Federal legislation was not the goal of the state commissions, however. With Breckel's help, the two commissions developed a plan of action that could be adopted without federal involvement. It recommended drawing boundaries around gorge towns to limit development, encouraging clustered rather than strip development, and restricting the siting of new industries in undeveloped areas. But those were just recommendations. Nothing required cities or counties to pay them the least attention.

Even as consensus was building for some level of state protection, plans by local boosters to draw more tourists to the gorge ratcheted up the debate. In 1978, a California consultant hired by the Mid-Columbia Visitors' Center recommended building a 200- to 300-bed resort and motel in rustic White Salmon, Washington. Consultant Allan Kotin said the gorge needed to become a destination, not just a day trip or a one-night stop. Though the gorge was a magnet for day-trippers, the region lacked the "major attractions, or image builders," that would be necessary to keep those visitors in the gorge and spending money, Kotin said. Hikers and campers were all

Clearcut, Burdoin Mountain, Washington. Photo by Darryl Lloyd.

very well, he said, but they brought their tents and groceries with them when they visited and generated no revenue for local communities.

No one was "selling" the gorge, he said. Travel agents and airlines had nothing to recommend to tourists beyond a tour of Bonneville Dam because there was no place for people to stay. He suggested building a 350-passenger sternwheeler to carry tourists into the gorge. He resurrected the idea of a tramway, this time at Cascade Locks, to hoist visitors to the rim of the Gorge. He also proposed building a $12 million cultural center in tiny North Bonneville, offering wagon trail rides in Klickitat County, and developing a Hood River-to-Parkdale excursion train on the Oregon side.

Gorge residents did not embrace this concept of a Gorge Disneyland. Advocates for protection declared that the various tourism schemes advanced by the ports and chambers of commerce posed a serious threat to the future of the gorge. At least two of those ideas did become reality, however. The sternwheeler *Columbia* was built; its cruises from Portland to Cascade Locks and back became popular day trips in good weather. And in 1987, the Mount Hood Railway began offering excursions from Hood River to Parkdale in the upper Hood River Valley.

By the mid 1970s, the extent of logging in the Washington foothills north of the gorge was on the public radar. The Washington Gorge Commission began discussing the need to preserve forested landscapes from clearcut logging. In 1976 it adopted guidelines that called for creation of small and irregular clearcuts that would blend in with the natural landscape, rapid reforestation, selective cutting near the Columbia River, and the retention of beauty strips of trees along heavily traveled roads. A reporter for the *Columbian* scoffed that those guidelines "are like a toothless bear running around this scenic trench through the Cascade Mountains."

That didn't stop timber companies from protesting. "I have some qualms that good intentions can add up to red tape and costly delays," said timber company owner Vernon Good. Commercial timber land should not be turned into parks, he said, and access roads should be kept primitive. "Let's not develop our county roads so well that they dump the public in our laps."

Mining proposals also were raising eyebrows in some quarters. An Oregon timber company provoked controversy when it proposed to mine 30,000 cubic yards of rock over two years at Government Cove, east of Cascade Locks, for use in the construction of a second powerhouse at Bonneville Dam. The Hood River County Planning Commission was on record as opposing surface mining in the gorge. Old quarries should not be reopened, commissioners said, if they would mar the natural beauty of the gorge. The proposed quarry also would violate the two state gorge commissions' voluntary standards on mining. Nonetheless, the commission ultimately granted a conditional use permit for the quarry, illustrating how little influence the gorge commissions wielded.

In 1979, as these controversies simmered, several forces converged to sharpen the discussion and add urgency to the gorge debate. In February, the National Park Service announced that its Denver regional office would undertake a six-month study of the gorge, from Washougal, Washington to The Dalles, Oregon and recommend options for federal protection. The study also would recommend ways to strengthen land use planning, which was then the responsibility of individual counties and largely optional under Washington's weak land use rules. "It doesn't mean the gorge is being proposed as a park, but for scenic management to prevent urban sprawl," Glenn Gallison of the Park Service stressed.

Nonetheless, the announcement sent tremors through gorge communities. Within weeks, port districts and the Mid-Columbia Economic Development District had lined up against a federal role in gorge land use. "The National Park Service study scares the hell out of my commissioners," said Larry Hendrickson, manager of the Port of Skamania County. Park officials sought to reassure gorge residents. They were not seeking a role in the management of the Columbia River Gorge, they said. The service itself had no agenda.

The idea for a Park Service study did not materialize out of thin air. Chuck Williams, a writer, photographer, and national parks advocate for the conservation group Friends of the Earth, had recently moved back to the small community of Skamania, Washington, where his family owned property. Williams had roots in the Northwest and in the gorge. He was a Cascade Chinook Indian on his father's side and the great-great grandson of an Indian chief who had signed the 1855 Grand Ronde Treaty with the U.S. government. Living in Skamania, Williams saw firsthand the evidence of clearcut logging on public and private lands. He warned that it was destroying gorge views. He was equally alarmed over the potential for residential development in Skamania County and along tributaries of the Columbia, especially the White Salmon and Klickitat rivers.

Williams had connections with national and regional conservation groups. In February 1979, he broke the news about the pending Park Service study with a story in the environmental magazine *Earthwatch Oregon*. He invoked the example of Lake Tahoe, which also straddled the border between two states, California and Nevada, and also was a magnet for runaway development. "Most conservationists agree that strong federal action will be needed to preserve the gorge," Williams wrote. "Like Lake Tahoe, the gorge is shared by two states that seldom see eye to eye, and nearly fifty local jurisdictions spread up and down both sides of the river have never been known to agree on anything." A national scenic area managed by the Park Service was the most likely solution, Williams said. He would soon co-found the Columbia Gorge Coalition to press the case for federal protection of the gorge.

Breckel traveled to the National Park Service's Denver office to help write the Park Service study. It was a unique exercise: How to design a study based on protecting something as intangible as scenery? Planners used a graphic information systems program that enabled them to view the entire gorge in 40-acre squares. They selected key viewpoints, evenly spaced, throughout the gorge, including Crown Point, Cape Horn, the major highways and the Columbia River itself. The GIS program allowed them to identify areas of the gorge that could be seen from these viewpoints. The higher the viewpoint's elevation, the larger the "viewshed." Those unique and highly visible landscapes would become the Special Management Areas in federal legislation, where development would be prohibited or tightly restricted on parcels smaller than 40 acres.

"We were trying to come to grips with the fact that the gorge was not pristine," Breckel recalled. Roughly 40,000 people lived in the gorge at the time. It was a major transportation and energy corridor. What kind of protection was practical? Planners looked to the regional parks in England's Lake District and to the vast Adirondack Park in upstate New York for ideas about how to integrate protection of natural areas into regions where people lived.

The gorge "didn't fit a national park model," Breckel said. "We needed to incorporate the history, the agricultural land, and orchards, the towns." He noted that it was relatively easy to identify the most visually sensitive areas. But how to protect them was subject to debate. For example, Archer Mountain in western Skamania County, a bowl of gradually rising forested slopes, was dotted with scattered houses in a rural setting. Planners thought it could be protected with zoning rather than by using the heavy-handed tool of Special Management Area designation. From the start, political considerations came into play. "There was concern about giving the federal government too much control over private land," Breckel said. "It was an emotional issue. People were terrified they were going to lose their land. You could show them the language, but they still weren't convinced."

As the Park Service study was being written, a new interstate freeway was approaching completion near the west end of the gorge. The Interstate 205 Bridge, formally the Glenn Jackson Bridge, would connect Portland's eastern suburbs with east Vancouver, putting western Skamania County within a twenty-minute commute of jobs in Portland. Skamania County had no zoning. Land speculators already were eying property between the county line and Stevenson. As if to put an exclamation point on that prospect, in 1979, George Rizor, a developer and a member of the Camas Planning

Commission, filed papers with Skamania County indicating his intent to divide 65 acres in Skamania County, directly across from Multnomah Falls, into as many as twenty-eight building lots.

Rizor's wooded tract along the Washington shore was visible from a number of gorge parks, viewpoints and hiking trails in Oregon, including Multnomah Falls, one of the state's most popular tourist attractions. He had logged part of the tract in preparation for dividing it into seven 10-acre lots and conveying title to his wife, daughter, and son-in-law. By beating a November 1, 1979, deadline, he figured he could divide each of those 10-acre plots into four $2\frac{1}{2}$-acre lots. After November 1, when a new county ordinance went into effect, he would be restricted to developing twelve building lots on his property.

There were obstacles to Rizor's plan, including an absence of public water and sewer systems nearby. Still, it raised a red flag. Rizor's property bordered land owned by John Yeon, whose father, John B. Yeon, had made his fortune in timber. In later years the elder Yeon was appointed Multnomah County's roadmaster and became a member of the team that designed and built the Columbia River Highway.

His son John occupied himself as a conservationist, art collector, and self-taught architect. In 1966, he bought 75 acres of waterfront property directly across from Multnomah Falls for $50,000 and set about creating a naturescape that met his exacting esthetic standards. Yeon restored creek beds and wetlands and replaced blackberry thickets with meadows of tall grasses. He preserved evidence of human activity on the site, including the pilings of an old railroad spur and remnants of a nineteenth century pear orchard. With landscaping, he created a sublime showcase for views of Multnomah Falls across the river. "My attitude toward building in landscapes was, and is, that of a landscape painter imaging what would look good in his landscape painting," the younger Yeon once said. He named his estate the Shire.

Through Yeon, word quickly got back to a core group of Portland conservationists that Rizor planned to build a large subdivision next to the Shire. The news instantly defined the decision facing the region in the starkest terms possible—and brought the Portland establishment into the fray. In August 1979, Yeon wooed Nancy Russell, a wildflower collector and a wealthy member of the Portland Garden Club and her stockbroker husband, Bruce Russell, urging them to help save the gorge from development.

He invited them to a private dinner at the Shire. Under a full moon he urged them to commit themselves to the cause—and bring their wealthy and influential friends on board as well.

The Rizor development scheme gave Oregon supporters of federal protection for the gorge plenty of ammunition for their cause. Chuck Williams called Rizor's plan an attempted end run around Washington's subdivision law. If fully developed, he said, the project would represent the largest concentration of people in the 20-mile stretch between Washougal and the hamlet of Skamania.

The promotional material for Rizor's project, called Columbia Gorge Riverfront Estates, did nothing to quell critics' fears:

The more than 60-acre site is located on...the Evergreen Highway about twenty miles east of the new I-205 Bridge. Local landmarks near the property include Multnomah Falls (directly across the river), Beacon Rock and Bonneville Dam (to the east) and Cape Horn Washington and the Oregon Vista House (to the west)...From the lots in the "upper parcel," spectacular views of the gorge are afforded through the dense forest cover...Outstanding views of the world famous surroundings are also afforded from lots in the "lower parcel," which is enhanced with many beautiful features.

Reaction from the Washington Gorge Commission was swift. Chairman Irwin accused Rizor of circumventing the subdivision rule and threatened a lawsuit. Skamania County officials backed Rizor, saying it was his right to develop his land as long as he met county codes.

Multnomah County Executive Don Clark jumped into the fray, calling for an environmental impact statement and public hearings before the Rizor project could go forward. Skamania County officials pointed out that this wasn't Oregon; no such actions were required under Washington law. Bob Leick, the sharp-tongued, longtime Skamania County prosecutor, recalls that Clark called him and asked him to "do something" about the proposed Rizor subdivision. "I suggested he and his group might want to buy the land and keep it pristine. In my view, that would have been the American way."

In 1983, Harriett Burgess of the Trust for Public Land would do just that. Today the Rizor subdivision is the Forest Service's Sams Walker Day

Use Area, a mosaic of fields and woodlands laced with trails and Native American artifacts offering a lovely pastoral view from both Cape Horn and Multnomah Falls.

At the end of 1980, as the Rizor threat continued to reverberate, the National Park Service released its gorge study. To no one's surprise, the service concluded that the western gorge was threatened by urban sprawl as the I-205 bridge neared completion. It also noted that increased demand for quarry rock, timber, and power production would inevitably damage gorge views.

The study offered several options: Maintain the status quo; expand the role of the two state gorge commissions and give them more power; establish a national recreation area administered by the Forest Service or Park Service; or establish a national reserve or scenic area run by a local commission with federal financing.

Appointing a multi-governmental commission to oversee the nation's first national scenic area was the preferred option, but that could happen only through federal legislation. The commission would need representation from local, state, and federal governments. The federal government would buy and hold land considered important to preserve. Most private land would remain private, especially where the natural landscape was in agricultural use. Buying the gorge and turning it into a national park was not on the table. Setting aside the obvious political implications, the Park Service acknowledged that Congress never would appropriate the money. Yet Park Service planners made it clear that they found the status quo unacceptable. "In the long term, tourism and its economic benefits would decline if the scenic quality of the gorge is noticeably deteriorated," they wrote.

Soon after, a new voice from Portland weighed in on the controversial Rizor project. "I am very distressed," Nancy Russell said in a statement to the press. Rizor's proposed subdivision "demonstrates the legitimacy of concerns raised in the National Park Service study. It is not fiction that the gorge is going to be developed. It is being developed."

Russell was particularly upset at the prospect of a subdivision across from Multnomah Falls and within view of Cape Horn on the Washington side. "This is the most pristine part of the gorge," she said. "You can stand on Cape Horn and see an idyllic scene. If you believe this is a special landscape, not another real estate property, you are appalled that this is

Hood River waterfront. Photo by Darryl Lloyd.

happening across from Multnomah Falls." A political neophyte but a quick learner, Russell would soon become the dominant voice in the move to protect the Columbia River Gorge.

The state gorge commissions took no position on the study when it was released. But over the preceding months, at Breckel's urging, they had attempted to preempt it. Breckel suggested that people could protect scenic views of the gorge by screening new houses, clustering development, requiring setbacks from bluffs and cliffs, retaining surrounding trees and bushes, and painting buildings in colors that would blend in with their natural surroundings. His suggestions would become the basis for future rules to minimize the visibility of new development.

Don Clark saw the National Park Service study shortly after it was released and determined that it would not gather dust on a shelf. A liberal Oregon Democrat with strong ties to labor and progressive leaders, Clark had long advocated for gorge protection. Multnomah County encompassed not only Portland and Gresham but also a large chunk of the rural gorge, extending east from Troutdale nearly to Cascade Locks. As county sheriff, Clark had waged a running battle with Troutdale Mayor Glenn Otto, who was trying to expand his tiny town eastward into the gorge.

"My political life, a good deal of it, was defending the gorge," Clark recalled in a 2012 interview. "It was an adversarial relationship. I always felt Multnomah County had a special relationship with the gorge and a special commitment to protect the gorge."

In the 1960s, when the Oregon Highway Commission proposed replacing some of the hand-crafted stone masonry railings along the historic Columbia River Highway with steel rails, Clark alerted Republican Gov. Tom McCall, who halted the plan. That marked the beginning of their bipartisan effort to protect the gorge.

Clark also had worked to help kill the Mount Hood Freeway, a signature 1970s battle led by then-Portland Mayor Neil Goldschmidt. The campaign saved a swath of residential southeast Portland along the proposed freeway's path from destruction. And Clark was the only elected official to have opposed construction of the new I-205 freeway. "It quadrupled the amount of land available for urban use in Clark County," he said.

By 1980, a regional intergovernmental panel with representatives from both sides of the river was discussing limits on development of the Portland-Vancouver metropolitan area. Members "really did begin to grapple with the concept of transportation driving land use," Clark said. "We needed to contain the growth or it was going to destroy our livability."

When the National Park Service study landed on Clark's desk, he sat down and read it. Then he called his staff together for a discussion of how they could advance the cause of winning federal protection for the gorge.

It was a presidential election year, and U.S. Interior Secretary Cecil Andrus came to town that fall. "He was drumming up support for the reelection of President Jimmy Carter and offering political largesse," Clark said. "I had supported Sen. (Ted) Kennedy, but I'm a loyal soldier." Clark agreed to publicly support Carter against Republican Ronald Reagan. In exchange, he asked a favor.

"I said, 'I have this study. The federal government has done nothing about it. It's a bistate gorge and we need to get federal protection. We need a solution as big as the issue.'"

Andrus promised to propose legislation after the election. Then Reagan won in a landslide. So Clark tried another tack. He called Oregon's most powerful member of Congress, Sen. Mark Hatfield, a former Oregon governor, a Republican, and the chairman of the Senate Appropriations Committee.

"We had a personal relationship, and we also had a gorge relationship that went way back," Clark recalled. "Hatfield also had a relationship with Reagan."

Clark asked Hatfield to support federal protection for the gorge. The senator, Clark said, responded with a fifteen-minute lecture "about how he was not appreciated. He had been a champion of land preservation and no one had given him credit for that. It had come back to bite him. I listened to that and I said, 'What are we going to do?'"

Hatfield told Clark, "'If you will get me an army, both sides of the river, both ends of the gorge, Democrats and Republicans, labor and management, if you will do that, and if it gets momentum,'" then he would agree to back legislation and get it through Congress, Clark recalled.

Hatfield set one more condition. He said, "'I don't want anyone to get in the way or interfere. I know how to do this.'" Clark readily agreed. "He was the master at getting things passed."

Clark asked his staff to begin recruiting someone impressive to lead the political campaign. He recalled that his administrative assistant, Sally Anderson, "came back to me and said, 'I have found a jewel, a top-drawer, high-class Republican, a member of the Portland Garden Club." When Clark met Russell, he was impressed. "She had class and she was smart. She wasn't afraid to say, 'I don't know how to do that.'" At their first meeting, he offered her the job of leading the campaign.

 Clark himself recruited members of a high-powered gorge steering committee: Former Oregon Governors Tom McCall and Bob Straub and Portland City Commissioner Mike Lindberg, among others. "These were friends of mine," he said. "We shared political agendas. I essentially told them what Mark Hatfield had told me. We needed a broad-based coalition, people of substance, to stand up."

While this was unfolding in Portland, Chuck Williams, the person most responsible for initiating the Park Service study, had been busy writing a book to make the case for federal protection of the gorge. In late 1980, Williams published *Bridge of the Gods, Mountain of Fire: A Return to the Columbia Gorge*, a 192-page coffee table book featuring numerous historical photographs and his own color photographs of the gorge. The book recounted in vivid detail the human and natural history of the gorge. Sierra Club founder and environmental icon David Brower wrote the introduction. For Williams, creating the book was a labor of love that communicated his deep affinity with the first inhabitants of the gorge, their cultural traditions, and the natural landscape of the region.

Williams, then thirty-seven, said he had written the book to make the general public more aware of the history and significance of the Columbia River Gorge. He called the gorge "by far the most historic site in the Northwest." It held his own family history as well; his paternal grandparents had raised their children on a farm at Cape Horn.

In the book's final chapter, Williams warned that the industrial development dreams of the gorge port commissions would threaten wildlife and salmon runs. He warned of the coming boom in home building. "The new interstate bridge to be completed in 1982 will make the most critically threatened stretch of the gorge— Washougal to Beacon Rock—a bedroom community of Portland."

The book was a richly illustrated manifesto that made a strong case for federal protection of a natural treasure. But by the time it was published, McCall, Clark, and other powerful politicians and community leaders in Oregon had planted the seeds for formation of a Portland-based organization to lead the effort. The momentum now was with Friends of the Columbia Gorge.

Bowen Blair, Friends' first executive director, believes the ascendancy of Friends of the Gorge and Williams' waning influence was a matter of timing. "Chuck took himself out of the campaign for a year to write his book and it was a great book. He came back, and suddenly you've got someone who is smart, well-connected, and focused like a laser on the issue. Nancy became the focal point for the press. Chuck felt the (Columbia Gorge) Coalition was not given sufficient credit. But they were instrumental in getting the National Park Service study done, and that was a major contribution."

Wilson Cady, a conservationist who lived in the west end of Skamania County, had worked closely with Williams as the Columbia Gorge Coalition was taking shape in 1979. In fact, the group's first meeting was held in his living room. At the time, grassroots groups were fighting dams on the White Salmon River, an industrial park at Steigerwald Lake and expansion of Mount Hood Meadows ski area in Oregon. They had convened to discuss their separate campaigns.

"Chuck said, 'What we need to do is stop fighting all these little fires and start fighting to save the gorge,'" Cady recalled. "That was the inspiration." Yet Cady also believed that despite Williams' passion, he was not the person to build a national campaign. "He was anti-establishment. He didn't play well with others. We saw that a few hippie environmentalists weren't going to change things. Chuck didn't have the power to stop subdivisions. We needed a Don Clark, a Nancy Russell. So we got involved with Friends."

There was another sticking point: Williams strongly favored protection of the gorge under the stewardship of the National Park Service. He believed the Park Service would be less influenced than the Forest Service by timber companies and their allies in Congress. Initially, Friends of the Gorge agreed. But Hatfield was adamant. The Forest Service, not the Park Service, would represent the federal presence in the gorge.

"Hatfield was unequivocal," recalled Blair, who spent much of his time in Washington, D.C., during the four-year campaign to win federal gorge legislation. "He was not going to support the National Park Service, and he wouldn't support the gorge legislation with that in it."

The Friends' new stance placed them at odds with Williams, who bitterly opposed what he regarded as a sell-out by the founders of Friends. He did not trust the Forest Service to protect the gorge. A schism opened between Williams and Friends of the Gorge that never healed.

Early on, Russell met with Richard Benner, a land use attorney with the group 1000 Friends of Oregon, which served as a watchdog to enforce Oregon's strict land use standards. Benner would become the first executive director of the Columbia Gorge Commission.

In some ways, 1000 Friends would serve as a model for Friends of the Columbia Gorge, though the new group would face the far more daunting challenge of working to enforce an unpopular law in two states with radically different laws and political players.

Clark wasted no time in taking Russell on the road. "Nancy didn't know much about organizing a political campaign," he said. He invited her to accompany him on a barnstorming trip to gorge communities to promote his vision of federal legislation to protect the gorge. The Portland politician delivered his message to a mostly hostile audience on both sides of the river. Port officials and county commissioners said they feared federal red tape would hamstring their plans to broaden industrial tax bases. Landowners said they worried that their private property rights would be trampled.

Clark stayed on message. "Unless we act with some deliberate speed, this could be the generation that lost the Columbia River Gorge," he said to crowds in Hood River and The Dalles. "And that's a burden I don't want to bear." He pointed out that the federal government already was heavily involved in the gorge through the Forest Service, the U.S. Army Corps of Engineers, and the Bonneville Power Administration, among other agencies. What was needed, he said, was a federal agency with jurisdiction over both states that could be held accountable for the gorge as a single unit. Its governing body should include representatives of federal, state, and local government.

At a rally in Hood River, Bill Hemmingway, manager of the Port of Klickitat, was openly skeptical after hearing Clark make his case. "Oh, he makes an eloquent presentation," Hemmingway said. "That's what I'm afraid of. There's no way people up here can deal with the politicians."

"I was used to dealing with hostile crowds," Clark said. "We had fired cannons across the gorge many times. I was pretty aware that there was a deep hostility. In some ways I was trying to protect them from becoming part of Portland, because they hated Portland."

Clark and Russell made the rounds of elected officials, too. They met with Oregon Gov. Vic Atiyeh, who initially opposed a federal role in the gorge but later softened his opposition. They met with U.S. Rep. Denny Smith, a conservative Oregon Republican who was hostile to any federal role in the gorge. Clark recalled that Russell scolded Smith, reminding him that President Theodore Roosevelt had been both a Republican and one of the great conservationists in American history.

"She was fearless. She was driven," Clark said. And not much of a diplomat.

Clark announced that he would meet with every member of the Oregon congressional delegation, including Senators Hatfield and Bob Packwood, and with Washington's senators, Democrat Henry "Scoop" Jackson and Republican Slade Gorton, to press the case for federal gorge protection.

In February 1980, Clark and other supporters of gorge protection announced the formation of a steering committee with more than 140 sponsors, including corporate heavy-hitters and political leaders, to push for federal legislation. The committee, Friends of the Columbia Gorge, would soon become the dominant player in the long congressional campaign to save the gorge.

At a Portland news conference, Robert Wilson, chairman of the board of Weyerhaeuser Company, and Tom McCall, who had famously invited Californians to visit Oregon, but please not to stay, urged congressional approval of a national scenic area in the gorge, to be administered by the National Park Service.

McCall had written to Washington Gov. John Spellman, who was still on the fence, urging him, "Don't be pushed around by the buffalo hunters on this one."

Among honorary members of the new steering committee were former Washington Gov. Dan Evans; Harriett Bullitt, owner of King Broadcasting Corporation in Seattle; and Susan Cady of Washougal, the co-founder of the Vancouver Audubon Society.

In May, Friends of the Gorge rolled out a proposal for a Columbia River Gorge National Scenic Area, to be administered by the Park Service and overseen by a thirteen-member regional commission. Russell, who had been named co-chairman of the new watchdog organization, said draft legislation had been in the works for four months. She expected it to be written into bill form for congressional consideration by June. She hired Blair, fresh out of law school at Lewis and Clark College's Northwestern School of Law, to become Friends' executive director.

At a meeting in Hood River, the founding members discussed how federal legislation might come together. "I said it wasn't going to be a national park," Clark recalled. "It was already a corridor of commerce and you can't undo that. I described it as a land use planning process."

The fledgling group had a tiny staff and no money at first. Then Russell stepped up. "Nancy almost immediately came up with the money," Clark said. "She came up with it out of her own purse and she had dinner with influential people who wrote checks." Most of the donors were well-heeled Republicans, he said. "If they had been Democrats, they would have written checks for $10."

With the clout of Portland's power elite behind it, the campaign to win federal protection for the gorge was launched.

Chapter 3
Saving Steigerwald

Wilson and Susan Cady bought their property at the top of Belle Center Road in 1972. Their seven-and-a-half acres, just inside the Skamania County line, sit at an elevation of 1,200 feet, with unbroken forest above. Deer, bobcats, and birds of every description inhabit the secluded property. Most of it lies within the Columbia River Gorge National Scenic Area. That's fine with the Cadys; they believe Congress intended for the Scenic Area to extend from rim to rim.

Cady is a third-generation resident of the western gorge. His pioneer grandmother, Katy Gill, ran the Gill Seed Company. A great-aunt came out on the Oregon Trail.

In the 1970s, before the campaign for federal protection of the gorge began, the forested slopes of eastern Clark County and western Skamania County were ripe for development. Several subdivisions were on the drawing boards. The Port of Camas-Washougal had big plans for the large wetland that bordered the Columbia River immediately to the east. And the port wasn't the only interested party.

Rudy Hegewald, owner of the Stevenson Co-Ply mill in Stevenson, enlisted Skamania County Prosecuting Attorney Bob Leick to help him get land along the Columbia River zoned for industrial development. Developers also had their eye on the forested slopes at Cape Horn, the unincorporated town of Carson, even the small community park at Home Valley.

Most industrial schemes proposed for Skamania County failed to win financing. But residential development in the county was virtually unrestricted. "In Skamania County, you could build on any two-acre lot anywhere in the county," Cady said. "There was so much development going on in this area that we went to the Skamania County Commission and asked for a moratorium on development. We didn't move out here to be in town."

View of the Gorge looking east from Cape Horn Trail. Photo by Darryl Lloyd

Getting a building permit was a simple matter, Cady recalled. "In 1976, all you had to do was take a napkin into the planning office and show the dimensions of the house so they would know how much to charge you. There was no real building inspection in Skamania County except what was required by the state, for electrical and plumbing. Later, when the state Uniform Building Code came in, Skamania County put it on the ballot, as if it were optional: 'Do you want a building code?'"

County commissioners even had the chutzpah to demand money from the state to implement the building code. "When they found out the state wouldn't pay, they wouldn't hire a building inspector," Cady said. Instead, commissioners gave the job to Bob Lee, the county forester. The county put out the welcome mat for homebuilders, surfacing the roads leading to new subdivisions with gravel and installing power lines from Belle Center Road. A federal grant helped pay for a new school to serve the county's west end, where commissioners envisioned hundreds of new families with school-age kids.

The Cadys, conservationists and amateur naturalists, had worked for federal protection of the Indian Heaven Wilderness in Southwest

Washington, donating the steelhead for the barbecue when the wilderness area was established. They soon set about turning their own seven acres into a wildlife haven. They joined the Portland Audubon Society because there was no local Audubon chapter in Clark County at the time. In 1975, local naturalist Hazel Wolf founded one and Susan Cady was named vice chair.

There was no shortage of issues facing the new chapter. At the top of the list was how to deal with the imminent threats facing Steigerwald Lake, the broad wetland bordering the Columbia River across the state highway from Washougal.

Like most Columbia River lowlands, Steigerwald Lake once had ebbed and flowed with the tide and the natural course of the undammed river, absorbing rich nutrients and providing fertile habitat for waterfowl and wildlife. Gibbons Creek, which fed the wetlands, flowed from hills to the east and spread across the flood plain. Ranks of cottonwoods sprouted along a high dike on the shore of the Columbia, built to hold the river back after 1938, when Bonneville Dam was completed.

The history of Steigerwald Lake is a history in microcosm of development along the lower Columbia beginning in the late nineteenth century. Livestock grazing turned the lake into an ecological wasteland. John Gibbons, for whom the creek is named, brought his cattle to the shallow lake from Illinois. They swam the Columbia and grazed on the natural wetlands. As the water level dropped, Gibbons grew potatoes and other crops. In 1906, the Steigerwald family began farming the property. The father, a Portland businessman, had made his fortune in the Klondike Gold Rush. His son David grazed dairy cows on both sides of the river. Milk from the dairy at Steigerwald Landing was sent down to Portland and sold at a store featuring a giant milk bottle.

Cottonwood Point, along the shore at Steigerwald, was a historical landmark. When British Captain George Vancouver arrived at the mouth of the Columbia in 1792, he sent a 22-foot boat, the *Chatham,* under the command of Lt. William R. Broughton, to explore the river. Broughton sailed as far upriver as Cottonwood Point in October 1792.

"He got out, stuck a flag in the ground and claimed all the land drained by the Columbia for Great Britain," Cady said. Broughton could see the tip of Mount Hood and decided to name the mountain for British Lord Admiral Hood. The peak's craggy summit is clearly visible on sunny days from the hiking trail atop the Steigerwald dike. Mount Hood's name remained, but the land claim eventually went to the United States of America.

In 1964, with a federal grant obtained by Washington's U.S. Representative Julia Butler Hansen, Steigerwald Lake was dredged and diked. "That upset Washougal, because it was their beach," Wilson Cady recalled. That same year, Clark County zoned Steigerwald for heavy industry in its comprehensive land use plan. Throughout the 1960s and 1970s, the property was owned by Don Stevenson, president of SDS Lumber Co., who leased it for cattle grazing.

In 1975, Keith O'Neill of the Washington Department of Fish and Game came to a meeting of the new Audubon chapter. He asked the members, "What are you guys going to do about Steigerwald Lake?"

"I said, 'You mean Robert's Bean Farm?' That's what they called the wetland, because it grew row crops," Cady said.

O'Neill had other plans for the wetland. "He wanted it preserved as a pheasant release site," Cady said. "Ducks were the main interest of the agency then. We started doing surveys out there. You needed to have data. So we did bird counts on a regular basis."

Steigerwald sits at the crossroads of several migratory bird routes. "The lake is on the Pacific Flyway," Cady said. "Migratory birds fly directly over the lake en route to the Willamette Valley, and the Columbia Gorge itself is a migration route." Losing Steigerwald would be huge blow to migratory birds, because 90 percent of wetlands in the Lower Columbia River already had been lost. It took Cady and his Audubon volunteers ten years to gather the data they needed to document the use of Steigerwald by migratory waterfowl. By 2012, they had confirmed that more than 200 bird species used Steigerwald and more than 300 species passed through Clark County on their migratory routes. That total "included a lot of birds not normally found in the area, such as prairie falcons and sage thrashers," Cady said. Sandhill cranes and ducks flew both west and east through the gorge. They also flew north and south through the Okanagan Valley between the Arctic and the Great Basin, and along the trough that divides the Coast Range from the Cascades.

Even Don Stevenson appreciated Steigerwald's value as waterfowl habitat, Cady said. "He liked to hunt for ducks there. He came in by helicopter and flushed the ducks out." But Stevenson and two business partners had other plans for the land. They wanted to sell the property to the Port of

Camas-Washougal, which owned adjacent wetlands downriver. The port was eager to acquire the land.

"We started going to all the port meetings," Cady said. Port commissioners were supremely confident, he said. "They knew it was going to be theirs. They were sure of it. They were considering a garbage incinerator for power generation. But that didn't happen. Then the port got itself declared a nuclear port in case they ever wanted to handle nuclear material coming from Trojan."

Trojan, on the lower Columbia near the town of Rainier, was Oregon's only nuclear power plant. It was decommissioned in the 1990s, but its spent fuel rods remain at the site awaiting a permanent storage solution.

By 1980, the campaign to save the gorge was heating up. Clark County Audubon volunteers decided it was time to take matters into their own hands. "We started a long campaign to save Steigerwald," Cady said. "We saw that the Port of Camas and Washougal had received an economic development grant for $2.5 million to expand infrastructure for an industrial park."

Cady read in the newspaper that Washington's U.S. Rep. Mike Mc-Cormack "had gotten rid of the environmental stuff"—apparently including language in the federal Clean Water Act that required no net loss of wetlands—"to speed up the process."

"We called the Environmental Protection Agency in D.C. They said the Presidential Wetland Act doesn't apply because there are no wetlands there."

"It's all wetlands," Cady told the EPA bureaucrats.

The agency sent a couple of employees to check out the situation. "These guys showed up in three-piece suits and wingtips to tour the refuge. We walked out into the fields. We were looking out over Steigerwald Lake. A bald eagle flew overhead. They said, 'No, this is a wetland, they can't build here.'"

It was a significant victory. But Steigerwald remained threatened. The Cadys joined with other grass-roots conservationists in the gorge to fight designating the wetland as a nuclear port. In the end, it was Oregon's Sen. Mark Hatfield who got Steigerwald set aside as a national wildlife refuge as part of the environmental mitigation the federal government required for the construction of a second powerhouse at Bonneville Dam. Cady recalled

that the Oregon Republican said "he was not going to have tourists standing at Vista House looking down on a cooling tower," Cady said.

Don Stevenson was not quite finished squeezing revenue from his
property. Before he sold it to the federal government, he cleared the willow
forest to ready the land for development. He even threatened to cut down
the cottonwoods that lined the Columbia River dike. In the end, he sold it
for its value as industrial land, pocketing $1.6 million for 900 acres.

Public sentiment, even then, was not with Clark County's tiny conservation movement. "We were getting phone calls at night," Cady recalled,
saying "Those ducks can go somewhere else!"

The Steigerwald National Wildlife Refuge was officially established in 1988
to help offset the loss of 1,122 acres of forest, scrub, lakes, marshland,
and sloughs destroyed in construction of the second Bonneville Power
Administration powerhouse.

Instead of becoming an industrial park, Steigerwald became a user-
friendly refuge, protected as a critical stopover for migratory birds in
the Western Hemisphere, and an outdoor classroom for students in Clark
County's Evergreen School District.

When the Trust for Public Land bought the property, providing bridge
funding until Congress could appropriate money for the purchase, it was
10 feet deep in blackberries. Cattle had eaten all the native tree seedlings.
With a federal grant, refuge manager Jim Clapp of the U.S. Fish and Wildlife
Service and Wilson Cady's volunteer corps, now organized as the Columbia
Gorge Refuge Stewards, began the work of transforming Steigerwald from
boggy pastures and blackberry thickets to a mosaic of restored meadows
and wetlands. Crews deployed a hydro ax and a huge mower to eradicate
the blackberries, then sprayed them with herbicides. Today, Steigerwald
is a refuge for people as well as waterfowl, with hiking trails, interpretive
signs, whimsical outdoor art, and plantings of native species.

The transformation did not happen overnight. Though the refuge is
federally protected, it's still a work in progress. Volunteers with Columbia
Gorge Refuge Stewards continue to plant between 3,000 and 4,000 shrubs
each year along a low grassy area known as the Audubon Swale. They also
plant native vegetation along Gibbons Creek to provide shade for fish.

The Fish and Wildlife Service built a small interpretive center at the
entrance to Steigerwald, just off Highway 14. The spot provides trail access

and also marks Washington's western gateway to the Columbia River Gorge National Scenic Area. The refuge has become a popular close-in nature hike, offering encounters with geese, ducks and bald eagles and expansive views to the east and south.

Cady would like to see it expanded to provide more information on the refuge and other nearby features, including the state's Washougal Oaks Natural Area and Cape Horn, and the Scenic Area as a whole. "Visitors enter the Scenic Area just east of Washougal and pass some of the most significant sites in the gorge without understanding what they are seeing," he said. Cady, now retired from the Camas pulp mill where he served as the mill's first environmental officer, has worked with the local school district to develop an environmental education program. Kids get a tour of Steigerwald and a talk on the history of the refuge. Then they go out into the field to count birds and install artificial nesting sites for purple martins. The rare birds nest in cavities at just four sites in Washington, primarily in dead cottonwood snags. They winter in Brazil. Only about 3,000 pairs survive.

Another subspecies of purple martin can be found east of the Cascades, but the westside birds are unique, Cady said. As a committed conservationist who walks the walk, he identifies with the winsome birds—and with the larger campaign to protect their boggy habitat along the shore of the lower Columbia River. "Our purple martins like to live by themselves and close to water."

Chapter 4
Balancing Act

The year 1981 was an inauspicious time to launch a major national conservation initiative. Republican Ronald Reagan had just defeated President Jimmy Carter, ushering in an era of environmental retrenchment. As a 1966 candidate for governor of California, Reagan had telegraphed his view of forest preservation with a widely quoted paraphrased quip, "If you've seen one redwood, you've seen them all." As his first Secretary of the Interior, he appointed James Watt, the most anti-environmental interior secretary in the nation's history.

A linchpin of Reagan's philosophy was protection of private property rights. He advocated a limited role for the federal government and adamantly opposed anything that smacked of federal zoning of private property. But Reagan did not have a free hand to dismantle environmental laws. He took office at a time when Oregon wielded extraordinary clout in Congress. Moderate Oregon Republicans Mark Hatfield and Bob Packwood held key leadership posts in the Senate, Hatfield as chairman of the budget-writing Senate Appropriations Committee and Packwood as head of Senate Finance.

The early 1980s also marked a rare period of bipartisan cooperation. In 1982, sixty U.S. senators—enough to break a filibuster—were considered "moderate," according to the *National Journal*. By 1994, that number had dropped to thirty-six.

Had the Columbia River Gorge National Scenic Area Act been introduced in a more partisan era, it would have been doomed, said Bowen Blair, who served as executive director of Friends of the Columbia Gorge during the four-year congressional campaign.

Instead, for a short time the political stars aligned. "I don't think that constellation ever lined up again, when Oregon had so much clout." Blair said. "That clout was critical to rolling President Reagan." Fresh out of law school, Blair spent most of those four years helping to shepherd gorge legislation through Congress.

Elected to the Senate in 1967, Hatfield had risen to command broad control over the federal purse strings. Widely regarded as a master of the deal, he knew how to get legislation through Congress. During his thirty-year Senate career, he walked a tricky line with constituents back home, sponsoring landmark conservation bills while remaining a staunch supporter of Oregon's timber industry and backing full funding of the Forest Service timber sale program, a mainstay of the state's rural economy.

Packwood, a former Oregon legislative leader elected to the Senate in 1969, was best known for the key role he played in winning passage of a massive 1986 federal tax reform bill. He ultimately left the Senate in disgrace after an ethics investigation revealed he had made inappropriate sexual advances to women in his D.C. office. But early in his Senate career, Packwood staked out a reputation as a friend of conservation causes. He led a Senate campaign to keep the proposed 670-foot High Mountain Sheep Dam out of Hells Canyon, the deepest canyon in North America. He championed an Oregon campaign to save French Pete, a much-beloved national forest roadless area east of Eugene, by adding it to the Three Sisters Wilderness. Though his committee assignments gave him no direct jurisdiction over public lands, Packwood was proud of his role in saving Hells Canyon, where the Snake River divides Idaho from Oregon and Washington, from the high dam proposed by a consortium of four private power companies. It was, he said, a far tougher challenge than the 1980s campaign to protect the Columbia River Gorge. "It started with no indigenous support and strong local opposition" in the rural counties of northeastern Oregon, he said. "All those counties are poor, and dams meant jobs."

The national conservation groups were on board, "but I couldn't get a hearing," he said. "I could not get anyone to cosponsor the bill." He finally prevailed upon Arizona Republican Sen. Barry Goldwater. "I said, 'This is deeper than the Grand Canyon.' I got Goldwater, and then I got (Massachusetts Sen.) Ted Kennedy." Typically, in those years, Senate colleagues would agree to cosponsor each other's bills as favors—as long as those bills weren't opposed by their own constituents.

Saving the gorge, in contrast, seemed like a slam-dunk. "It never occurred to me that the gorge needed to be saved," Packwood said. He was a frequent visitor at the family compound of Nani Warren near Prindle on the Washington shore. Warren, a wealthy heiress, chaired the Oregon Gorge Commission.

Oregon politics were clearly on the side of federal protection. An October 1981 memo analyzing the prospects for success of a gorge bill concluded that "from an Oregon standpoint, this is a no-lose proposition," Packwood said in a 2012 interview. As for the Washington delegation, "we thought of them the way we thought of Wallowa County. You aren't going to win them over."

The Washington delegation was a mixed bag. Senator Henry "Scoop" Jackson, a moderate Democrat, represented Washington for thirty years in the Senate and a dozen years in the House. He died in office in September 1983, just as the Scenic Area Act was gaining momentum. He was succeeded by Sen. Daniel Evans, a moderate Republican, who would play a key role in negotiating the final bill. Republican U.S. Sen. Slade Gorton of Washington supported gorge protection in the end.

Liberal Democrats dominated the House delegations in both Washington and Oregon. Representative Tom Foley, a moderate Democrat who represented an eastern Washington congressional district, held House leadership positions from 1965 until his defeat in the 1994 Republican takeover of the House. Representative Don Bonker, a moderate Democrat, represented Southwest Washington, and Rep. Sid Morrison, a moderate Republican, represented the Washington side of the Columbia Gorge.

In Oregon, Democratic House members Les AuCoin, Jim Weaver, and Ron Wyden all supported a federal role in managing the gorge to varying degrees. The state's two conservative Republican House members during this time, Bob Smith and Denny Smith, were intractable foes of the legislation.

In the Northwest, the nascent campaign to win federal protection of the gorge continued to stir up controversy. As Don Clark took his Save-the-Gorge show on the road, another player entered the fray. Chuck Cushman, a rabid foe of the National Park Service, had established the National Inholders Association to raise the red flag over potential threats to private property rights posed by the Park Service. His organization defended the rights of those who held private land inside the boundaries of a national parks and national recreation areas. He had once been a member of the Sierra Club but he had changed his politics after the federal agency tried to buy private inholdings, including his family's property, within California's Yosemite National Park.

Cushman relocated to rural Clark County to fight the Scenic Area Act. He warned that the Park Service would pressure gorge landowners to sell even if their property was not actually needed for a new Scenic Area. A General Accounting Office report buttressed Cushman's argument when it criticized the Park Service's tactics in the purchase of private land at Stehekin, a settlement of private landowners at the remote north end of Washington's Lake Chelan, within a national recreation area.

In January 1981 Cushman invited local gorge officials to a meeting at Cascade Locks, where he told war stories about the Park Service and other federal agencies. Once you let legislation in, he warned, "they will nibble you and nibble you." To stave off federal meddling, he advised local officials to "get out front, pass the zoning laws, and show that you are working to protect the gorge." The seasoned warrior offered to help by alerting sympathetic members of Congress across the nation, raising money, and digging out information under the Freedom of Information Act.

Meanwhile, state Sen. Hal Zimmerman, whose Washington Senate district included most of the gorge, proposed asking voters to approve a money measure that would enable the state itself to buy the most sensitive tracts on the Washington side of the gorge. The idea was modeled on one in King County, where in 1979 voters had approved a $50 million bond measure to buy prime farmland in the county's east end to preserve it from development as Seattle's suburbs spread east. Skamania County Commissioner Bill Benson had approached Zimmerman with the idea of a similar approach in the western gorge. People should be fairly paid for their land if the state declared it to be of scenic significance, Zimmerman said. But that idea went nowhere. In the end, it would be the federal government that would pay to preserve private land in the gorge from development.

As Don Clark stumped for federal protection, he insisted that any legislation would be "subject to negotiation" and invited those who wanted to make sure local interests were represented to join his steering committee. He also predicted that it would take ten years to resolve all the competing interests and enact federal legislation. In fact, it would take five.

Clark held up east Multnomah County as a cautionary tale of what might happen if the future of the gorge was left to local governments. After World War II, the unincorporated east end of the county, between Portland and Gresham, had been transformed from strawberry fields and vegetable farms to a vast suburb. There were virtually no brakes on sprawl until the state's land use law took effect. As a result, wells in the area had been contaminated by a plume of groundwater pollution that would ultimately force annexation of nearly the entire unincorporated area to the cities of Portland and Gresham.

At the state level, there was no consensus about how to proceed with protection of the gorge. Oregon's Governor Atiyeh, a moderate Republican, said he was open to discussion of a bistate compact approved by the two state legislatures that would establish a common land use policy for local governments in the gorge. Washington's new governor, Republican John Spellman, said he would not take a position on what level of gorge protection to support until he had had time to study the issue thoroughly. Atiyeh changed positions four times on gorge protection over the next two years, while Spellman played a game of delay and indecision.

In late 1981, Sally Newell, then a resident of The Dalles, was invited to a party where she met Nancy Russell, orchardist Barbara Bailey, and other members of Friends of the Gorge. They were shopping a Gorge Scenic Area bill around. It was the first time she had seen a draft bill.

"They had this legislation. It was just kind of a twinkle," Newell recalled. "I just went nuts. I thought this was the most awful thing, a terrible abrogation of private property rights. I felt Oregon had very good land use laws. It just seemed crazy to me." Newell later met with Jeff Breckel of the Gorge Commission, Wasco County planner Dan Durow, and Klickitat County planner Steven Anderson, among others, to discuss whether the counties themselves should create zoning overlays to protect special areas, with the goal of preempting federal legislation. "The thought was, if all the counties would do that, we could head it off," Newell recalled. "There was an ad hoc committee formed to create a set of rules. We knew you'd have to paint your house brown and get rid of all the trailers. All the counties were on board except Skamania. They were up in arms."

1981-82

As the curtain opened on a four-year congressional campaign to bring federal protection to the gorge, the politics of the issue had not begun to jell. Crafting the legislation would become a textbook exercise in compromise, negotiation, and hardball politics. Hatfield was in charge. As was his style, he proceeded carefully and strategically, leaving the early negotiations to other members of the delegation and the two governors' offices. The effort was slow to gain traction, as the Reagan administration pursued an agenda bent on weakening a raft of environmental laws passed in the 1970s. Negotiations over the shape of gorge legislation were contentious. Compromise was the key to holding a shaky coalition together.

Friends of the Columbia Gorge quickly became an inside player. Executive Director Blair tracked every twist and turn as members of the delegation sought to put their stamp on a bill.

Two politically powerful Washington timber companies with extensive gorge holdings, SDS Lumber Company in Bingen, and Broughton Lumber Company in Stevenson, recognized early on that federal legislation was coming. They met with the congressional delegation and helped negotiate language that exempted private timber land from new restrictions on logging. With a few exceptions, the Scenic Area Act would require owners of private timberland in the General Management Area only to abide by the states' existing forest practices laws.

Bob Leick, Skamania County's prosecuting attorney, fought federal legislation tooth and nail. He still resents the fact that SDS and Broughton took care of their own interests and left the counties to fend for themselves. "We didn't get any help from the timber industry," he said in a 2012 interview. Company officials didn't attend public meetings or give opponents money to wage a campaign against the legislation.

After the Scenic Area Act became law, SDS and Broughton negotiated large land trades with the Forest Service that held them largely harmless in their ability to log—and even to convert timberland to residential development.

Politics inevitably came into play in the drawing of boundaries. A Klickitat County orchardist fought drawing the eastern boundary of the Scenic Area to include the Maryhill Museum, a landmark in the eastern gorge, because that boundary would take in his own land too. He prevailed; in the final maps, the museum lies just outside the Scenic Area boundary. Late in the game, Skamania County Commissioner Ed Callahan won language that included the small timber community of Home Valley, where he lived, as the thirteenth designated urban area.

Liberal Oregon Democrats Jim Weaver of Eugene and Les AuCoin of Portland were the first to formally raise the prospect of federal legislation to protect the gorge. In 1981, they announced that they would undertake a study to lay the groundwork for introducing legislation to designate an 85-mile-long stretch of the Columbia River as the nation's first national scenic area. But the real campaign kickoff occurred in 1982, when Hatfield and Packwood introduced the "Columbia River Gorge Act of 1982," essentially the bill drafted by Friends of the Columbia Gorge.

Packwood already was thinking strategically. Addressing what he knew would be a major obstacle for the Reagan administration—potential claims that the federal government was unconstitutionally "taking" private land by depriving its owners of economic use of that land—Packwood came up with a solution to shield the federal government from such "takings" claims: "Let the Forest Service draft a plan and submit it to a regional commission." The commission, with members appointed by the six counties and the two governors, would have the last word on the plan, he said. But local control would go only so far. "We were not going to let local counties have a veto."

At the same time, Washington's governor and U.S. senators would have to be brought on board. "Washington could have stopped it," Packwood said. "You don't ride roughshod over another state." On January 26, 1982, Packwood went to Hatfield's office to bring him on board as well. "It was easy," he said.

The Hatfield-Packwood bill proposed a balanced approach. The Forest Service would administer the law, with advice from the regional commission. Six members would be chosen by the governing bodies of the six counties, two by each governor, and three by the U.S. Secretary of Agriculture. The Forest Service chief, with the commission's advice, would select a team to prepare a management plan, which would be implemented through local zoning ordinances. The general goal of the legislation would be to "protect, maintain, and enhance the scenic, natural, and cultural values" of all the lands in the National Scenic Area, and to designate appropriate uses for those lands. The Forest Service would have complete discretion to make those decisions.

Hatfield introduced another bill, with the same title, on the same day. This one bolstered the management authority of the regional commission and reduced the role of the Forest Service by giving the counties' appointees a majority vote and the primary responsibility for writing the management plan. It incorporated comments by gorge residents, many of whom saw the Oregon lawmakers' bill as a federal takeover of private property.

Hatfield said he was introducing both bills so that the various ideas for managing a new national scenic area could be discussed and debated. Neither bill got a hearing in the Ninety-seventh Congress and no member of the Washington delegation introduced legislation in 1982. But this was the beginning of an effort to balance federal, state, and local control of the gorge—an effort that would occupy Congress for four years to come.

1983

By early 1983, congressional intent to confer some form of federal protection on the gorge was set. Hatfield and Packwood introduced a new bill identical to their 1982 bill, which proposed to put the gorge in the hands of the Forest Service and a regional commission. The alternative version, giving most of the power to the commission, was not resurrected.

Packwood introduced his own bill as well, which gave federal agencies clear lead authority over the Columbia River Gorge National Scenic Area. His bill focused on governance issues, proposing that the new Scenic Area become part of the national forest system. It downplayed the role of the proposed regional commission. In a nod to the fears of many gorge residents, Packwood's bill also minimized the use of the federal government's powers of eminent domain to acquire private land, instead authorizing land exchanges. Still, it provoked fierce resistance, especially from the Washington delegation.

In a Senate floor speech, Packwood expressed "renewed commitment and an increasing sense of urgency" about the need to counter the threats facing the gorge from unregulated development. Hatfield struck a more cautious note. "A great deal of discussion and cooperation with state and local governments, as well as gorge residents on both sides of the Columbia River, will have to take place before the legislation moves forward," he said.

Back in the Northwest, Skamania County residents who opposed federal protection organized as Columbia Gorge United and vowed to fight to keep the federal government out of the gorge. Packwood held the first field hearing on his legislation in Hood River, Oregon. It drew a large and fractious crowd. Conservationists supported federal legislation; most gorge residents were bitterly opposed. The lines were drawn. Packwood had accomplished his goal. "The hearing went excellently," he recalled. "It was black and white," with each side staking out its ground.

Meanwhile, Governors Atiyeh and Spellman announced that they had reached an informal agreement to protect the Gorge without federal intervention. They proposed to create a twenty-three-member commission that would develop and enforce a management plan for the gorge. The plan would be binding on local governments. The Forest Service would not play a major role. Despite its emphasis on local decision-making, this plan failed to win favor either with environmentalists or with gorge residents. Fifty-four witnesses testified at a Portland hearing over the course of seven hours on the day of the bill's release. Some of the most colorful testimony came from Skamania County Commissioner Bill Benson, who called the plan a "misbegotten agreement."

The governors' plan "seems an innocuous document that harms no one," Benson said. But he predicted it would undergo a transformation when it arrived on Capitol Hill. "When it reaches the houses of Congress, the Sierras, Audubons, 1000 Friends of Oregon, the garden clubs, the Friends of the Columbia Gorge...and they finish cutting, slashing and amending it, they will have accomplished their original goal: To put Skamania County under an onerous, unreasonable, unheeding, uncaring, unfeeling, unthinkable bureaucracy, which will toll the death knell for life as we know and love it."

Skamania County never wavered in its opposition. In 1984, county commissioners demanded that Governor Spellman disband the powerless Washington Gorge Commission. In 1986 they evicted the state commission's staff from a county building.

Conservationists led by Friends of the Gorge and the Columbia Gorge Coalition also opposed the governors' concept. A twenty-three-member commission would be unwieldy, they said. The Forest Service would have no meaningful role, and there was no provision for interim protection for scenic gorge lands. They preferred the Hatfield-Packwood bill, but proposed substituting the National Park Service for the Forest Service as the administering agency. They also wanted protection for tributary streams in the gorge.

The two state gorge commissions weighed in in favor of the governors' plan, as did some trade associations and Hood River County.

The governors formally unveiled their bill in August. At their request, Senator Hatfield of Oregon and Senators Jackson and Gorton of Washington introduced it. Senator Packwood refused to sign his name to it, saying it lacked adequate protections for the gorge. And indeed, it was a far cry from the 1982 Hatfield-Packwood bill. For one thing, it proposed a scenic area one-third smaller than the one envisioned in the earlier bill. Its drafters had used the original boundaries established in the 1950s by the two state gorge commissions, which encompassed 190,500 acres. Packwood's bill used the boundaries established in the 1979 Park Service study, drawn to encompass the entire "viewshed" of the gorge—all the lands that were visible from the Columbia River, Washington's Highway 14 and Interstate 84 (then Interstate 80) in Oregon, a total of 260,260 acres.

The governors' bill barely addressed the critical issue of how to provide interim protection for gorge lands while a management plan was being written. It required no interim guidelines, instead merely directing the commission to review certain developments on a case-by-case basis. One irony: It gave the Gorge Commission just sixty days to review proposals for development, yet it required the commission to meet only every ninety days.

In contrast, the Hatfield-Packwood bill required the Forest Service to adopt and enforce interim rules that would stay in place for three years, until a formal management plan was in place.

Logging got a pass in the governors' bill, which flatly exempted commercial forest activities in the Scenic Area from regulation. Those forests constituted about 20 percent of the proposed Scenic Area. Gorge logging was in the headlines at the time, in the wake of a 1982 clearcut on steep slopes that had destroyed a section of Oregon's Columbia Gorge Highway. The governors' bill also exempted the pending development of new locks at Bonneville Dam from regulation, despite widespread controversy over where spoils material from the site would be deposited. In spite of these weaknesses, Oregon Rep. Ron Wyden agreed to introduce a bill almost identical to the governors' bill in the House.

The bill was weak, but it offered a path out of the morass. Only Packwood stood in the way. "Had I been willing to cosponsor that bill," he said in a 2012 interview, "the governors' bill would have become law."

1984-85

In 1984, Democrat Booth Gardner succeeded Spellman as Washington governor. He initially favored a primary role for the federal government in protection of the gorge.

But the big conservation campaign in Congress that year revolved around passage of wilderness bills in several states, including Washington and Oregon. Gorge legislation was put on hold pending passage of those wilderness bills.

In the meantime, Packwood's position in favor of a strong federal role began to lose favor with members of the Oregon and Washington delegations. Both the Packwood bill and the governors' bill died at the end of the session.

Senator Dan Evans began a search for a balanced approach to gorge protection. He brought together his staff and Packwood's staff and asked them to conduct an inventory of gorge lands and define critical areas that warranted protection. When the inventories were nearly complete, the four Republican senators met to discuss the findings with local and state officials. Their recommendations were highly controversial. They signaled that the future of gorge legislation was shaping up as a contest between Packwood and Evans.

Evans' staff proposed reducing the size of the National Scenic Area by 18,700 acres, leaving out lands not visible or minimally visible from key viewpoints. The Evans proposal also identified 35,700 acres on the Washington side for "possible federal acquisition"—lands east of Beacon Rock, north of North Bonneville, and along the face of Burdoin Mountain all the way east to Catherine and Major creeks in Klickitat County.

The hope of finding agreement among the four senators evaporated when it came to the question of who would control management of the new scenic area. Earlier in the year the lawmakers had pledged to work together. But by mid-summer, it was clear that Evans' attempt to narrow differences by concentrating on defining which lands actually would be subject to management was on the brink of collapse. Packwood was poised to reintroduce a bill vesting broad management powers over the Scenic Area with the federal government. He said he didn't care whether the Forest Service or the National Park Service administered the Scenic Area as long as the federal government was in charge.

"I've gone about as far as I am going to go," he told the *Oregonian's* David Whitney. "I don't see any point in negotiations and meetings and further frustrations...This is not a time to talk compromise. There's no point in retreating at the start. And I would prefer not to retreat at all." Virtually every conservation group backed Packwood's bill. A skilled campaigner, he was not about to risk losing those supporters as he launched his 1986 reelection campaign.

Evans' boundary maps generated their own controversy. Voters in the liberal Puget Sound region might accept federal purchase of 37,500 acres, but his fired-up constituents in the gorge opposed any land acquisition. Evans took a typically moderate view. He said he supported shared management, with the feds in charge of the lands it owned and the counties, under federal guidelines, in charge of the rest.

Packwood called that inconsistent. He favored giving state and local interests advisory authority only, with the federal government having the final say.

Evans' process had succeeded only in establishing that legislation was needed and that urban areas in the gorge should be exempt from the act.

Electoral politics was a player in the impasse. In Hatfield's 1984 re-election campaign, he had co-sponsored Packwood's bill. The pro-federal stance was the politically correct thing to do back in Oregon. But with Evans now actively involved, Hatfield might be reluctant to make a move that would divide the two states' delegations, Whitney wrote. He might decide to remain neutral in 1985.

Both Packwood and Evans needed Hatfield's support. But it appeared that to get it, Packwood would have to give ground—a hard call as he faced his own 1986 election challenge.

In August 1985, Governor Atiyeh and Booth Gardner, Washington's new governor, held a retreat with congressional staff members and their own staffs at St. Martin's College near Olympia. "Real deliberations didn't start until Booth Gardner was elected," recalled Jeff Breckel, staff director of the two state gorge commissions, who helped organize the meetings. "Gardner sequestered all the congressional staff and Pat Amadeo from Atiyeh's staff. He said, 'Okay, are we getting on board with this? Are we going to have legislation or are we not? Can we decide we are going to have legislation?' He wanted an agreement; he wanted Washington to buy in."

Out of that meeting, the participants reached agreement on a two-tier government structure for the scenic area, with designated critical areas and a development authority to provide grants and loans to gorge communities. After the meeting, John Stevens from Packwood's staff, Joe Mentor from Evans' staff and Breckel started roughing out a map of the scenic area and its boundaries. Where there was disagreement between Stevens and Mentor, Breckel mediated.

At one point, the three recessed the meeting, went out and bought a half case of beer, and brainstormed. "We speculated on what we could do to make this more palatable" to the gorge counties, Breckel recalled. They came up with the idea of including funding for a conference center in Washington and an interpretive center in Oregon to draw tourists and economic development. When they floated the idea to members of Congress, it won immediate support. This carrot for gorge counties, backed by $5 million in federal subsidies for each project, became one of the few uncontroversial provisions in the final law.

1986

Evans took the lead in crafting a compromise. In February 1986, he introduced a bill that won support from all four senators. But both Evans and Packwood said they viewed the bill as merely a starting point. It divided the gorge into areas to be managed directly by the Forest Service, areas to be managed by the regional commission, and twelve—later to become thirteen—urban areas that would be exempt from any restrictions on development. Controversy quickly erupted over the urban area exemptions. There were questions about why the small rural communities of Corbett and Bridal Veil in Oregon and Underwood and Home Valley in Washington had been excluded.

Responding to pressure from Friends of the Gorge and the Columbia Gorge Coalition, the bill was rewritten to designate portions of the White Salmon and Klickitat rivers as wild and scenic rivers. However, this language provided only illusory protection. Both river segments were bordered by private land, much of it zoned by Klickitat County for development. The only authority the Forest Service could wield to protect the river corridors would be through voluntary land exchanges.

Public hearings on the new draft bill were stormy, especially in Skamania County. U.S. Rep. Sid Morrison, whose district encompassed the proposed Scenic Area lands, was one of the few politicians willing to brave angry crowds in the county. At an April meeting in Stevenson, he was met with shouts and jeers as he explained that the reason he had signed onto a House gorge protection bill was so that he could influence the final legislation. "Political pressures are driving this bill," he said. "I wish I could tell you it's going away, but it's real." County Prosecuting Attorney Leick dismissed Morrison and Senators

Dan Evans and Slade Gorton, who also attended the hearing, as "flimflam people." "What we need and expect is a champion," he said. "What we expect are Wheaties; what we are getting is Frosted Flakes."

Morrison loved the gorge and got there frequently. Yet, in a 2012 interview, he said that Hatfield was always the driver on Scenic Area legislation. "I felt that it was going to happen regardless of what the Washington side thought or wanted, and so my legislative style was to do everything I could to make the process work with as much local involvement as possible."

There was no question that Skamania County would feel the greatest impact from federal legislation, Morrison said. "The folks in Skamania were organized and vocal." County Commissioner Callahan "was a gentleman in opposition to inviting more government than most local folks wanted," he said. "Bob Leick was what an attorney should be, verbally harsh and on the attack. They felt that their congressman could end the perceived threat by screaming loud enough, even though I was more inclined to buy what I could for them by reaching for accord on the best, most flexible package."

He recalled a town hall meeting held at the Rock Creek Grange in Stevenson during this period. It was one in a series he had scheduled to discuss Social Security issues. The anti-scenic area group Columbia Gorge United crashed the event. "Even though I paid to rent the hall, some of the audience insisted on presenting a slide show they had prepared in opposition to the scenic area designation, and I insisted on sharing the latest information on Social Security, which I did while the slide show played out on the front of my white shirt," he recalled. "My guess is that we covered both subjects and were able to laugh about it later."

On Capitol Hill, Morrison's staff worked to influence the process for selecting members of the new regional commission, a key piece of the balancing act. "I want to believe that I helped find a balance that protects the scenic values of the gorge without doing great damage to the folks who own the property and live there," he said.

He strongly favored using the Forest Service, "the most flexible of federal agencies," to administer the scenic area. "My experience with the Park Service was that they were used to ruling with an iron hand." In the end, Morrison would join the majority of the bipartisan delegation in voting for the final bill.

Hatfield took the lead in guiding an amended version of the Evans bill through the Senate and trying to bring the Reagan administration on board. But on the House side, obstacles raised by western Republicans slowed things down and nearly derailed the legislation.

Northwest Democrats introduced three gorge bills in early 1986. One, sponsored by Representatives Jim Weaver of Oregon and Mike Lowry of Washington, was modeled on the Packwood bill. It called for a strong federal role in managing the scenic area. Another, from Representatives Les AuCoin of Oregon and Don Bonker of Washington, attempted to capture the middle ground. A third, introduced by Representatives Ron Wyden and Sid Morrison, contained the weakest standards. For example, it allowed residential development, surface mining, and hydroelectric projects to proceed if those activities did not "substantially impair" gorge resources.

The various bills also differed on the matter of enforcement. The new Senate bill made enforcement of the act's standards and management plan entirely discretionary. Both the AuCoin/Bonker bill and the Weaver/Lowry bill made it mandatory.

The AuCoin-Bonker bill included the clearest and most protective standards. It included a six-month moratorium on development in the Special Management Areas while the Forest Service adopted interim guidelines. Those guidelines would remain in place until the Gorge Commission adopted and the U.S. Secretary of Agriculture approved a formal management plan.

Hearings

The congressional clock was ticking by the time June hearings were held on the House and Senate bills. Nearly one hundred witnesses flew to Washington, D.C., for the June 16, 1986 House hearing; Eighty testified at the Senate hearing the following day.

At the Senate hearing, Packwood was the first witness. He said he doubted that the bill before the Senate Subcommittee on Public Lands would effectively protect the scenery and natural values of the gorge. He called on the committee to amend it to make clear that enforcement of the management plan must be mandatory, not discretionary.

The Reagan administration weighed in at this hearing in opposition to the very premise of the legislation. Peter C. Myers, deputy secretary of agriculture, said the administration opposed the bill's creation of "an overriding federal presence" in the gorge, any imposition of federal authority over private lands, the enforcement of the law through federal fines, and the expenditure of federal funds authorized in the bill.

Bill Benson, the Skamania County commissioner, was in fine form, denouncing "flatland carpetbaggers" and "dilettante nongorge residents and nongorge taxpayers who wish to steal our birthright by making the gorge their scenic playground."

Conservationists, meanwhile, focused their efforts on winning amendments to require mandatory enforcement of the management plan, a high bar for overriding a federal veto of the management plan, and strong interim protection for undeveloped lands.

It was clear that with just ten weeks remaining in the Ninety-ninth Congress, basic disagreements remained to be worked out. On adjournment of the Senate hearing, Evans pleaded with those who were calling for stronger legislation to recognize the concerns of gorge residents who had traveled to Washington, D.C., to testify. "These are not bad people; they are good citizens, good citizens who are frightened about what might happen," he said. He urged lawmakers to find a way to preserve the unique qualities of the gorge while also reassuring its residents that their lands and livelihoods would not be taken from them. Evans also took a dig at those who were spreading "outrageously wrong information" about how people would be affected by the legislation. "They are creating fear where fear should not occur," he said.

The Senate bill cleared the Senate Energy and Natural Resources Committee on a unanimous vote. But on the Senate floor, opposition surfaced from Republicans James McClure of Idaho and Malcolm Wallop of Wyoming. Both opposed federal regulation of private land within the Special Management Area. The bill remained in committee.

Meanwhile, in the House, the Weaver/AuCoin bill ran into a solid wall of opposition, led by Oregon Republicans Bob Smith and Denny Smith. The bill remained bottled up in two House committees. Then House Majority Whip Tom Foley of Washington stepped up. Foley convinced the House Rules Committee to forward the bill to the House floor. He won unanimous support among Washington House members. Bob Smith of Oregon attached an amendment that required one of the gubernatorial appointees in each state to be a gorge resident, to which Foley agreed. The legislation then passed 290-91, with both Smiths still opposed.

The bill then went back to the Senate, where McClure and Wallop still objected; they wanted assurances that the federal government would not use its powers of condemnation to acquire private land. Hatfield, Evans,

and Gorton negotiated a compromise that removed Forest Service jurisdiction over private lands in the Special Management Areas, a significant
weakening of the bill. With that done, the Senate passed the bill on a voice
vote.

Packwood agreed to amend his own more protective Scenic Area bill to
make it more palatable to conservationists and local counties. But schedul-
ing a vote to move the Packwood bill out of committee before the August
recess looked to be impossible. On August 14, Hatfield wielded his power to
win a highly unusual waiver of Senate rules. That afternoon, the committee
voted to move the Packwood bill out. No committee report accompanied
the bill, which had been completed only hours earlier.

On the House side, the machinations were far more complex. Denny
Smith in particular was determined to disrupt the bill's movement out of
committee by any means necessary. On September 23, after the summer
recess, most of the House delegation from Oregon and Washington united
behind a new Scenic Area bill with several strengthening provisions.
Because Congress was preoccupied with passing a major tax overhaul,
it agreed to extend its adjournment from October 3 to October 10, even
though it was an election year and members were anxious to get home and
campaign. The first House subcommittee markup on a gorge bill, in the
House Interior Subcommittee, ran into an ambush. Denny Smith proposed
eighty amendments to the bill. Republican members demanded a quorum
vote on each one.

After three hours, Subcommittee Chair Bruce Vento ended the exercise,
saying it was apparent that because of tactics employed by Republicans,
"the subcommittee will not be able to conclude deliberations." An attempt
by the full Interior Committee to discharge the bill failed as well.

When the subcommittee reconvened on October 7, Denny Smith again
planned to block a vote on the bill by offering his eighty amendments. But
this time he was foiled by House Democrats. Over the previous weekend,
the Democratic leadership had won commitments from enough members
to reach a quorum in favor of discharging the House bill from the subcommittee. Vento moved to do so. Weaver then moved to substitute a five-line
placeholder bill containing no provisions that would be vulnerable to Republican amendments. Later the language in the original bill could be restored. But passing the substitute bill would require a larger quorum of the
subcommittee. A recess was called until 4:00 p.m., when the subcommittee

reconvened. At 4:15 p.m., with no Republicans yet present, Democrats moved Weaver's substitute bill out of committee by unanimous consent.

When Denny Smith appeared and learned of the ploy, he shouted to Subcommittee Chairman John Seiberling, an Ohio Democrat with strong conservationist credentials, "Is this that important to you, to railroad it through like this?" Seiberling retorted, "If you didn't get here, that's tough."

Meanwhile, the House Agriculture Subcommittee discharged the bill with a single amendment, requiring that all of the gorge county appointees and two of the governors' six appointees to the Gorge Commission live within the boundaries of the National Scenic Area.

Congress' adjournment date was again pushed back. The House Agriculture Committee met to consider the bill, but again two Republican members sought to block it. After several quorum calls, Committee Chair Kiki de La Garza, a Texas Democrat, banged down the gavel and adjourned the committee, stating, "It's regrettable that action would get stalled when we're trying to preserve that beautiful area."

The Reagan administration then weighed in with a series of amendments to limit the federal government's control, reduce the cost of the bill, and make other clarifying changes. There was no time to enact such sweeping amendments in the waning days of the Ninety-ninth Congress. Instead, the personal staffs of the Northwest senators and the relevant committees began a series of round-the-clock negotiations to try to resolve the Reagan administration's concerns.

The administration's main objection was straightforward: the federal role should be limited to providing advice to the Gorge Commission. There would be no direct federal control over zoning of private lands. But this view undercut the foundation on which the compromise rested. Without federal authority over the Special Management Areas, which included the most valuable and sensitive lands in the gorge, the coalition supporting federal legislation would collapse. The administration also believed the Forest Service's interim powers, which would remain in effect for several years, were too extensive.

At the last minute yet another compromise was struck—a kind of arm's length weakening of the Forest Service's authority. The Secretary of Agriculture would retain authority over the Special Management Areas, but the Gorge Commission would serve as an intermediary between the federal government and the counties, with authority to override the secretary's interpretation of whether a county's land use ordinance was consistent with the management plan guidelines.

By October 7, the Senate bill had been amended and the Reagan administration had softened its opposition to the latest version. On October 8, Northwest senators rushed to the floor to try to pass the amended version. But because of Senate end-of-session rules, they needed unanimous consent to bring the bill to the floor for a vote.

Hatfield stepped in. Using a procedural rule, he and the other three Northwest senators spent an hour delivering floor speeches that summarized the amendment and stressed the importance of protecting the gorge. The Senate voted in favor of the amendment, with three dissenting votes. But the House failed to muster the votes to bring the amended Senate bill to the House floor.

Congress postponed adjournment to October 14. Sponsors believed they now had the votes on the House floor to pass the bill. Getting it out of committee was the last hurdle. Despite a direct appeal from Hatfield, Rep. Bob Smith refused to budge in his opposition.

The *Wall Street Journal* weighed in at this point, declaring in an editorial that the gorge bill "offhandedly sacrifices people's homes, jobs and communities and casually supersedes elected governments with appointed 'managers' accountable only to Washington, D.C." The U.S. Department of Justice voiced its own concerns, which it said were "fundamental and serious enough to warrant consideration of a veto recommendation from this Department should the Congress now pass the legislation." House members still had to deal with the five-line bill that had passed out of the Interior Subcommittee. But Congress was now two weeks past its adjournment date. Even if a bill should emerge from the full House Interior Committee, it faced an all-out battle on the House floor.

At this point Vento, the House Agriculture Committee chair, raised a series of relatively minor changes to the bill before his committee, eating up precious time. During the few remaining days until adjournment, no more bills could be moved to the House floor without a two-thirds vote. Only the House Rules Committee could allow a vote on the new version addressing Vento's concerns. But the Rules Committee was not scheduled to meet during the final week.

On the morning of October 14, Weaver set a hearing on the bill before the Rules Committee. He sought to limit debate on the bill and prohibit amendments to it. Bob Smith objected, saying he had ten amendments he wanted to submit for debate. Weaver's proposed rule was defeated, and he pronounced chances of the bill's passage nil. After four years of congressional effort and months of intense negotiations, the Scenic Area Act appeared dead.

But hours later, AuCoin, Bonker, and Wyden rounded up Rules Committee members and asked them to reconsider. At that point, House Majority Whip Foley saw an opening. He intervened directly with Rep. Claude Pepper, the Florida Democrat who chaired the Rules Committee. House rules required a legislative day to elapse between issuance of a rule and debate on that rule. Two days remained. Foley asked Pepper to schedule a Rules Committee meeting at midnight, which would technically allow debate on the second-to-last day of the session.

Bowen Blair, who was present, described the midnight meeting in a law review article as "explosive." The three Republican opponents, Bob Smith, Denny Smith, and Rep. Ron Marlenee, stomped out of the room after being denied a chance to present their amendments. At 1:00 a.m. the Democrats mustered a majority to approve Weaver's rule.

Later that day, the House met for four hours to consider the rule. "Raucous debate ensued," Blair wrote. "Opponents emphasized, often vitriolically, the bill's failure to pass cleanly through committee, its controversial provisions regarding federal authority over private lands, costs, and the resistance of gorge residents."

Proponents emphasized the bill's widespread grassroots and political support. They pointed out that Bob Smith and Denny Smith were the only Northwest House members to oppose the bill, that it was the product of years of compromise, and that the unorthodox committee process was the fault of conservative Republicans' "dilatory tactics.'" The rule passed 252-138.

After Bob Smith presented three amendments, one of which was adopted, the act itself passed the House on a final vote of 290-91.

Hatfield brought the amended bill back to the Senate floor on October 17, the last full day of the Ninety-ninth Congress. After some discussion, a vote was called for. The Columbia River Gorge National Scenic Area Act passed unanimously.

At the news, the American flag at the Skamania County Courthouse was lowered to half-staff for a week. But the battle was not yet won.

Reagan's Call

Supporters hoped Reagan would sign the bill before the November 4 general election in an attempt to help fellow Republican Slade Gorton win reelection. But the bill did not reach the President's desk until November 5. Because Congress had adjourned, Reagan would have to sign the bill by midnight, November 17, or it would die of a pocket veto.

The signs were ominous. The bill still faced stiff opposition from within the Reagan administration. Reagan's Interior Secretary, Don Hodel, opposed it and advised the president not to sign it. Attorney General Edwin Meese declared it unconstitutional. The Office of Management and Budget also recommended a presidential veto. Only the Department of Agriculture, which oversees the Forest Service, recommended approval. Gorge residents launched a mail campaign urging a veto.

It was now up to Hatfield to persuade President Reagan to sign the bill. In the days leading up to November 17, he met with the president on almost a daily basis. Though he did not speak publicly of their conversations, rumors circulated that the powerful Senate Appropriations Committee chair at one point asked Reagan how badly he wanted Congress to fund his Strategic Defense Initiative, better known as "Star Wars." In the press Linda Keene, a reporter for States News Service, was one of the few to report the rumor, which Hatfield never confirmed or denied.

On November 17, hours before the Scenic Area Act was to expire, and with one hand holding his nose, Reagan signed the Scenic Area Act. In his signing statement, he expressed concern that the law "could lead to undue federal intervention in local land use decisions" and expressed "grave doubts" as to its constitutionality. "I believe that the regulation of private land use is generally not a responsibility of federal government," he wrote. "While I am strongly opposed to federal regulation of private land use planning, I am signing this bill because of the far-reaching support in both states for a solution to the longstanding problems related to management of the Columbia River Gorge."

The Columbia River Gorge National Scenic Area Act truly was a balancing act. It gave the Forest Service, the states of Washington and Oregon and the six counties bordering the gorge a shared role in managing 282,000 acres of public and private land. The Forest Service would manage public lands in the four highly visible Special Management Areas, located primarily in the western gorge, and would write land use regulations for those areas. Development of the remaining lands, except those within the thirteen urban areas, would be governed by a bistate commission, made up of twelve voting members, with three appointed by each governor and one appointed by each of the six gorge counties. A Forest Service official would serve as a non-voting member.

The commission would be required to write a land use plan protecting the gorge's scenic, natural, cultural, and recreational values. The plan would prohibit new industrial and most commercial development in the rural gorge, outside urban areas, and would strictly limit residential development, especially in the Special Management Areas.

The bill authorized money for land acquisition, recreation and economic development: $40 million for Forest Service land purchases; $2 million to offset lost tax revenue to local governments; $10 million for economic development projects in the two states; $5 million each for a convention center in Washington and an interpretive center in Oregon; $10 million for construction of recreation facilities by the Forest Service; and $2.8 million to restore abandoned sections of the Historical Columbia River Highway as a hiking and cycling trail.

To provide the legal authority for state involvement, the Oregon and Washington legislatures would be required to sign a bistate compact directing their agencies to carry out their respective functions in accordance with the Scenic Area Act. And, in a decision that would give legislative opponents outsized clout, the Gorge Commission's operating budget would come entirely from state appropriations, divided equally between the two states.

The stage was set for a titanic land use battle. A great experiment in uncharted legal territory was about to commence.

Part II
THE LAUNCH

Mouth of the Klickitat River in December. Photo by Darryl Lloyd.

Chapter 5
Writing the Rules

The job of launching the new Columbia River Gorge National Scenic Area fell to the U.S. Forest Service. It was not a task for the faint-hearted. In early December 1986, days after the act was signed into law, Forest Service Chief Max Peterson visited Portland. He predicted that tourism would blossom and property values would soar as the new Scenic Area designation brought national recognition to the gorge. But he stressed that his first job, even before implementation of the act began, would be to ease the fears of gorge residents. Outsiders must recognize that local residents have a "very legitimate concern about their need to keep the gorge commercially viable," Peterson said. "It's going to require that people on both sides put aside past fights and move forward." He predicted that the effort to protect scenic values without hurting the local economy would be "a real test of cooperation."

The Scenic Area would not be a national park or a wilderness area, yet Peterson said he'd already heard one newscaster declare that the federal government would acquire all the land in the gorge and move all the people out. Within weeks, the Forest Service began getting inquiries from property owners interested in selling their land to the federal government. Most of these offers came from people whose land lay within the Special Management Areas, where the minimum lot size was 40 acres. They could not build houses on their land. But the agency had no money yet to purchase it.

"Those folks, in my view, are between a rock and a hard spot," said Forest Service official Gene Zimmerman. "I don't know what alternative they have except maybe to buy some of their neighbors' land to get up to 40 acres."

Art DuFault, a twenty-five-year Forest Service veteran, was named the first Scenic Area manager. In January 1987, he and a small staff moved into offices in downtown Hood River, Oregon. They had just six months to complete their first assignment: writing interim guidelines to help them evaluate proposals for new development in the gorge. Hundreds of applications were in the pipeline.

Jurgen Hess was among the first Forest Service employees to move to the gorge. He and his wife arrived from Medford, Oregon, in December 1986. He helped set up the Hood River office and became the Scenic Area's landscape architect. The political climate was volatile. "It was a firestorm, especially on the Washington side," Hess recalled. "We had bomb threats at our office. We told our staff after meetings to check their vehicles. There was so much animosity and vitriol, it was kind of scary. We coached our employees to be careful, to listen to people's concerns. We had a job to do. We needed to explain the Scenic Area Act."

Columbia Gorge United, the property rights group formed to fight the act, was "beating the war drums, warning of condemnation," Hess recalled. "There was so much fear about condemnation. We said, 'We are not going to be using condemnation.'" Still, Forest Service employees were faced with making decisions that would affect the use of private property, an unfamiliar and uncomfortable role for an agency accustomed to administering the federal timber sale program in the Pacific Northwest.

The cultural shift was not easy, Hess recalled, especially when it required him to say no to people who had invested years and money in dreams of building a home in the gorge. He remembered meeting with "a big guy from Multnomah County, who explained the work he had done on his house. He broke down and cried. He came back later and said, 'I haven't done that since I was in Vietnam.'"

In the first year, staffers reviewed a backlog of about 500 residential building permits. They conducted a vested rights analysis on each one to determine how much the property owner had invested and whether construction could proceed under the interim rules. If someone's proposed development didn't meet the test, Hess said, "we sent them to see about the Forest Service purchasing their land."

Line staff members working in the Scenic Area office got no direction from Portland or Washington, D.C., Hess said. They were on their own. "The regional office, the national office, didn't really know how to guide us. We talked to congressional staff members, to Friends of the Gorge, to the counties. We asked, 'What's your take on the situation?' We had to work hard to understand the landscape, the communities."

Key staff members were required to live within the Scenic Area. Not all of Hess's colleagues were comfortable with the rule. "We had everybody watching over our shoulders. We had Friends of the Gorge, the *Oregonian*, county commissioners, local people. I couldn't walk into a grocery store without someone saying, 'I want to talk to you about my house.'"

During the early months, Hess discussed the challenges of establishing the scenic area with Russell Dickinson, director of the National Park Service, who told him his agency had not wanted the job. "It was going to be extremely controversial and we were glad to have the Forest Service do it," Dickinson told him. Despite those challenges, Hess grew to love the job and the gorge. "There were times I'd go to the top of Dog Mountain and ask myself, 'What am I doing here?' Then I'd come down and get back to work."

Gorge property owners began feeling the impact of the new law within weeks. Those hoping to build in the Special Management Areas were desperate to learn whether they could proceed. There were winners and losers in this early lottery. To many gorge residents, the decisions the Forest Service made seemed arbitrary.

Mike Parkins owned 28 acres, including 12 acres in an SMA about three miles north of the town of Skamania. He'd paid $18,000 for the property in 1985 and hoped to build an A-frame house on it. When he learned he couldn't build, he applied for a permit to put a double-wide mobile home on the lot. But he was told the 40-acre minimum lot size applied to mobile homes, too.

Terrance Wasinger had a 40-acre lot in an SMA on which he hoped to build an airstrip, a restaurant, a small lodge, and a recreational vehicle camp. The Forest Service found his plan "inconsistent" with the intent of the law. But because Wasinger had obtained a building permit just weeks before the act was signed into law, his project was grandfathered in.

Leanna Herndon owned four acres in a SMA in Multnomah County, east of the Sandy River. She had hoped to build there, next to her parents' house. But the 40-acre-minimum lot size ruled that out.

Jim Gentry had six wooded acres northeast of Cape Horn in Skamania County, where he had planned to build a house for his family. But the boundary of the National Scenic Area ran right through his property. Part of it was outside the Scenic Area; the rest was in the SMA. No one had an immediate answer to his dilemma.

By February 1987, the Forest Service had received seventy-seven in-quiries from land owners offering to sell a total of 3,200 acres. Once money began flowing from Congress, the agency tried to accommodate just about everyone who walked in the door—even if it made no sense for the federal government to acquire specific patches of land. Under the Scenic Area Act, the agency also was allowed to grant hardship exemptions in cases where health or economic issues made it necessary for landowners to sell immediately.

"Whoever had land in the SMA could get it purchased immediately, and at its current value," said Michael Lang, conservation director for Friends of the Columbia Gorge. The hardship provision remained until the Gorge Commission adopted a management plan for the Scenic Area. "It relieved a lot of tension among landowners," Lang said. "It kept the temperature down in the gorge."

Residential development wasn't the only issue percolating in the early months. Near North Bonneville, a Port of Skamania commissioner proposed to mine for gold on 40 acres, a project that would involve hauling sand and gravel near the Columbia River. The advisory state Gorge Commissions, soon to disband, asked the Washington Department of Natural Resources to study the project's impact on noise, dust, water quality, and the supply of water to a nearby hot spring. Nancy Russell took a harder line, calling the proposal "absolutely incompatible with the goals of the National Sce-nic Area." She vowed that Friends would fight the gold mine. The project eventually was abandoned.

As the Forest Service scrambled to deal with a crush of issues, the two state legislatures faced a November 1987 deadline for approving the bistate compact that would give the Scenic Area Act the official stamp of approval under state law. With bipartisan ambivalence, both states met the deadline. The alternative—handing the entire Scenic Area over to the Forest Service to manage, thereby disrupting the delicate balance of local and federal decision-making that had been so carefully written into the act—was unacceptable.

If federal control was the stick, money for economic development (in-cluding a conference center in Washington and an interpretive center in Oregon) was the carrot that got the states to sign on. There was no wiggle room; under the act, the states had to approve identical language in order for the compact to be legally valid. Also, they had to make identical biennial appropriations to fund the Gorge Commission. If one state budgeted less than the other, the Gorge Commission would get the lesser amount.

The siting of the Forest Service National Scenic Area office was an early issue. Should it be in Hood River, where the agency had temporary offices, or across the river in Washington? Despite their unshakeable opposition to the new law, Skamania County officials actively courted the Forest Service and its payroll. "We've had a change of heart and we'll milk it for everything we can get out of it," quipped County Commissioner Bill Benson.

"Now that we have a law, we're not lawbreakers," agreed County Commissioner Ed Callahan. It made sense to base the Forest Service in Skamania County, he said, because that's where 99 percent of its work would be done.

Cities and port commissions up and down the gorge were wooing the agency too, but the Forest Service elected to stay put in Hood River. It faced the urgent task of developing interim guidelines that would govern development applications in the Scenic Area until a new Columbia River Gorge Commission adopted a formal management plan. Those guidelines would remain in place for nearly five years.

A twelve-member team was appointed to draw up the Forest Service's interim guidelines. Agency planners from Idaho's Sawtooth National Recreation Area and California's Mono Lake Basin were enlisted in the effort, along with local planners.

Disagreement quickly surfaced over how specific the guidelines should be. Local planners argued for very specific guidelines to back up case-by-case decisions on development proposals. Without specific rules, they warned, the Forest Service and Gorge Commission would have to justify each land use decision on its merits.

Initially, Forest Service planners were uncomfortable with this by-the-book approach. They were used to managing the national forests under a multiple-use mandate and exercising broad discretion in allocating resources on public land. They had limited experience regulating private land. Eventually, they adopted the local planners' view. They submitted detailed, specific guidelines to Forest Service headquarters in Washington, D.C.

But those standards hit a wall at the U.S. Department of Agriculture, the Forest Service's parent agency. Reagan administration officials were loathe to see the federal government control private land use, even on an interim basis. Reagan officials also feared that detailed, highly specific guidelines would produce a rash of nonconforming uses, forcing the agency to reject permits, and generating pressure to condemn land. They rejected the planners' work and demanded that all specifics be eliminated from the Scenic Area guidelines.

When the Forest Service released its draft interim guidelines in April 1987, it was obvious they had been extensively rewritten. All sides criticized them for lacking critical detail. Friends sent the Forest Service a thirty-seven-page response to its eight pages of guidelines. The governors and members of the Northwest congressional delegation also objected.

Bowen Blair, executive director of Friends of the Gorge, warned that the lack of specifics "makes it highly unlikely that counties will incorporate the guidelines into their zoning ordinances," or that the gorge would be adequately protected during the interim period until a detailed management plan was in place.

Reagan administration officials did an about-face. In July, the Forest Service returned with a set of specific guidelines for managing land use in the gorge. The new guidelines identified twenty-two key viewing areas from which the scenery of the gorge would be protected, twice the number in the initial draft. They called for developments not to "detract from or impair views from key viewing areas" or to break the skyline.

Still, Blair and Jeff Breckel, who was now serving as acting executive director of the Gorge Commission, had reservations. They argued that the guidelines would allow the Forest Service to take a pass on controversial land use decisions, essentially abdicating most of its responsibility and leaving the Gorge Commission to review proposals for surface mining, commercial development, land subdivisions, and other hot-button issues. The interim guidelines would leave the Gorge Commission with 95 percent of the work and a much smaller staff than the Forest Service to accomplish it, Blair agreed. As a result, he warned, the commission might not be able to give development proposals more than a cursory review.

Blair also announced that the role of the Friends of the Gorge would be shifting as well, to that of an aggressive watchdog. More than 250 development proposals had been brought before the Forest Service in the first six months, and all but seventeen of them had been approved. Friends would have to monitor future development proposals closely to determine whether they complied with the standards, Blair said. In some cases, the organization would have to sue. In fact, litigation already was proving to be Friends' most potent weapon. The organization had brought lawsuits to block George Rizor's Riverfront Estates subdivision across from Multnomah Falls; to kill the proposed Hidden Harbor subdivision and a private marina downriver from Beacon Rock State Park; and to open Wells Island, in the Columbia River near Hood River, to commercial development. In each case, Friends ultimately prevailed. "Eternal vigilance is truly required if the timeless scenic, natural, cultural, and recreational values of the Columbia River Gorge are to be preserved for ourselves and for future generations," Blair declared.

As the wheels of the new bureaucracy began to turn, the Columbia Gorge Coalition closed its office, citing financial distress. Coalition founder Chuck Williams was furious over stepped-up logging in the National Scenic Area that had begun in 1987, with the ink barely dry on the Scenic Area Act.

In early 1987, the governors of Oregon and Washington and the six counties began making their appointments to the Gorge Commission. In June, the panel held its first meeting, though two of its twelve members, from Multnomah and Clark counties, had yet to be appointed.

Friends had been busy recruiting candidates who would support the act's mission. According to Blair, that wasn't a problem in Portland. "But we didn't have any clout in Skamania or Klickitat counties, and only a little in Wasco County."

The new Gorge Commission's role would be to make tough decisions. But the commission represented views and backgrounds as diverse as the gorge itself. Oregon Gov. Neil Goldschmidt appointed three strong advocates of land use regulation: Wasco County orchardist Barbara Bailey, former Multnomah County Executive Don Clark, and former state legislator Stafford Hansell, an eastern Oregon farmer widely regarded as the father of Oregon's land use laws. Hansell was elected the first chairman. Washington Gov. Booth Gardner appointed Dave Cannard, a Vancouver insurance agent who had served as co-chairman of Friends of the Gorge; retired university professor and urban planner Stuart Chapin of White Salmon, and Gail Rothrock of Vancouver, a former member of the Washington State Shorelines Hearing Board.

At the county level, appointments were even more diverse. Clark County appointed businessman Bob Thompson. Skamania County chose

Nancy Sourek, director of the county's emergency management program. Klickitat County picked Pat Bleakney, a cattle rancher and former county commissioner who opposed the National Scenic Area Act.

Joyce Reinig, a nurse and a member of the Hood River planning board, represented Hood River. Wasco County appointed former county commissioner Ray Matthew. Multnomah County appointed attorney Kristine Olson Rogers, a specialist in cultural resource law and Native American issues, who would later become U.S. attorney for Oregon.

Nancy Russell lobbied for a seat on the commission, but Multnomah County commissioners declined to support her after they received a letter signed by 250 gorge residents who said they feared she would give little consideration to the economic health of their communities. Reinig, who became the longest-serving commissioner, called the diversity of the new commission a good thing. "A lot of commissioners at the beginning were from outside the gorge and had a national perspective. I wanted them to know that we had 50,000 people in the gorge and their voices and concerns needed to be represented, too."

As the commission began hiring staff and searching for an office, it too faced the question of where to locate. Should it move into the Forest Service office complex in Hood River to allow for close coordination and communication? Or put down stakes across the river in Washington, to underscore the bistate role in managing the Scenic Area? Don Clark favored a Washington site for what he called "some very valid political reasons." Chairman Stafford Hansell said the commission and the Forest Service should be "close but separate." Eventually, the commission found offices in White Salmon, across the bridge from Hood River.

In the summer of 1987, as the machinery of the National Scenic Area Act began to gear up, Friends of the Gorge celebrated the passage of the Scenic Area Act with a big party at the Shire, John Yeon's riverfront estate on the Washington shore. Friends publicized the soiree in its newsletter with an illustration depicting French post-impressionist artist Georges Seurat's famous painting "Sunday Afternoon on the Island of La Grande Jatte."

Members were encouraged to "Bring your family and friends to our annual Bring-Your-Own-Picnic at John Yeon's gorgeous nature preserve facing Multnomah Falls....There's a lovely bay to swim in, broad lawns to lounge on, a mile of riverfront to explore, birds to watch, and a view of the Oregon cliffs across the river that you'll never forget."

There was cause for celebration. But organizers also appeared tone-deaf to the message they were communicating. Living in a place like the Shire was a dream many who loved the gorge had nurtured. That dream, for all but a wealthy and lucky few, was now out of reach.

The Gorge Commission took charge and immediately launched a search for an executive director. In September 1987 the commission chose Richard Benner, a Portland land use attorney who headed 1000 Friends of Oregon, a statewide watchdog group that worked to enforce Oregon's strict land use law. Benner advocated strict enforcement of the interim guidelines in the gorge. He, rather than the commissioners, would become the lightning rod for complaints about the new rules.

Benner was no stranger to controversy. Legal challenges of Oregon's pioneering land use law had begun in 1974 and continued until 1982. Oregon's land use wars had prepared him, at least in part, for defending the Scenic Area Act. One of the state's most astute land use attorneys, Benner understood that his task was to help the Gorge Commission implement the law, hire a staff, and write a budget. The commission would not have the final word on implementing the law, however; that would fall to the courts.

In a 1997 interview long after he had left the Gorge Commission, Benner conceded that he was probably the wrong person to build local cooperation in the gorge. "We had to communicate that Congress meant what it said in the act. When Congress said, 'Protect agricultural lands,' it meant that. It didn't mean give up half of it. It said the same thing for forest land, cultural resources and scenic resources. The commission felt very strongly that it had to send a signal that this is a national scenic area, Congress has enacted legislation, and the act means what it says."

In Oregon, where residents had been living under strict land use laws for fifteen years, that wasn't difficult. But Washington had no such laws. In Washington, the Scenic Area Act triggered culture shock. And Benner's decision to live in Portland and commute to White Salmon, a daily two-hour round trip, meant he remained somewhat distant from the concerns of gorge residents.

By December 1987, the Gorge Commission was ready to assume responsibility from the Forest Service for carrying out the interim guidelines.

Bowen Blair of Friends of the Gorge continued to have misgivings. "If development continues at the rate of the past eleven months, the impact on the gorge would be devastating," he said. "At the very least, key areas of the gorge will have been lost forever before the management plan and implementing ordinances are even adopted."

Forest Service officials countered that they had justifiably treated all development proposals approved by gorge counties prior to the act's passage as vested. They believed the federal government had no power to reverse the counties' actions.

Benner walked into the regulatory environment the Forest Service had created. His job would be to apply its guidelines to address a swarm of controversial development proposals. Benner and Forest Service Scenic Area Manager Art DuFault faced some high-profile decisions right off the bat. In September 1987, DuFault confronted the touchy issue of gravel mines and rock pits in the Special Management Areas. Stevenson Co-Ply, a worker-owned mill in Stevenson, had for years been mining rock from the base of Wind Mountain along Highway 14 just east of Home Valley, and hauling it to log yards in Home Valley and Stevenson. The rock was prized because it came out of the mountain in fractured chunks that could be spread on pavement without further crushing.

But pulling rock from the bottom of Wind Mountain had caused the south slope to cascade down on itself, creating a scar that could be seen for miles. One Forest Service official called it "the most visible gravel use site in the gorge." Rock pits had long been a blemish on the face of the gorge. DuFault told the company that hauling rock from the mountain was inconsistent with the act, which prohibited surface mining in SMAs unless the rock was to be used for logging road construction nearby. He said the law would likely shut down many existing rock pits.

DuFault proposed a compromise that would involve locating another source of rock for the mill. But Skamania County Commissioner Ed Callahan said the ruling endangered expansion plans for the plywood company. "It's a matter of jobs compared to what some people perceive as scenic," he said. "One or two little rock pits ought to be left alone." The Gorge Commission prevailed.

Also in September, DuFault told Klickitat County commissioners they would have to close a county landfill because the use conflicted with the Scenic Area Act. The county had hoped to attract large amounts of garbage from Clark County to the 80-acre dump. Ironically, the county was leasing the landfill property from rancher Pat Bleakney, Klickitat County's appointee to the Gorge Commission. Bleakney was incredulous when Benner informed him the landfill would have to go.

The city of Washougal, at the west end of the gorge, had its hopes pinned on Gates of the Gorge, a woodland subdivision northeast of the city limits. City leaders hoped to persuade Congress to move the scenic area boundary to let the city expand. Several meetings ensued between the city and the Gorge Commission about the complexities of moving the boundary. "The bottom line was that the urban area boundaries and the National Scenic Area boundaries were determined by Congress," Benner said. "It took them a long time to understand that." Asking Congress to reopen debate on the act could open the floodgates to other proposed changes and provoke a congressional backlash, he warned.

During debate on the Scenic Area Act, some people had advocated letting the Forest Service draw boundaries to correspond to watersheds or other geological features rather than leave the boundary decisions to Congress. That would have been an unworkable process, Benner maintained, because the Forest Service never would have been able to reach consensus on what was ultimately a political decision. "We might not have a Gorge Commission today if Congress had not set the boundaries," he said.

Even his extensive experience in land use law did not prepare Benner for how difficult it would be to direct a bistate commission. He had to explain the bistate compact to legislators. He had to try to persuade the states, particularly Washington, to adequately support the Gorge Commission budget. Some lawmakers just didn't get it. "I was two months into the job when I got a call from state Sen. Dean Sutherland," Benner recalled. "He said, 'Can you stop by?' He looked me in the eye and said, 'Make sure it doesn't get controversial.'" Benner laughed, but Sutherland wasn't joking. Benner told him, "We'll do our best, we'll listen, but ultimately we will have to make decisions. It's going to be highly controversial."

Yet as the Gorge Commission and its staff set about writing a management plan for the Scenic Area, an amazing thing began to happen. The commissioners—ranchers, environmentalists, business owners, and local gorge officials—came together to create something brand new: A blueprint for managing more than 280,000 acres of public and private land in the nation's first national scenic area.

Don Clark was pleasantly surprised. "Some of those people were appointed because they were opposed to the Scenic Area Act," he recalled. "As it turned out, this group of people, even those on the Washington side who were not supportive, sat down and started liking each other and respecting each other. They were still able to argue their positions, but they didn't make it personal." Benner was key to bringing the commissioners together, Clark said. "He was very professional. He was staff and he had to carry out the mandates of the Gorge Commission."

Writing the management plan was very much a hands-on exercise. Gorge Commissioners were assigned to committees tasked with writing the various sections dealing with scenery, recreation, economic development, forestry, agriculture, and more. The committees met twice a month for four years in sessions staffed by Benner and his three planners. "It was an incredible commitment of time," Benner said. "No sooner would we be done with one meeting than we began planning for the next one. There was a great deal of commitment and it lasted for a period of time. Until the plan was adopted, nobody peeled off, nobody left. None of my staff left. I had never been through anything so intense." Only after the plan was adopted, Benner said, did local governments start reacting to it in the appointments they made to the Gorge Commission.

Bleakney, the Klickitat County rancher, "was among the people who grew in vision over the four years," Benner said. Even though the Gorge Commission's decision to close the Klickitat County landfill had hit close to home, Bleakney came to support the act wholeheartedly, Benner said.

Protection of archaeological resources was a legally complicated and politically fraught issue for the Gorge Commission. Because Benner was not well-versed in tribal and cultural resource law, Commissioner Kristine Olson Rogers took the lead. But Benner soon got on-the-job training.

"We got an application from a guy from California who was proposing a campground adjacent to Horsethief Lake," Benner said. The area was rich in Indian petroglyphs and pictographs. The interim guidelines required Benner to notify the four treaty tribes. "We got a letter from the Yakama Tribe saying, 'We have resources, so you have to deny the application.' I told them, 'There have to be specific descriptions of the resources.' They said,

'Of course there's evidence, but we're not going to give it to you because we don't trust you or any other white person to protect these resources.'"

Benner asked staff attorney Larry Watters to research the issue. Watters came back with a recommendation that the Gorge Commission hold a public hearing to discuss the application and then go into executive session to let tribal leaders present their site-specific evidence that cultural sites and artifacts would be disturbed by development of a private campground. Yakama tribal leaders agreed to the plan and agreed to show Benner and Watters the site.

The two drove up Dalles Mountain Road to the proposed campground site. The tribal elders were waiting. "It's a wonderful spot, a wetland, with a high point where Indians did their vision quests," Benner recalled. "There was a rock outcrop that was sacred, with wild foods they gathered every spring." The tribal leaders started speaking, Benner said—in their traditional language of Sahaptin. "I didn't understand them. I asked them to speak English, but they refused." Later tribal chiefs agreed to submit their report in writing.

They must have been persuasive. Benner considered the evidence and denied the permit. The California developer demanded more information. With permission from tribal leaders, Benner provided the full report. Soon after, the developer called Benner to let him know he was withdrawing his application.

Benner also was unschooled in the complexities of the federal government's treaty relationships with Columbia Basin tribes, and with the tribes' governing structures. One day Johnny Jackson, a member of the Klickitat Band of the Yakama Nation, arrived unannounced at a Gorge Commission meeting to educate him. Jackson was a river Indian. He lived and fished at a traditional site near the mouth of the Klickitat River, far from the Yakama Reservation. He spoke without notes. "He just spoke to the Gorge Commission for thirty-five minutes straight," Benner recalled. "He spoke of thousands and thousands of ways that white people have violated their treaty rights. He said, 'We have rights in those treaties, to the sacred lands.'" Jackson also made it clear that he did not speak for the Yakama Tribe. Some river Indians were affiliated with the Yakama, some with the Confederated Tribes of Warm Springs, he said, but those were arbitrary decisions made by white men. "I am affiliated with the Yakama, but not because that was my decision."

Benner and the commissioners encouraged Jackson and other tribal leaders to come to their meetings and serve on their committees. But tribal government offices were distant from the Gorge Commission headquarters in White Salmon. Participation was an expense they could not afford. "We have a staff of three," one Yakama leader told Benner. "We are dealing with Hanford," the federal nuclear site in Eastern Washington. "We are trying to protect the water. We have many obligations. Now that we have a new one, you had better pay us to participate." Benner and the Gorge Commission took the issue to the Forest Service, which won a congressional appropriation of $100,000 a year, $25,000 for each tribe, to help the tribes cover the cost of participating in National Scenic Area issues.

Building trust between the Gorge Commission and the tribes was essential if the commission was to fulfill one of the goals of the management plan: developing an inventory of Native American cultural sites in the gorge so that the commission could protect them as it considered development proposals.

But at times the tribes themselves were less than cooperative, as Louie Pitt Jr., a Gorge Commissioner and an official with the Confederated Tribes of Warm Springs, acknowledged at a commission meeting in 2000. Treaty tribes could do a better job of helping strengthen protection for hundreds of cultural sites within the Scenic Area that were vulnerable to development, he said. "We're trying to get the tribes back on board. They are key players. I'm wondering, where are the people who give a damn about these resources? They really need to step up their efforts."

As the Gorge Commission geared up "to bite into meaty things," in Benner's words, there was a period during which people would show up at commission meetings with all kinds of ambitious ideas about what the panel should do "People would come in and talk about tourist trains coming through the gorge, or a shuttle service." One group came to testify about the need to preserve rare oak forests. Wildflower expert Russ Jolley offered to tell the commissioners where the best gorge wildflowers were.

Carried away by all this enthusiasm, Gorge Commissioners decided they needed a logo to put on stationery and publications. Some suggested that Tsagaglalal, the iconic petroglyph of a woman's face carved into a basalt boulder near Horsethief Lake, should be that logo.

Benner felt the commission had enough on its plate. Nonetheless, he had a rendition of the image drawn up. To his surprise, "Out of the blue came a letter from the Skamania County Historical Society, addressed to the Gorge Commission. They said they had filed for copyright on the image." Though Tsagaglalal was located in Klickitat County, the Skamania County Historical Society had taken the audacious step of establishing it as a trademark to promote a $9 million interpretive center in Skamania County. Already, the image, widely known as "She Who Watches," was appearing on the society's stationery, tee-shirts, and bibs. The county's centennial committee also had its eye on Tsagaglalal to mark its upcoming celebration.

Bennett called Kristine Olson Rogers. "She blew her stack," he recalled. "She said, 'This is outrageous. If anyone has a copyright on She Who Watches, it's the Yakama Nation.'"

Commission Chair Stafford Hansell and Commissioners Kristine Olson Rogers and Bob Thompson arranged to meet with Skamania County Commissioner Ed Callahan and Prosecuting Attorney Bob Leick over the matter. Also present was Sharon Tiffany, director of the proposed new interpretive center. (Skamania County had quietly appropriated the name; under the Scenic Area Act, the Columbia Gorge Interpretive Center was to be built in Oregon.) "The hope was that we could work this out," Benner said. "But this was a meeting I dreaded."

The Skamania County representatives started the meeting by demanding to know, "Why did you choose 'She Who Watches'?" Thompson, the Gorge Commissioner from Clark County, began to diplomatically explain that from time immemorial, according to Native American legend, "She Who Watches" had looked out over the gorge and protected it. In passing the National Scenic Area Act, he said, Congress had asked the Gorge Commission to take on that mantle of protector.

"If you think you're taking over the gorge now, why don't you put your face on the logo?" Leick demanded.

Upon which Chairman Hansell said, "You know, I think this meeting is over."

A few months later, the Gorge Commission decided it had more important matters on its plate than to fight this particular battle. After due consultation with the Yakama Tribe, it chose instead to use the image of Spedis owl, a well-known pictograph found at sites throughout the gorge.

Under the Scenic Area Act, the Gorge Commission was supposed to produce a management plan by 1990. But one distraction after another delayed the process. In public hearings on the plan, some interest groups demanded things that were far outside the authority of the commission to provide. The fast-growing Hood River-based windsurfing community wanted the Gorge Commission to go to the railroads and demand that they provide better access to the river. Benner inquired of Union Pacific, owner of the tracks on the Oregon side, whether it would be willing to provide an overpass or underpass. He quickly learned that the Gorge Commission was no match for the railroad. "It was a slammed door," he said.

Resolving appeals of decisions made by the Forest Service years before was time-consuming. After a couple of years, some Gorge Commissioners asked Benner to develop a plan that would allow them to spend less time on appeals. Benner and his staff came back with a suggestion that a subcommittee handle appeals so the full commission could devote all its time to writing the management plan. "The Gorge Commission discussed the idea, but ultimately they decided against it," Benner recalled. "They said, 'We need to understand that these rules are going to affect people and their property. We are learning a lot. As much as we hate it, we think we should continue to hear these appeals.'" And so they did.

Meanwhile, communities on both sides of the river began gearing up to compete for the big chunk of federal money that was on the table: $5 million for a conference center on the Washington side, and $5 million for a museum or interpretive center on the Oregon side.

In January 1988, county commissioners met with Benner and his staff to learn about the process the Gorge Commission would follow in choosing the sites. The goal was to select both sites by the end of the year. "We decided to start with the Interpretive Center because everyone knows what an interpretive center is," Benner said. Every national park and national monument has a center where visitors can obtain maps and learn about the history and features of special places set aside by Congress.

A conference center, on the other hand, required investment by the private sector, and neither the Forest Service nor the Gorge Commission had experience in developing such a facility. Benner invited several experts to visit the gorge and led them on tours. "They said, 'We advise you against doing a conference center unless you do it at the west end. You're not going to get people to drive 50 miles in the gorge to go to a conference."

Each of the three Oregon counties was invited to develop a proposal for an interpretive center. Competition was intense. Initially, Oregon proposed thirty-nine sites. Multnomah County did not have a practical site to recommend. Hood River County offered a stunning location, a slope directly across the river from Coyote Wall in Klickitat County. What killed it, Benner said, was opposition from The Nature Conservancy. "They said, 'This is one of the jewels of the gorge.'" Also, the site was isolated, with limited access to Hood River in case of a fire or other catastrophe.

That left the Wasco County site, a former cement plant at Crate's Point, a promontory a few miles west of The Dalles. "We had a theory it would bring people deeper into the gorge," Benner said.

The Columbia Gorge Discovery Center, which also incorporated a Wasco County museum, was architecturally striking. It was situated on a 54-acre site that included walking trails, a pond, scenic overlooks, and one of the oldest continuously occupied areas in North America. It eventually won a prestigious American Institute of Architects Honor Award for its design. But it would not succeed in attracting large numbers of tourists. It did not pass the Rule of Ten, Benner said. "If you want to attract tourists to a place, you have to offer at least ten nearby destinations. The Dalles didn't have that."

On the Washington side, Clark County's Washougal made a pitch for a large conference center, but the contest soon narrowed to one pitting Skamania County against Klickitat County.

Early on, Benner conferred with John Gray, the Portland developer of two of Oregon's most handsome and best-known resorts, Salishan on the Oregon Coast and Sunriver south of Bend, in the shadow of the Cascade Range. Benner took Gray to the Skamania County site, a boggy open area surrounded by forests. Gray initially told him, "I'm not interested in this project." The developer stressed that a substantial investment in the gorge was really risky. For one thing, Skamania County was wet, with an average annual rainfall of 69 inches. Gray told Benner, "I think you could make it go as a resort, but if you do it, I recommend you do it in conjunction with a hotel." He added, "No golf course, no resort."

Skamania County officials decided to make an all-out bid for the conference center. "We were not looked upon favorably by the Gorge

Commission," Leick said. "We were looked on as backward." To upgrade the county's image and draw visitors and up to 200 jobs to the economically depressed area, Leick and others contacted Gray independently and asked him to be involved. They got the Washington Legislature to grant an exemption to a state law so the county could build a destination resort. They agreed to put up $5 million of county money to match the $5 million from Congress. Gray's firm, GrayCo, ultimately agreed to invest $10 million.

County commissioners gave Leick an additional $1 million to acquire land for the conference center on a bluff overlooking Stevenson and the gorge. He bought several parcels, including land owned by the local public utility district, an undeveloped subdivision, and the county dump—120 acres in all, enough to encompass a resort hotel and conference center and an eighteen-hole golf course.

In Klickitat County, the Port of Klickitat took the lead, forming a consortium to put together a project at Bingen after county commissioners bowed out. Benner said County Commissioner Joan Frey told him, "This is a taxpayer subsidy and we don't want any part of it."

It fell to Benner and his staff to invent a process for selecting the conference center site. Each county would have to submit a detailed plan. Despite early interest from Washougal, Clark County ultimately decided not to compete.

The process culminated in a huge public hearing before the Gorge Commission. Both counties made excellent presentations. When Gray spoke, "you could hear a pin drop," Benner recalled. "He said, 'I'm seventy-four years old. This is my last project. And we're not going to make a profit, because we are going to dedicate the proceeds to the community.'"

Even the resort's swimming pool would be open to the public, he said.

"My own view was, 'There's no comparison,'" Benner said. "I thought, 'This is a slam dunk.'"

Instead, the commission vote was a 6-6 tie that fell largely along county lines. Those opposing the Skamania County site argued that it would be better to draw people further up the gorge, to Klickitat County.

Gorge Commissioners were stunned. Chairman Hansell asked whether anyone wanted to change his or her vote. Someone suggested that the two counties could form a team to combine the proposals.

Benner called for a recess. "We quickly dismissed the idea of a team. I said, 'Let's work on the process. That will take a couple of months. What do you think would break the logjam?'" The staff decided to hire three resort development experts and underwrite the cost of bringing them to the gorge for a three-day visit. "I called the Urban Land Institute. I said, 'Here's our mess. Can you help us out?'"

The three arrived in the gorge and went off on their own for a while. Meanwhile Skamania County officials strategized about how to impress the out-of-town experts. "We were told we needed to look good," Leick said. County officials considered hiring a local Native American to paddle a canoe on a pond at their site to provide regional color, he recalled. Fortunately, that idea fell through. County employees were encouraged to sit on the courthouse grounds with signs saying, "We support the lodge." Locals who opposed a conference center on the river at Bingen because it would displace a log dump were mobilized.

Benner and his staff took the out-of-town experts to the two sites. At the Port of Klickitat, as they were looking around, the visitors heard the roar of log truck engines. Several of the big trucks had parked across the railroad tracks, gunning their motors and blocking the exit.

"It had a psychological effect," Benner said. "The consultants realized, 'Oh, there are people who don't support this.'"

At the future site of Skamania Lodge, it was raining. Still, it was an easy call. "We had another meeting of the Gorge Commission," Benner said. "The consultants made their presentation. It was strongly supportive of Skamania Lodge. Their recommendation broke the logjam. It was 9-3."

Skamania Lodge became a successful addition to John Gray's legacy. It restored an old dump site. It was built with recycled wood. It was a model of environmental sustainability. It won design awards and soon became the largest private employer in the county. "By the second year it was making a profit," Leick said. County commissioners were not interested in holding the lodge for the long term. After a couple of years, they sold it to GrayCo, which later sold it to another private resort manager.

But county commissioners became impatient as they waited for Congress to reimburse them the $5 million it had promised for the project. It was Leick who came up with the idea of attaching several conditions to the county's Scenic Area ordinance, to ensure that it would get the economic benefits promised—and to protect the county from future "takings" lawsuits.

Leick proposed that the ordinance be sunsetted—allowed to expire—if by November 1995 the federal government had not disbursed the promised

$5 million toward the construction of Skamania Lodge, appropriated funds for economic and recreational development, amended the management plan to allow counties to grant variances, established jurisdiction for litigating "takings" claims brought by property owners, and passed laws to protect the county itself from takings lawsuits.

At a November 1995 meeting in Stevenson, Leick's successor, County Prosecuting Attorney Bradley Andersen, said he had run out of patience with the federal government. "Enough is enough, we've tried to be a good partner and they haven't even met a quarter of their obligations," he declared.

The concept that the county could retain any local control of land use was "illusory" at best, Andersen said, because the management plan offered no flexibility. He complained that Friends of the Gorge routinely appealed every decision the county made in favor of landowners and that the cost of administering land use applications under the Scenic Area ordinance had mounted to $140,000 in just the first two years.

He also argued that the arrangement placed the county in a legally un-tenable situation, because it would be "first in the firing line" in the event of a takings lawsuit filed by any landowner who was unable to develop his land.

Kathleen Butcher, Skamania County's representative to the Gorge Commission, agreed. She said her four years of service had led her to conclude that the county never would be allowed to exercise discretion or allow variances in its Scenic Area ordinance to help landowners. "We worked diligently, in good faith, to put together the ordinance and found that what we were told by the government one day would change three days later," she said.

After that bit of theater failed to win over the Gorge Commission, Skamania County collected its money and proceeded to implement its ordinance.

Skamania Lodge put the Washington Gorge on the map. It became a regional destination, boosted the local economy and remains one of the most successful tangible results of the National Scenic Area Act.

As Benner and the Gorge Commission raced to meet their 1990 deadline for producing a new management plan, another distraction surfaced—a lawsuit challenging the legality of the plan under Washington law.

In 1990, SDS Lumber Co. and Broughton Lumber Co. joined with Klickitat County in filing suit against the commission. They argued that the management plan must pass muster with Washington's weak State Environmental Policy Act.

A U.S. District Court judge approved a preliminary injunction blocking the commission from taking any action to adopt the management plan. "They found a friendly judge who said they would shut us down unless we followed SEPA," Benner recalled. He turned to Watters, his staff attorney, who persuaded the judge to step up hearings on the case by several months. Benner told the judge, "Your honor, we are under a federal deadline to adopt a management plan."

Benner and Watters found a comparable case on which to base their argument. The Seattle-based Master Home Builders Association had sued the Northwest Power Planning Council, a federal body made up of representatives from Washington, Oregon, Idaho, and Montana. They had argued that its regional energy plan, required under the federal Northwest Power Planning Act, must comply with SEPA. The homebuilders had lost that case in the Ninth U.S. Circuit Court of Appeals.

The lesson Benner and Watters took from that precedent was to look to the Scenic Area Act and the Bistate Compact. Neither mentioned SEPA. "Larry and I wrote the brief and prepared all the documents," Benner said. We had our trial in Yakima. I didn't know the judge. I was pleasantly surprised. He made his decision very quickly."

But though the judge ruled in its favor, the Gorge Commission lost several months of progress. Benner asked for more time to complete the management plan. The clock was ticking. The deadline was a powerful motivator. "If it drags on," Benner feared, "people will resign."

As the Gorge Commission plowed ahead, in October 1990 the Forest Service released its draft management plan for development of public lands in the Special Management Area and its recreation plan. Both drew fire.

The Forest Service plan designated some of the most sensitive areas in the gorge, including high-elevation lands in the Mount Hood National Forest and sensitive wetlands along the shore, for high-intensity recreation. Under that designation, parking lots with up to 200 parking slots and campgrounds with as many as 150 units could be allowed. Forest Service planners went back to the drawing board.

In the fall of 1991, as the Gorge Commission prepared to adopt the final plan, commissioners got emotional. Some voices broke as the commissioners made their closing statements. "We voted on each element of the plan and on the plan itself," Benner said. "Pat Bleakney gave a wonderful speech on how much he had learned, how much he respected the views of people he disagreed with."

The commission's vote came, nearly two years past its deadline. The vote was 9-3. Commissioners Bleakney, Sourek, and Reinig voted no.

"As far as I was concerned, it was the best land use plan in the United States at that time," Benner said. "And I don't think there has been a better Gorge Commission."

Chapter 6
Early Friction

By 1992, the first Columbia River Gorge Commission had completed four years of hard work on the Scenic Area Management Plan and the U.S. Department of Agriculture had signed off on the plan. Executive Director Richard Benner left to accept a job as director of the Oregon Department of Land Conservation and Development. Several commissioners, burned out by the arduous task, chose not to seek a second term. Change was in the wind.

Jonathan Doherty took the reins of the commission as a new batch of commissioners came on board. Doherty had worked previously as chief of park planning for the Mid-Atlantic Region of the National Park Service, supervising a staff of twelve, and overseeing a dozen planning projects. New to the Northwest, he would serve a tough seven years implementing the new gorge plan. Doherty immediately set a new tone by deciding to live in the gorge. Unlike Benner, he didn't consider commuting from Portland. "I had no interest in spending two hours a day in a car," he said. He moved his young family to White Salmon. He recalls returning from long days at the office to pick raspberries with his children in the soft alpenglow of Mount Hood.

Reaction to his decision came quickly, he said. "I got the distinct impression that some people"—including Gorge Commissioners and members of Friends of the Gorge—"felt my living in White Salmon was a mistake; that I would become too sensitive to the concerns of gorge residents."

Tension came from the other side as well.

"One day, a few months after moving to White Salmon, my wife, two young daughters, and I were driving on Interstate 84 and had car trouble," he recalled. "We called a tow truck from White Salmon. The truck operator hitched up our car and we climbed into the truck for the drive back."

The driver, at first friendly, asked what Doherty did for a living. His wife flashed him a warning look, which Doherty chose to ignore. "I said I was the Gorge Commission director. The driver's tone immediately changed. He snarled, 'I ought to throw you out of this truck right now.' His feelings were sincere, but fortunately he didn't act on them!"

Those extremes dominated the public debate, Doherty said. "On one end there was the small group of gorge residents associated with Columbia Gorge United, who were still extremely bitter about the enactment of the Scenic Area Act, and who simply refused to move on. These folks regularly showed up to complain, though with decreasing frequency as time passed."

At the other extreme was Friends of the Columbia Gorge, dominated by Portland voices, which in Doherty's view advocated for a hard-line, legalistic approach to enforcement of the new management plan.

Occupying the middle ground were ordinary gorge residents who came before the commission to appeal its decisions on their development applications. "Some of those appeals were reasonable," Doherty said. Others were intent on testing the law's reach. Also in that middle group were the majority of gorge residents who were not directly affected by the act because they lived in the thirteen urban areas, which were exempt from restrictions on development.

An immediate task facing Doherty and the commission was to persuade all six gorge counties to make the new management plan their own. That would require them to incorporate the new rules into their own land use ordinances and agree to enforce those ordinances. In effect, the counties would become responsible for administering the Scenic Area Act, with the Gorge Commission looking over their shoulder and resolving appeals.

The Gorge Commission had both carrots and sticks to nudge the counties toward compliance. Counties that adopted their own ordinances would get money for economic development projects as well as money and technical assistance to help them write the new rules. Counties that refused to enforce the law would get no economic development money and their constituents would be forced to deal directly with the Gorge Commission and its staff on land use issues.

Politically, these decisions were critical. Counties that complied would be able to review development proposals under their own rules rather than bow to a rule book enforced by an impersonal bureaucracy.

Between 1992 and 1994, five of the six gorge counties adopted their own Scenic Area ordinances. Oregon's Wasco County was the first to do so; Skamania County, the county most affected by the new plan, was second.

Sparsely populated Klickitat County, in the eastern gorge, was the sole holdout. The county's elected officials had fiercely opposed the Scenic Area Act. They announced early on that they would not participate in implementing the law. Klickitat County leaders had no reservations about forfeiting federal economic development grants. They were pinning their economic hopes on a large regional landfill at the county's east end, development of the Dallesport urban area, and a nascent energy boom.

But their decision would carry real consequences for property owners with land in the Scenic Area. They would have to deal with Gorge Commission bureaucrats—a dynamic that would feed resentment and opposition.

Doherty and the new commissioners had old business to attend to as well. The commission was still hearing appeals of decisions issued under the Forest Service's interim guidelines. Trying to maintain continuity was a challenge. "Transitions are generally hard for everyone, particularly those who feel put out," Doherty said. In 1993, he visited Great Britain to learn how property owners there had accepted the imposition of national land use planning rules in the 1950s. "They said it took a decade or so for people to move beyond the anxiety of the new regulations."

Many rural gorge residents still feared that the federal government would condemn their land. Chuck Cushman of the National Inholders Association and other property rights groups continued to fan that fear. Technically, the government did have the power to condemn land in the Scenic Area, but only if that became necessary to head off an imminent threat that the land would be used in a way that violated the law. To remove the terror from the word "condemnation," the act clearly stated that the government could not condemn land if its use had not changed.

The Scenic Area Act authorized the Forest Service to buy private land from willing sellers who were unable to develop it. But that raised another concern: County officials feared they would lose property tax revenue as their tax bases shrank. The act had addressed the issue on a short-term basis by authorizing $2 million in federal compensation, to be split among gorge counties that lost property tax revenue due to federal land acquisition. For five years, counties would get annual payments equal to one percent of the fair market value of the land purchased. This was supposed to give them time to diversify their economies. But it was hardly enough time to turn around economies built on a century of logging and other resource extraction.

In 1989, the northern spotted owl raised its feathered head, becoming an instant symbol of a changing land ethic on federal forests across the Northwest. Conservation groups sued the Forest Service and the Bureau of Land Management to require protection of the forest-dwelling owl as a threatened species under the Endangered Species Act. Attorneys for national and regional conservation groups argued successfully that a century of logging in Northwest forests had decimated the owl's habitat. In 1990, under court order, the first Bush administration listed the owl as threatened throughout its range, from the Canadian border to northern California and from the Pacific Ocean to the crest of the Cascade Range. The owl's listing, coming on the heels of the new Scenic Area rules, hit gorge timber towns with a double whammy. It virtually shut down the federal forests that provided their major source of raw material. Rural timber towns throughout the Northwest turned their wrath on the government, environmental activists, and the owl.

The listing was only the beginning of a major shift within federal land management agencies. Under the leadership of Forest Service Chief Jack Ward Thomas, those agencies entered a new era of ecosystem management. In the early 1990s, the federal government listed several species of wild salmon and steelhead in the Columbia River Basin as threatened or endangered. The listings required land managers and hydroelectric dam operators to change the way they managed dams, rivers, streams, and riparian forests and meadows across the Northwest—or face the prospect of taking out four Lower Snake River dams. Timber companies, commercial fishermen, and farmers with salmon streams running through their land reeled from the new restrictions.

Meanwhile, the aluminum industry, which had flourished with cheap power from the Bonneville Power Administration, was on its last legs, no longer able to compete with foreign aluminum smelters that relied on cheap labor. Eventually, smelters in Troutdale, The Dalles, and Klickitat County would close, dealing another blow to the Northwest's natural resource-based economy. It was through this lens of change and uncertainty that gorge communities reacted to the new layer of regulations the Scenic Area Management Plan imposed.

Skamania County was the hardest hit. Nearly 90 percent of the county was managed by the Forest Service and the Washington Department of Natural Resources. For a century, timber had fueled the county's economy, providing its major source of jobs and revenue. Worker-owned Stevenson Co-Ply in Stevenson had to shut down because the large old conifers it depended on were scarce after the shutdown of federal timber sales. "In the 1960s and 1970s, there were five or six sawmills in Skamania County, and that's all there was," recalled longtime county prosecuting attorney Bob Leick. By 2012, he said, just two mills remained in the county. "I give credit to the National Scenic Area and the spotted owl."

Jonathan Doherty, like Richard Benner before him, was frustrated by the quasi-judicial approach under which the Gorge Commission heard appeals. The rules required the staff to maintain an arm's-length relationship with commissioners to ensure that landowners coming before the commission would get a fair and unbiased hearing. That angered some gorge residents, who were used to talking problems through in a less formal context. It also meant the commission staff was prohibited from discussing the issues surrounding individual projects with its policy-making body.

Friends of the Gorge and the Columbia Gorge Coalition urged the commission to stiffen its spine and enforce the rules. Instead, they said, commissioners were bowing to pressure from property rights advocates.

Chuck Williams believed that compromises on logging struck by Congress to win support for the act had produced fatal flaws that could never be remedied. He did not hide his bitterness. "All you have to do is drive around and see all the new clearcuts in every direction, or drive to Rowena or up to Belle Center Road or Seven Mile Road to see suburban sprawl the legislation was supposed to end," he wrote in 1997. "Go to the Rowena viewpoint and notice that the rim across the river has been lined with houses since 'protection.'"

Many property owners, and Doherty himself, were frustrated over the Forest Service land acquisition program, which lacked an overall strategy for prioritizing which gorge properties to buy. The Scenic Area Act gave the agency authority to buy land in the Special Management Areas, where many landowners had lost all ability to develop their property. But some of those lands were effectively protected from development already by their

The Rowena loop on the historic Columbia River Highway. Photo by Darryl Lloyd.

zoning as agricultural land or open space. Doherty argued that other properties were far more vulnerable. "There was no solid rationale for this," he
said. "Its sole effect was largely to compensate SMA landowners for the
downzoning created by the act, which made landowners in the General
Management Area feel they were being treated unfairly." Doherty wanted
the Forest Service to use some of its money to buy visually sensitive land to
protect the government from future litigation over "takings" claims. There
were many such properties, up and down the gorge, that had been zoned
as Open Space in the management plan.

"It became apparent to me and the commission staff that the Forest Service's land acquisition program did not have a strategic relationship to the rules the Forest Service had set out for the SMAs in the management plan," Doherty said. "The Forest Service was buying land or conservation easements on parcels designated for large-scale agriculture or forest use." He believed the agency should instead be spending its money to buy critical lands, including visually jarring rock quarries and commercial timberland zoned as Open Space. He was convinced the federal government was legally vulnerable to lawsuits over "taking" if it restricted commercial activity on those lands. Buying them would make the problem go away. "In each of these cases, there was concern that the regulations could have been successfully challenged in court," Doherty said. "As a result, we spent some considerable time with the commission and the Forest Service advocating for development of a land acquisition strategy with rational objectives and criteria."

Such approaches were commonplace in other parts of the country and used by many major conservation organizations. But Doherty said the concept was fiercely opposed by the Friends of the Gorge and only grudgingly accepted by the Forest Service. However, the agency did ultimately buy out the operator of a controversial rock quarry east of Hood River after the Gorge Commission ordered that it be phased out. The site eventually became the Mark O. Hatfield State Park and the trailhead for the Hood River-to-Mosier segment of the Historic Columbia River Highway Trail.

Doherty and the commission had no shortage of fires to put out on the Washington side of the gorge. In December 1994, Clark County commissioners adopted the county's first growth management plan, required of urban counties under Washington's new Growth Management Act. The plan, adopted by a unanimous vote, designated about 250 acres of the National Scenic Area for dense urban and industrial development. The vote represented a political shift for the fast-growing county, which generally supported the concept of a National Scenic Area during the battle for federal legislation.

Friends of the Gorge joined Clark County's small environmental community in appealing the plan to a regional hearings board. It was a slam-dunk. The board ordered Clark County to pull back its urban growth boundary so that it did not intrude into the National Scenic Area. Friends also found itself fighting a proposal by a timber company to log 75 acres of steep, forested bluffs on state land above the Columbia River next to a spring that was the sole source of water for residents of Underwood. The unincorporated community's water supply had been declared inadequate by the state, a finding that restricted new development. The logging plan also appeared to violate Skamania County's own gorge ordinance, which prohibited timber harvests on land zoned for open space, including the springs.

Animosity toward the Gorge Commission boiled to the surface with the state budget cuts of 1997. Clark County's Seventeenth Legislative District was a conservative bastion in the late 1990s. Its Republican legislators saw an opportunity to score points over the uproar in the gorge, though not a single acre of the Scenic Area lay within the seventeenth district. State Reps. Marc Boldt and Jim Dunn, and State Sen. Don Benton led the charge to slash the Gorge Commission's biennial budget. They succeeded in getting both the state house and senate to pass legislation reducing Washington's share of the budget from $550,000 to $155,000. Under their legislation, some of the money slated to go to the Gorge Commission would be diverted to the three gorge counties. Each would receive $80,000 for planning and monitoring. Meanwhile, the commission's staff would be slashed from eight to two.

Under the Bistate Compact, if appropriations from the two state legislatures differed, the Gorge Commission was permitted to spend only the lower amount. That meant the commission was looking at a budget cut of nearly $800,000.

The Clark County lawmakers went further, sponsoring a bill aimed at drastically changing the way the commission operated. They proposed to force the panel to issue a single-house building permit to any applicant who had owned gorge property before the National Scenic Area Act took effect on January 1, 1987. Under their bill, a new appeals board would be established to handle protests of Gorge Commission land use rulings. And voters in the six gorge counties would be allowed to elect their representatives to the Gorge Commission directly, rather than through appointment by county commissioners.

The bill was a clear violation of the Scenic Area Act and the Bistate Compact. Only Congress could change the governance of the Scenic Area. The bill died in committee, but the Republicans of the Seventeenth District had made their populist point.

The deep budget cuts forced staff layoffs and threatened the commission's ability to keep up with its work load—an issue that would come back to haunt it in 1999. "Prior to the cuts, I believe we had a planning staff of four: two full time administrative staff, a two-thirds-time counsel and the executive director," Doherty said. "I had to let two of the planners go; I reduced the hours of one of the administrative staff to part time; I reduced our counsel to half time; and all staff—including me—agreed to take a voluntary 10 percent reduction in pay in order to avoid any further layoffs."

The cuts were demoralizing for his staff, Doherty said. "Part of the attack on the commission was fueled by misperceptions that appeared to me to have been created early on. Some members of the state legislatures said they had even been led to believe that once the plan was complete and the county ordinances adopted, the commission would only have a token staff. It actually seemed like some of this had come from early commissioner members who had not really thought it through."

But Doherty was not naïve. "Of course, the real attack on the commission's budget was led by members of the legislature who completely opposed the Gorge Act and the commission," he said. "They saw attacking the funding as the 'starve the beast' solution."

In reality, Doherty and his staff always had a much larger workload than could be realistically accomplished. "Even before the cuts, the commission's budget was literally puny," he said, in comparison to the budgets of the only two comparable agencies in the nation, the Tahoe Regional Planning Agency on the California-Nevada border and the Pinelands Commission in New Jersey.

Legal challenges continued to dog the commission. In 1995, a case arose that tested its power to override state law in Washington land use rulings. Scott Anderson, a resident of Skamania County, applied to the county for a permit to expand a run-down trailer park near Beacon Rock Moorage that had existed at the time the Scenic Area was established. It was on property where the management plan prohibited new development that would be visible from key viewpoints. The trailer park was grandfathered into the management plan as a "nonconforming use." But the issue was more complicated than that.

The county had originally permitted ten sites at the trailer park, but only three had ever been occupied. Anderson wanted permission to develop the other seven. The county approved the expansion. Citing state legal precedent, prosecuting attorney Brad Andersen argued that the permit remained valid because there was no evidence the owner had intended to discontinue its use as a trailer park.

A neighbor, Chris Woodall, appealed to the Gorge Commission. He argued that Scenic Area rules governing land use took precedence over state law. The Gorge Commission agreed and overturned the county. Andersen appealed the commission's ruling to Washington Superior Court and lost. He appealed to the State Court of Appeals, which overturned the ruling and found in his favor.

The state of Oregon and Multnomah County joined the Gorge Commission in seeking a ruling from the Washington State Supreme Court. By then Scott Anderson had put the property up for sale, but the litigation moved ahead.

The Woodall case was worthy of the Supreme Court's attention because it raised the larger issue of whether the Bistate Compact or any Gorge Commission ruling trumped state law. In general, the court had ruled that unless a Bistate Compact specifically invoked state law, the compact was the final word. But the issue was complicated by the fact that the two states treated land use law differently. Much of Oregon's land use law was statutory; it had been adopted by the legislature. Much of Washington's land use law was common law; it had evolved from court rulings.

Oregon law said that when nonconforming uses were discontinued, they ceased to exist. In Oregon, the Scenic Area Act trumped statutory law. But the situation was muddier in Washington. The Gorge Commission ended up applying the Scenic Area Act in Oregon and state law in Washington. "I don't think this is what Congress intended," gorge staff attorney Jeff Litwak remarked. "How are we supposed to have one uniform management plan if we have to apply two states' laws?"

Skamania County lost its case in the state Supreme Court in 2003, and a key legal question was clarified.

Another challenge to the Gorge Commission's legal authority first arose in 1997. Two unbuilt Skamania County subdivisions that had been platted almost ninety years previously were suddenly back on the books and scheduled for construction—one across from Hood River in Underwood, the other across from Multnomah Falls in Prindle. Nothing had been done to develop the subdivisions in the eight decades since they had been platted. But that made no difference to Skamania County planners, who pointed out that there was still a legally recorded document in the auditor's office, signed by the appropriate county officials of that time. Friends of the Gorge vowed to appeal. It took the position that state law and the 1986 act essentially eliminated the old undeveloped subdivisions in rural areas. "You can't grandfather the old plats," Friends Conservation Director Michael Lang said. The county could not resurrect a high-density subdivision from 1908 and be able to develop it at that density today, he insisted.

Doherty agreed that the county's interpretation would undermine the act. "The downside is what happens to the gorge itself," he said. "The whole regional approach falls apart. We will have no long-term permanent guarantee that the character of the gorge will be maintained."

The Gorge Commission eventually prevailed in the "ancient subdivisions" case.

With all the litigation and political friction, there were reasons to celebrate. A decade after passage of the Scenic Area Act, the gorge economy was robust. The unemployment rate in the four rural counties had declined from 15 percent to 10 percent since the early 1980s, after peaking in the early 1990s with the shutdown of logging on the national forests.

By 1995, two new major retail stores had opened in The Dalles, Cascade Locks had a new hotel, and windsurfers had transformed Hood River into a recreation boomtown. Skamania Lodge, an instant success, had undergone an expansion. It was now the county's largest employer, though Gorge Commissioner Bud Quinn scoffed that the low wages it paid did not make up for lost timber jobs. The Columbia Gorge Discovery Center west of The Dalles had been less successful. When it opened its doors in May 1997, some boosters predicted that it would draw 150,000 visitors annually. That projection proved wildly optimistic.

Two Gorge Commissioners who served during this period—Bud Quinn, a Skamania County property rights warrior, and Steve McCarthy, a Portland conservationist—offered sharply contrasting views of how the Scenic Area Act was working at the ten-year mark. Quinn lived on 38 hillside acres east of Washougal. A retired millworker in his seventies, with silvery-gray hair and beard, he enjoyed his hobby farm, where he kept a menagerie of five llamas, several shaggy dogs, a pet macaw, and a pot-bellied pig. He motioned to the woods that surrounded him—woods that would never be developed under the Scenic Area Management Plan—and joked that he was a Rockefeller. "That's what the Rockefellers did, you know—they'd buy a piece of land and then make all the land around it into a park."

Twice an unsuccessful candidate for the Washington Legislature, Quinn represented Skamania County on the Gorge Commission and also chaired the Skamania Board of Equalization, which heard appeals of local property tax bills. He was active in the Wise Use movement and had helped lead the unsuccessful campaign by Columbia Gorge United to get the Scenic Area Act overturned in federal court. In February 1996, when the county appointed him to the Gorge Commission, Quinn made his agenda clear. "I've watched major decisions being made without input from local citizens and I think that's wrong," he said. "I also felt the Gorge Commission should work harder to get Congress to uphold the economic promises made to the gorge counties when the act was passed." Quinn supported the deep state budget cuts the Gorge Commission had suffered in 1997. He argued that the county needed those state dollars more than the commission did. "It costs us $150,000 a year to administer the Scenic Act," he said.

But after serving on the commission for a while, Quinn no longer supported overturning the law. "I have no fault with the act itself," he said. "I think the act was good, to keep the gorge from being developed the way Clark County was developed. My problem is with the way the act has been implemented." He objected to the way the Forest Service had handled land purchases. Political pressures, not clear objectives, had too often determined which land parcels the agency bought, he said. "I think the Forest Service should have made a list of the priority lands and let property owners know whether their land would be purchased at some point in time."

He also maintained that the Scenic Area Act had created financial hardship for both property owners and local governments. "Land purchased by the Forest Service leaves the tax rolls, and other property owners have to pick up the slack." At the same time, the assessed value of Quinn's own land had climbed by $42,000 in a single year.

Quinn personally hated development and the pressure that growth brings. He was not in favor of disbanding the Gorge Commission. "Down the road at some point in time the commission should become smaller," he said in an interview. "I would say it should happen today, except there is so much unfinished business. But if the people in this state want the commission to exist, they should be willing to support it through their taxes."

Steve McCarthy had a different view. An Oregon baby boomer with a renaissance resume, he was Quinn's opposite on the Gorge Commission His mother, Kate McCarthy of Hood River, had been a strong advocate for protection of the gorge and of national forest land surrounding the Mount Hood Meadows Ski Area. McCarthy graduated from New York University Law School and worked for New York Mayor John Lindsay before coming home to chair the land use watchdog group 1000 Friends of Oregon and the Ralph Nader-inspired Oregon State Public Interest Research Group. He served on the board of Tri-Met, the Portland area's transit agency, then moved up to general manager. He owned a sports equipment business for a while then took a leap and founded a distillery that produced an acclaimed pear brandy.

His frustrations began on the day he attended his first Gorge Commission meeting, in 1994. By July 1997, he was ready to unload them before a large, influential audience at the weekly City Club of Portland lunch.

"When I arrived at my first Gorge Commission hearing, I expected to find an agency carrying out the act," he said. "I didn't expect it to be perfect, but I thought I'd find a clear commitment to protection. What I found was very different...The commission and the staff strategy seemed to be to get along with everyone, to be fair, to try to be liked. It's a timid, almost apologetic approach to protecting the gorge."

McCarthy's frustration extended to what he regarded as a lack of vision about economic development. Money earmarked by Congress for diversifying gorge communities was funneled to two state investment boards. It was going to pay for curbs and gutters, he said. Why not investigate ways to capitalize on caviar from Columbia River sturgeon, on the red alder and vine maple in gorge woodlands, on the edible mushrooms that flourished in its damp western valleys? "I'd hoped to see an effort to work with the sustainable development people, to identify some projects. Nothing has happened."

The deep budget cuts the commission had suffered that spring called for a reevaluation of the Scenic Area Act itself, he said. "Recent action convinces me the act is flawed. We had a shootout in the last legislative session and we lost. The ability to protect the gorge has been severely damaged." McCarthy resigned from the Gorge Commission soon after.

Quinn shared McCarthy's frustration about how economic development dollars were being spent, but for a different reason. "It's a joke," Quinn said of the commission's role. "The money is not being used like it should be used. It's not our job to decide whether these proposals meet the standard. We just rubber-stamp. At the last meeting, the Mural Society of The Dalles asked for $147,000 to paint murals on buildings," he said, shaking his head in disbelief. "I was the only one who said no."

Lauri Aunan, executive director of Friends of the Gorge at the time, worried that in an effort to get along with rebellious local officials, the Gorge Commission had lost its momentum. Without an adequate staff or budget, she said, it might be incapable of fighting off developers and their allies. "I really don't have a sense that most people understand how much land is available for development," she said. "Every lot that can be developed will be developed. In the gorge, here's what people want: They want the biggest home with the best view."

Yet Aunan, a California transplant who had moved to rural Corbett, admitted that everything was relative. "I lived in Southern California, where sprawl ate the world," she said. "When I came out here and saw the gorge, I said to myself, 'How on earth did they save this much?'"

In September 1996, two months before the tenth anniversary of the National Scenic Area Act, U.S. Sen. Mark Hatfield convened an oversight hearing in Hood River. The Senator who had pushed the act over the finish line reminded his audience that President Reagan had signed the bill over objections from his interior secretary, his agriculture secretary, his energy secretary and his budget director. "Someday," he said, "I would like to write a memoir on how President Reagan came to appreciate the importance of signing the bill into law." Hatfield seemed unruffled by the controversies that continued to roil the waters in the Columbia River Gorge. "The gorge, and how we have chosen to manage it, reflects the values that we as a region and as a nation have placed on environmental protection and stewardship," he said.

The Scenic Area Act had required Congress to balance conflicting values, he said. "To some, any government involvement in land use decisions is an affront, and to others total lockup is the only way to ensure adequate environmental protection."

The Forest Service had acquired more than 28,000 acres in the gorge through purchase or exchange, and not one acre had been acquired through condemnation, he stressed. Every property had been purchased from a willing seller. "Some still question the constitutionality of the Gorge Act," Hatfield said. "To them, let me say this: It has been upheld by the Federal District Court of Oregon, the Ninth Circuit Court of Appeals, and the Supreme Court of the United States. That argument ought to be laid to rest."

Hatfield then reeled off statistics on the investments Congress had made in the gorge during the Scenic Area Act's first decade, largely through his own clout as Senate Appropriations Committee Chair. Of $74.8 million authorized under the Act, $52.2 million had been appropriated, and millions more for land purchases were on the way.

"Congress has taken its role as a partner in the management of this area very seriously, both in the areas of land protection and economic development," Hatfield said. The scenic and natural character of the gorge had been preserved and in some cases improved; more people lived in the gorge; businesses had diversified; recreational projects had been developed, and sensitive lands had been protected.

"I realize that the act, like anything else in life, may not be perfect," he said. But ten years after his grand showdown with President Reagan, Hatfield's gorge legacy was secure.

Chapter 7
The Too-Tall House

On the morning of June 19, 1998, Gorge Commission planner Allen Bell and Forest Service landscape architect Jurgen Hess were leading a tour of the National Scenic Area for county officials when they stopped at Dalton Point on the Oregon side, near Multnomah Falls. As they gazed across the river, they were startled to see the unmistakable shape of a large house, fully framed, perched midway down a steep bluff. The three-and-a-half-story structure broke the tree line, calling attention to itself in a clearing carved into the forested slope. Members of the tour began peppering Bell and Hess with questions. At first, the two had no answers. They knew only that something had gone terribly wrong. A house of this size, in this place, was flatly prohibited under Skamania County's own Scenic Area ordinance and the Scenic Area Management Plan. Both required that new structures visible from key viewpoints be "visually subordinate" to the surrounding landscape.

Jonathan Doherty and his staff at the Columbia River Gorge Commission had interpreted that language to mean that, in general, new buildings must blend in with the natural environment through siting, landscaping, and the use of dark, non-reflective paint and roofing materials. Further, they required that developers "minimize visibility" of new structures by placing them where they would be the least visible from key gorge viewpoints. Clearly, that had not happened here.

Hess turned to a tour member, Skamania County planner Kari Fagerness. "Wow, what's that?" he asked her. In his notebook, he jotted down the time and place and their brief conversation.

"That's the Bea house," she replied.

"What happened?" Hess asked.

Fagerness told him County Commissioner Judy Carter had put pressure on county planners to approve the house even though it violated the county's own Scenic Area Ordinance. "We're not very happy about it," she said.

The controversy over the Bea house, clearly visible in this photo from the Oregon side of the Gorge, triggered a heated court battle over whether the Gorge Commission had the power to order the house moved to a less visible site. Photo by Milan Chuckovich of *The Columbian*.

She explained that the county had initially approved a one-story house on the site, with a daylight basement and loft. Its total height was not to exceed 25 feet. Yet the Bea house rose 38 feet on the bluff, dominating the view for miles around.

Bea's county permit also required him to leave a 200-foot setback from the south property line; instead, the newly framed house sat just 15 feet from the boundary. A follow-up investigation by County Prosecuting Attorney Brad Andersen revealed that, immediately after getting his building permit, Bea had cut down several large Douglas firs that were supposed to screen the site and had bulldozed 100 cubic yards of vegetation to assure an unobstructed view of the Columbia River to the south.

Thus began the saga of the Bea house, a dispute that raged for five years, drew national media attention and cast the Columbia River Gorge Commission as an overreaching, insensitive bureaucracy. Eventually, the case reached the Washington Supreme Court on its way to a negotiated resolution.

A Naked Challenge

The "visually subordinate" language in the management plan had not been tested until the Bea house began rising on the wooded bluff. And those who knew the Bea family were not surprised that they had decided to challenge it. The Bea family, third-generation landowners in the gorge, held title to property near Cape Horn that offered some of the most spectacular views in the Scenic Area. And they were not inclined to be pushed around by the federal government.

Brian Bea's great-grandfather had homesteaded near Cape Horn in western Skamania County in the 1860s. His parents, Richard and Sally Bea, built their house on the family property. In late 1986, as the Scenic Area Act was awaiting President Ronald Reagan's signature, sixteen-year-old Brian wrote a letter to the president inviting him to come to dinner and see for himself how the law would infringe on private property rights. He asked Reagan not to sign it.

In 1992, six years after the law took effect, Richard and Sally Bea applied to the Gorge Commission for a permit to build a house for Brad Bea, their older son. The commission gave them permission to build on a section of the property that was screened by large trees. For financial reasons, that house never was built. The following year, Brian and Jody Bea approached the Gorge Commission about building their own house on the family homestead, but they did not pursue a formal application at the time.

In 1996, just before the permit for Brad Bea's house was to expire, the Beas asked permission to move it 700 feet, to a more visible site. Doherty denied the request. If the Beas wanted to move the house, he said, they would have to reapply to Skamania County. (By then the county had adopted its own Scenic Area ordinance and was processing its own land use applications.)

In December 1996, Brad Bea contacted the Forest Service with an offer to sell a scenic easement on his property for $110,000. Because it was within a Special Management Area, the agency had the authority to buy it outright or purchase a conservation easement restricting its development.

Brad Bea gave Scenic Area Manager Art Carroll two weeks to accept or decline the offer. Otherwise, he said, he would clearcut the forested portion of the land "and proceed with subdividing the property to the maximum extent allowed."

"The inevitable result," he wrote, "will be a significant degradation of the Cape Horn view shed which will be noticed by many people." After January, Brad Bea said, he would seek "top dollar" for the property, which could cost federal taxpayers an extra $100,000.

Carroll refused to respond to the threat. An appraisal would be required to determine fair market value, he said. After that, the property would be ranked in importance according to its natural, cultural, and scenic values. Brad Bea responded that unless the Forest Service purchased the easement, he would build his house at the tree line between forest and pasture, where it would mar the expansive Cape Horn view.

Eventually, the Forest Service agreed to pay Brad Bea $216,000 for a conservation easement. In exchange, he agreed to save the trees. He had time on his side; if the agency failed to buy the conservation easement within three years, the property would be downzoned and Brad Bea would be free to cut all the trees.

Brian and Jody Bea did not have that option. Their property was not within a Special Management Area. So in 1996, they set about getting the necessary permits to build their own dream house with a million-dollar view. Brian applied to the county to build a modest house. He drew his site plan by hand on a piece of notebook paper. It showed trees screening the building. When questioned later, he said he had drawn the trees at random. County officials visited the site, reviewed his application, and ultimately attached thirty-three conditions to the permit.

But Brian Bea heard nothing from the Gorge Commission, which was supposed to review the application to make sure it complied with the Scenic Area management plan and the county's own ordinance. There were reasons for this; at the time, in 1997, the commission's staff was stretched thin and struggling to keep up with a flood of development applications after hostile legislators in both states cut the commission's budget in half. When Skamania County forwarded Bea's permit to the Gorge Commission, planners there gave it only a cursory review. They assumed that the large trees indicated on the site plan would in fact screen the house and that the Beas would comply with the thirty-three conditions. Instead Brian Bea, permit in hand, hastened to remove all the large trees on the house site prior to construction. The framed structure, with its white Tyvek insulation, was unscreened and visible for miles.

County Prosecuting Attorney Brad Andersen was returning from Portland to Stevenson when he spotted the Bea house. "I looked across the river and I said, 'Omigod, how did that get there?'" he recalled. He told his wife, "I bet I'm going to hear from someone about this." Sure enough, he soon got a call from Gorge Commission attorney Larry Watters asking what the county planned to do about the Bea house. "Right away, Watters came to meet with me and said they were going to come after the county because that house was in that location," Andersen said.

Andersen had done some initial investigating of his own. He had concluded that the county had followed its Scenic Area ordinance to the letter, even attaching findings of fact and conclusions of law as required. He recalls telling Watters, "'The problem is that Brian Bea is out of compliance with his building permit. If you're going to sue anyone, sue Brian Bea. This is an enforcement action and the county will take action to enforce the permit.' We weren't going to prejudge what the remedy would be."

Watters, he recalls, responded that the Gorge Commission's issue was not with Brian Bea but with Skamania County. "We don't have jurisdiction over Brian Bea," Watters told him. "We want the house moved. We're going to sue you, we're going to fine you, we're going to get an injunction." Andersen had some history with Watters, who had represented the Gorge Commission in a case that had forced Andersen's father to close a restaurant he owned in Skamania County.

Doherty said there was plenty of blame to go around. "When the commission staff investigated the case we found both compliance problems by the landowner and major issues with the county's decision," he said. "We viewed the latter as the bigger problem." The Bea house "stood out like a sore thumb," he said. "It was visible for miles along Interstate 84, even in the distance from Multnomah Falls." His office was besieged with calls asking, "What is that?" and "How could that have been permitted?"

A key issue for Doherty was that the Scenic Area Management Plan and the county's ordinance both required landowners to use existing topography as the main way to screen new development. "There was good reason for this," Doherty said. "Generally topography doesn't change over time. Trees, whether there at the time of the development or planted afterwards, do. They die, they get trimmed or cut, and often are not replaced. This becomes a real compliance issue in the long term."

Skamania County had failed to require that Brian Bea build his house on a site where natural topography would screen it. Instead, Doherty said, "The county allowed the house to be sited right on the most prominent location." As he and his staff studied options for after-the-fact screening of the house, they worried about setting a precedent that would permanently weaken the Gorge Commission's authority to enforce the Scenic Area Act.

A Painful Decision

In late July 1998, Doherty took the unprecedented step of issuing a stop-work order on the Bea house. He noted that with exterior work on the house nearly completed, it was now visible from Interstate 84, the Columbia River, and the Historic Columbia River Highway. Issuing a stop-work order while the commission decided on the next step was not an easy decision, he said, and it was his alone to make. He could not engage in a detailed discussion of the issue with commissioners, because they were required to base their decision on evidence presented in a formal hearing. "In fact, (the decision) was painfully difficult, because I was well aware of the stakes involved and the potential ramifications for the Commission," Doherty said. "Speaking for myself, and I was the individual who made the decision to bring an action against the county, there was no arrogance involved. I will never forget the soul-searching I went through in making the decision. It felt like the necessary choice at the time."

Into the Courts

The notion that the Beas might be required to move their house to a less visible site, at a cost of tens of thousands of dollars, struck many people as extreme. Bea vowed he would never move the house unless ordered to by the U.S. Supreme Court. Skamania County officials insisted that Bea's only infraction had been his failure to submit a landscaping plan. The county also contested the Gorge Commission's authority to issue a stop-work order. And the impasse was joined.

Andersen wanted to know how the three-story house rising on the bluff had managed to sidestep rigorous controls. He learned that when Brian Bea brought his plan for a single-story house with a daylight basement and a loft to the county, planner Mark Mazeski refused to approve it because it showed, in addition, a full second story with three bedrooms and two bathrooms. "Mark said, 'I'm not signing off on the conditions of approval. This is not a loft,'" Andersen recalled.

Mazeski's denial of the building permit quickly came to Commissioner Judy Carter's attention. She put pressure on Mazeski's boss, planning director Harpreet Sandhu, to approve Brian Bea's permit. Mazeski was told that his job was on the line.

In an interview in 2012, Andersen finally confirmed Carter's role. But in 1998, as he set about defending the county in the Bea house case, Andersen did not disclose that high-level political pressure had been brought to bear. Both Carter and Mazeski denied it at the time, but Gorge Commission planner Allen Bell went public with the revelation, which resulted in a bitter public dispute between Bell and Mazeski.

The public was quick to weigh in on the Bea house imbroglio. Conservationists painted Brian Bea as a selfish scofflaw who had executed an end-run around the Scenic Area Act. Conservative talk-show host Lars Larsen took up Brian and Jody Bea's cause on the airwaves. The national media portrayed Bea as a wronged property rights hero.

Meanwhile, the staff of the Gorge Commission searched for options. The tall trees that would have screened the house were gone. Without them, the house on the bluff would be hard to hide, given its size, location, light-colored cedar siding, and blue-green roof. The staff proposed three alternative home sites, all tucked behind existing trees or hidden by the topography. Bell raised the possibility that the house might need to be moved at least a few hundred feet back from the edge of the bluff.

Bea was defiant. "I am not going to put my house in some hole," he said. "I want full views. This isn't some mobile home park people are going to see."

In November, the Gorge Commission held hearings on whether the house should be moved. The hearings quickly became a media circus. Doherty argued that if the Beas were allowed to complete the house and move into it, a damaging precedent would be set. Other property owners would feel free to build luxury houses along the rim of the gorge, he said—the very scenario the Scenic Area Act had been passed to prevent.

"I'm sure hundreds of landowners would like a house out on a bluff, but they don't get one," Bell said. "It's about treating people equally."

Testimony at the hearings did not help the Beas' case. Fagerness testified that when she first visited the site in 1997, she was surprised. She had assumed the house would be much smaller and partially screened from view. A county building inspector admitted he did not know where the property line was located when he visited the site. He said Brian Bea had told him it extended all the way south to Highway 14. Bea countered that he didn't think the property line was an issue because his parents owned the land south to the highway. He insisted that the house had been built exactly where he had said it would be built back in 1993. Andersen argued that Doherty was too late in his appeal of the building permit because the house was substantially complete. "We cannot legally and practically go back and undo the decision," he said.

At the end of the public hearings, the commission ruled unanimously that the building permit was invalid and that the Bea house must be moved. A Clackamas County business offered to move it at half the standard cost.

At that point, the Beas had spent about $250,000 on their dream home, including worker wages paid in advance. Brian Bea estimated that moving the house to another site would cost more than $100,000. A new foundation would have to be poured, a new septic tank system dug, a new road built. And he was worried about how he would protect the unfinished house from winter weather.

He was hardly ready to concede defeat. Nor was Skamania County, which joined with the Beas to challenge the Gorge Commission's authority in court. The Pacific Legal Foundation, a property rights advocacy group, agreed to represent the Beas for free.

A Clark County Superior Court judge upheld the Gorge Commission's order and said the house must be moved. But in June 2001, the Washington Supreme Court reversed that verdict. It ruled 7-0 that the Gorge Commission had exceeded its authority in trying to undo a county building permit. In effect, it found that a county building permit carried more legal weight than the Scenic Area Management Plan. The court's ruling directly challenged the Gorge Commission's authority to enforce the Scenic Area Act.

The Ruling

Andersen still believes the Bea house issue could have been resolved without litigation, because the act clearly empowers the Gorge Commission to take action against individuals who violate it. "I think it was more political than legal," he said. "They wanted to beat up on Skamania County. Our argument was, 'There was a final land use decision. We require people who apply for permits to go through a full public process. A final decision is a final decision.' It was unbelievable to me that they could come in at any point and say, 'You have to move your house.'"

The state Supreme Court ruling "clipped the wings" of the Gorge Commission, Andersen said. "It was a blow to the Gorge Commission's ego. Everything had been a fight before then. This decision told the Gorge Commission it had to work with the counties." The relationship between the

Brian and Jody Bea listen intently as the Washington Supreme Court hears arguments against their attempt to build a three-story house on a bluff in violation of National Scenic Area rules. The Beas' attorney, John Groen, is in the foreground. The court ruled that the Gorge Commission overstepped its authority when it issued a stop-work order on the house and ruled that it must be downsized or moved. Photo by Troy Wayrynen of *The Columbian*.

Gorge Commission and the counties "became more of a partnership," he said. "That didn't happen until after the Bea house case."

Friends of the Gorge Conservation Director Michael Lang disagrees that the resolution of the Bea house case improved relations between the Gorge Commission and the counties. He remains convinced that Andersen sued the Gorge Commission in a deliberate and cynical campaign to weaken implementation of the Scenic Area Act and frustrate the law's purpose.

When the Gorge Commission announced that it would not appeal the ruling to the U.S. Supreme Court, the issue faded from the headlines. But though the state Supreme Court ruling had clarified the limitations of the Gorge Commission's authority, it had not given the Beas a pass on their non-conforming house. Without the county's approval, the Beas could not finish the house, which was still in violation of its building permit. The couple and their three young sons continued to camp out in a workshop on the property.

Attorneys for the Beas, the county, and the Gorge Commission began behind-the-scenes negotiations to resolve the Beas' claim for damages resulting from the stop-work order. Those negotiations continued for two years. Brian Bea remained defiant. "I didn't choose this fight but I'll end it," he told one out-of-town reporter. "I don't care about the battles. I want to win the war."

In May 2003, the parties reached a settlement. The Beas agreed to reduce the height of their house, install new siding and roofing, build an earthen berm in front of the house and plant more trees to help hide it from view. In exchange, the county and the Gorge Commission agreed to pay the Beas $300,000—with a stipulation that the couple would not get the money until all the work was completed to their satisfaction. Brian Bea estimated that would take at least two years. The press release he issued the day Skamania County commissioners approved the settlement was more conciliatory than defiant. "This settlement represents a true compromise," he said. "We need to do whatever we can so that we can finally move into our house."

The Bea house case proved a critical turning point, Lang said. "To our organization, what matters is, the landscape is protected. Ultimately, the outcome was that the house had to be redesigned. It had to be knocked down 12 feet and it had to be screened to achieve visual subordination."

"The Bea house was all about politics getting in the way of good land use decisions," the Forest Service's Jurgen Hess said. "In the long run, it helped the county. They do a good job of planning now. They have a professional staff."

A Farmhouse in Lyle

As the Bea house dispute played out in the courts, an imbroglio over another gorge house flared, this one in the small Klickitat County town of Lyle. Gail Castle, a sixty-year-old widow and lifelong Lyle resident, just wanted to replace her rundown, uninsulated farmhouse. For ninety years the weathered two-story house had stood at the base of a bluff that offered stunning views of Mount Hood and the gorge. It had been in her late husband's family since the 1940s. All those years of hot summers and cold winters had taken their toll. The foundation was crumbling. The plumbing and wiring needed replacing. The ancient linoleum was worn bare. The poorly insulated walls offered little shelter from bitter gorge winds.

But when Castle looked into renovating the old place, contractors told her it would be cheaper to build a new house. So she had plans drawn up for a one-story structure 10 feet east of her existing house. In December 1999, she applied to the Gorge Commission for a permit to build a new house and tear down the old one after the new one was completed. In March, the answer came: No.

Gorge Commission planner Gary Pagenstecher informed Castle that because her house was in a Special Management Area, she could replace it only with another house that sat on the exact footprint of her existing house.

Pagenstecher offered Castle three options: She could "minimize the visibility" of her new house by building it on a remote section of her 1,500-acre ranch. She could build a new house exactly where her present house stood, leaving her homeless during construction. Or she could add on to her dilapidated house.

Widowed since 1995, Castle made her living growing hay and raising a few horses and about thirty head of cattle. Her house was barely visible from Rowena Crest, across the river in Oregon. She didn't understand how replacing it with a lower-profile one-story structure would hurt the view. After all, she pointed out, she could have subdivided her farm into 20-acre lots long before the establishment of the National Scenic Area. "All of us who have been here longer than the Scenic Area, we seem to have taken pretty good care of the land," Castle said. "I think they should thank us."

Pagenstecher stood his ground. The management plan did allow for "in-kind replacement" of buildings that had existed prior to establishment of the Scenic Area. But he maintained that if the footprint was not identical, "it's a new building, and you review it as if there were no existing building there."

Claire Puchy had been on the job as executive director of the Gorge Commission for only a few months. She had stepped in as interim director in the summer of 1999 after Doherty resigned and moved back to the East Coast to accept a position with the National Park Service. Puchy arrived to find a demoralized staff, antiquated computers and a shortage of phones. "There was no voicemail, no decent conferencing capacity, no web site," she recalled. One of her first acts was to order business cards for her staff.

She had taken a leave of absence from her job with the Oregon Department of Fish and Wildlife. She ended up applying for the executive director's job, and a few months later the Gorge Commission offered it to her. During her twenty-one-month tenure, she commuted daily from Portland as she set about trying to turn around a politically embattled and woefully underfunded agency. When the Gail Castle case landed in her lap, she stood by her planners. They had worked with Castle, she said. They had offered her six options for an alternative home site.

But Castle was not mollified. She believed her civil rights as well as her property rights had been violated. She also understood that her situation would win her public support. She turned to Klickitat County for help. The county was only too glad to comply.

Castle's dilemma, and the Gorge Commission's perceived intransigence, triggered an outpouring of support in the county, where anger over the Gorge Commission's authority to dictate land use was especially intense. A county building official helped Castle prepare an appeal. He also advised her to file two additional applications to protect her right to build an attachment to her existing house. A new group, Gorge Reality, formed almost overnight and collected 297 signatures on a letter supporting Castle, which it mailed to members of the Gorge Commission, county commissioners, local legislators, the governor of Washington, and even members of Congress.

"I just think it's deplorable that a common-sense compromise hasn't been reached," said Klickitat County Commissioner Joan Frey. "It's a relatively simple issue."

Coincidentally or not, the county had recently hired a Seattle attorney to work exclusively on land use issues in the Scenic Area. "Our prosecuting attorney feels a lot of these issues are ready to be settled in court," Frey said.

Janis Sauter, one of the organizers of Gorge Reality, had her own ax to grind with the Gorge Commission staff. The Sauter family had been doing battle with the commission since the early 1990s over the division of the family property among five siblings after their father's death. Her husband John had waited eight months for permission to build a small hay-storage shed on the couple's property west of Lyle. The commission attached several detailed conditions to the permit. One required the family to plant ten eight-foot ponderosa pines in front of the shed to screen it and fence the trees to protect them from livestock. The Sauters appealed for permission to plant Douglas firs instead of pines, noting that pine needles can be toxic to pregnant cows. The Sauters also expected a battle over the color of the shed. They had painted it the exact buff color of the surrounding grasslands, but they'd been warned that under Scenic Area rules, buildings visible from key viewing areas had to be painted in dark earth tones.

Their experiences seemed to point to another example of regulatory overreach And it was against that backdrop that the Gorge Commission heard Castle's appeal.

Steve DiJulio, a Seattle land use attorney, agreed to represent Castle at Klickitat County's expense. He argued that unless his client was allowed to build a new house, "she can't continue to live and work on her property." At the appeals hearing, DiJulio reminded commissioners that one goal of the Scenic Area Act was to preserve historic uses and the cultural heritage of the gorge. The house Castle proposed to build, he said, "does not dominate its surroundings. It looks pastoral. It looks like what it is—a ranch."

A neighbor, Dale Swann, said what many in Klickitat County were thinking: The Gorge Commission appeared to be more concerned about protecting the views tourists saw driving through the gorge than about the rights of longtime landowners. Several commissioners signaled that they would be looking for a compromise. At the end of six hours of legal arguments, Commissioner Jim Luce of Vancouver, a moderate, was uneasy. "I'm trying to read as much flexibility into the rules as I can and still maintain the integrity of the National Scenic Area Act," he said.

Puchy herself later had second thoughts about the line she had drawn. "I knew there would be political fallout," she said in 2012. "I didn't appreciate the flexibility I had legally and that my staff had. I felt I had to be strict."

A few days before Christmas, Friends of the Gorge announced that one of its members had offered to provide Castle with temporary housing on her property at no cost to her while she built a new house. Nancy Russell, the group's co-founder, had made the offer. Castle declined it. She said she wanted to let her appeal work its way through the process.

In late December, the commission voted 8-3 to reverse its staff decision. The majority found that Puchy had erred in failing to exercise the discretion allowed under gorge land use rules to grant the permit. A crowd of fifty Castle supporters burst into applause, cheers, and whistles after the vote was taken.

The Castle case was another wake-up call for the Gorge Commission. Should its staff enforce the "minimize visibility" rule to the letter, regardless of specific circumstances? Or should the commission be an arbiter of what constituted reasonable regulation? The split was between strict constructionists, who held that allowing the house to be built outside its exact footprint would set a dangerous precedent, and those Gorge Commissioner Katharine Sheehan called "judicial activists," who looked for a way to give Castle what she wanted within the law.

Commissioner Joe Palena warned that planners' "rigid interpretation" of the rule had exposed the Gorge Commission to ridicule. Making those judgment calls was the reason Congress had established the commission in the first place, said Commissioner Joyce Reinig. In the Castle case, she said, the staff had gone too far. "It was never our intent to impose the restriction that 'minimize' meant 'eliminate.'"

What Compromise Looks Like

Lyle and Debbie Nelson thought they were home free when they broke ground on their dream house east of Washougal in the spring of 2002. They didn't count on resentment over the outcome of the Bea house case, which was still simmering in Skamania County. The Nelsons went through months of red tape before they started building their house. When Friends of the Gorge raised concerns about how visible the 10,500 square foot structure would be from the Oregon side, they agreed to scale the house back to 5,600 square feet and reduce its height from two stories to one. They also agreed to tear down the existing two-story house on the property and plant twenty Douglas firs in front of the new house to screen it from view.

Clark County approved their revised application. Friends agreed not to appeal it. But when the house was halfway built, in early 2003, the Nelsons found themselves caught in an ongoing feud involving Clark County, the Gorge Commission, and Skamania County.

The Nelsons had complied with their building permit. No one was talking about making them move the house. That would be difficult, because the presence of wetlands and unstable slopes left only two buildable acres on the 50-acre lot. Clark County declined to issue a stop-work order.

True, the Nelson house was clearly visible from the Oregon side. Its roof broke the skyline near the Interstate 84 Corbett exit, and the house could be seen from along the Historic Columbia River Highway. Yet instead of running afoul of scenic area rules, the Nelsons found themselves the targets of Skamania County Planning Director Harpreet Sandhu, who had let the Bea house go forward in violation of its building permit.

When she saw the Nelson house under construction, Sandhu contacted Puchy and demanded to know why the Gorge Commission had not intervened in Clark County's decision to permit the Nelson house. She attached digital photos of the house as seen from the Oregon side. Why was it, Sandhu demanded to know, that landowners in Skamania County could not get the same consideration as those in Clark County? Unsure of the answer, Puchy contacted Clark County and asked county officials to reconsider their decision to permit the Nelson house on the site. She asked them to undertake a "post-decision review."

Clark County agreed to propose landscaping changes to the Nelson house to reduce its visibility from Oregon. Debbie Nelson said the couple would be willing to plant more trees behind the house, but not to construct a berm in front. She said the issue of the house's profile on the skyline "was never addressed during the appeals process" by the county or by Friends. "Do we really want to open up this can of worms?" she asked.

Michael Lang of Friends of the Gorge conceded the view of the partially framed house gave him pause. "Looking at that house today, it's difficult to see how it can be screened within two years" as required, he said. "Considering how visible it is, I think it would be good for all parties to step back and assess whether it will comply with the law when it is completed."

But Debbie Nelson said Gorge Commission planner Allen Bell had assured the couple before they bought the property in 1999 that they would be able to rebuild the existing house there or replace it with a larger one. The Nelsons already had invested $300,000 in their dream home. They ultimately got their way.

Debbie Nelson sympathized with Brian Bea. "I do feel for him," she said. "That is why we have gone to such great lengths to do this properly. We would rather have built a two-story house. It's cheaper and it required less foundation and less wood. I believe we've done everything we can. We love the gorge too."

Chapter 8
Fear and Loathing

By 2000, Klickitat County was engaged in open warfare with the Columbia River Gorge Commission. Commissioners in the long, skinny rural county, populated by just 19,300 people, had refused to adopt their own Scenic Area ordinance. Because of their decision to opt out, development on 75,000 acres fronting 90 miles of the Columbia River was regulated not by the county, but by the Gorge Commission's staff.

County officials had their own vision for economic development. Thanks to its wide open spaces, lax environmental enforcement, and the efforts of an aggressive new economic development director, the county had set its sights on becoming a magnet for big industrial development projects, from gravel pits to natural gas turbines. Klickitat County also had a major revenue-generator in its Roosevelt Landfill, located in the county's sparsely populated east end, which had opened in 1990 and drew solid waste from across Washington and from as far away as California, Canada, and Alaska. The landfill generated $6.3 million in dump fees annually, providing 21 percent of the county's operating revenue.

Its major employer was an aluminum smelter near the John Day Dam, which faced an uncertain future.

As relationships with the Gorge Commission soured, Klickitat County was working on creating an energy overlay zone to encourage the development of natural gas-fired plants and a fast-track process for permitting their approval. The concept, conceived during the Northwest energy crisis of 2000 and 2001, was strongly opposed by local conservationists.

At the other end of the gorge, Clark County was embarking on a period of explosive growth. Developers had their eye on wooded parcels within the 6,000 acres of the county that lay within the National Scenic Area, and some county officials were eager to accommodate them.

Controversies over permitting of the Bea house in Skamania County and the Gail Castle house in Bingen had inflamed many Klickitat County residents. Gorge Reality sought to publicize what its members saw as the hidden agenda of Friends of the Gorge, founder Nancy Russell, and the Gorge Commission itself.

Gorge Reality's website posed pointed questions about how the Scenic Area Act had been written and how it was being implemented. It listed the past and present affiliations of key players in gorge politics and suggested that conflicts of interest were widespread. It vilified the Russells for purchasing property in the gorge and taking it off the tax rolls. Gorge Reality even challenged claims by Columbia Basin treaty tribes to their traditional fishing sites.

Founder Janis Sauter said she hoped to expose "blatant misuse of power" by the Gorge Commission and its staff. She called on U.S. Interior Secretary Gale Norton to hold congressional oversight hearings into the workings of the commission. Tim Southworth, a former Gorge Commissioner from Klickitat County, believed the county's decision to defer development decisions to the Gorge Commission staff contributed to the tension. "The Gorge Commission was never supposed to be doing this," he said. "It creates a negative effect on the people who live in the Scenic Area."

Goldendale Mayor Mark Sigfrinius acknowledged that passions ran high in the county over the role of the Gorge Commission's role in regulating development. "This is kind of a different county, a different town," he said in a 2001 interview. "There are people here who would rather the government go away."

The Gorge Commission was not the county's only target. Many were bitter over what they considered obstructionist tactics by local environmentalists Dennis and Bonnie White, who had filed numerous lawsuits to block economic development projects. "We tend to call them extortionists with binoculars," Commissioner Joan Frey quipped.

The Whites, who lived on an apple orchard near the White Salmon River, had been a thorn in the side of Klickitat County developers for a quarter-century. They had fought the regional landfill, defeated plans by the Klickitat County Public Utility District to build eight dams on the White Salmon River, and killed two wind power projects in the Columbia Hills. They had become scapegoats for the county's problems, including the Goldendale aluminum smelter's threatened shutdown.

Goldendale, the Klickitat County seat, was a quiet town of well-preserved Victorian houses in the shadow of Mount Adams. Its dominant feature was a complex of concrete grain elevators on the edge of town. A new natural gas-fired electrical generating plant was rising on the town's outskirts. But the town was anxious about the fate of the smelter down on the Columbia River. Once the county's largest private employer, it had contributed 700 high-paying jobs with an annual payroll of $50 million before it furloughed most of its workers and reduced production by 90 percent in 2000. The county's 2001 unemployment rate was 14.6 percent, tied for the state's highest.

The local weekly, the *Goldendale Sentinel*, had recently entered the fray. A new editor, Becky Blanton, arrived in September 2000 and quickly allied herself with the radical fringe. Her news articles and editorials inflamed anti-environmental passions.

In one editorial, she asserted that the county was being subjected to "ongoing political terrorism" by litigious environmentalists. She disclosed to county commissioners that the Forest Service "is partially under United Nations control now." Her comments were so over the top that some citizens had formed Goldendale Citizens for Balanced Journalism to publicize the paper's biased coverage. "The newspaper has created this atmosphere where the word 'environmentalist' has become equivalent to what the word 'communist' was in the 1950s," said Tim Young, a Goldendale filmmaker. "This is green-baiting, as opposed to red-baiting."

Klickitat County had parted ways with other rural Washington counties in choosing to go after new industry aggressively and to fight anything that stood in its way. Not only had it refused to adopt its own Scenic Area ordinance, it was one of only eleven counties that had declined to voluntarily comply with the Washington Growth Management Act, thereby passing up hundreds of thousands of dollars in state and federal economic development funds. It had joined Skamania County, its neighbor to the west, in fighting the removal of Condit Dam on the White Salmon River. For nearly a decade, it had ignored a Growth Management Act rule that required it to identify and protect wetlands and sensitive fish and wildlife habitat. And it had gone on the attack against the Trust for Public Land over its effort to protect 35 acres at Lyle Point, a grassy, windswept peninsula on the Columbia River, from becoming an upscale subdivision.

Kevin Gorman, the newly hired executive director of Friends of the Columbia Gorge, predicted in 2000 that the county's prickly relationship with the Gorge Commission would backfire. "They're not fully participating, so they play the role of throwing bombs from the outside," he said. "In the short term that may win them notice, but in the long term it won't gain them respect."

County Commissioner Frey said she had once worried about the perception that Klickitat County was against the National Scenic Area Act. No more. "In the last 10 years, the other counties have experienced high litigation costs, high administrative costs for the ordinances, all the things that Klickitat County knew would affect us," she said. "They are looking at us and saying, 'We sure envy your position.' They are looking at us with respect."

In 2000, several dozen Goldendale-area residents frustrated with Dennis and Bonnie White and with the Audubon chapter's tactics decided to stage an environmental coup and start their own development-friendly chapter.

Goldendale dentist Lyle Ferch, who helped spearhead the attempt, said he wanted to impress on the chapter's leaders the consequences of their lawsuits and appeals. "You are not suing a rock or a tree," he said. "We hurt. We have families. Is this responsible behavior, to destroy someone else's life with a piece of paper?" At the time, the chapter, with a dues-paying membership of about 380, had five pending lawsuits against the county. It was challenging a proposed gravel mining operation in Dallesport, a small wind-generation project in the Columbia Hills, and the natural gas-fired energy plant in Goldendale. Together with the Yakama Tribe, the chapter had helped defeat two other wind power projects in the Columbia Hills in the 1990s.

Meghan Sapp, a county outreach worker, contacted the National Audubon Society office in Seattle to ask what it would take to start a new chapter to serve sparsely populated eastern Klickitat County.

Jeff Parsons, director of the Washington state office, told Sapp to submit a petition with at least thirty-five signatures of people who would join a new chapter and support Audubon's mission. The signatures were collected, but Parson ultimately turned down the bid. "They have to support the mission of the National Audubon Society, which is to conserve and restore natural ecosystems," he said. Yet most of the applicants weren't even Audubon members. Besides, he said, Columbia Gorge Audubon was doing a good job serving its territory—advocating for birds and wildlife, offering field trips, putting out an excellent newsletter, and holding regular chapter meetings.

Rebuffed, Ferch then advocated a takeover of the local chapter as a way to fight the lawsuits and save the Goldendale energy plant. "It's only $30," he said in an interview with the *Goldendale Sentinel*. "Thirty dollars to have a chance to make a difference in your town, your county, and your state."

About sixty new members signed up with Columbia Gorge Audubon, but their attendance was spotty. When they did show up for meetings, they were disruptive. The last straw came when Ferch and a companion tried to videotape board meetings and wrote letters published in the *Sentinel* that opposed Audubon's mission.

"They don't understand that our mission is to actively advocate for the habitat of birds and wildlife," Dennis White said.

Though Klickitat County's tiny environmental community had once shown a united front, a schism over tactics had opened in 1995, when half the members and all the officers of Columbia Gorge Audubon split off and formed a new group, the Central Cascades Alliance. With about 200 members, the new group focused on education, research, and ecological restoration in the heart of the gorge, between Mount Adams and Mount Hood. Though both groups favored protection of the National Scenic Area, the breakaway group steered clear of the Whites' often confrontational tactics.

Jay Letto, a founder of the alliance, said the volatile political climate in Klickitat County made it harder to get people to support environmental efforts at a time when the county was under siege from development proposals. "The brush fire approach, while effective at stopping individual projects that would be harmful to the environment, takes away from the greater effort to protect sustainable ecosystems into the future," he said. Dennis White stood his ground. He accused the county of rubber-stamping new projects on behalf of outside companies with virtually no environmental scrutiny. "This story is about big business wanting to get control of our little county," he said.

Embracing the Wind

In March 2005, Klickitat County shifted gears. It adopted a first-of-its-kind Clean Energy Economic Development Zone covering 1,000 square miles, about two-thirds of the county deemed suitable for wind development. The zone included the Columbia Hills, known for their abundant populations of golden eagles, hawks, and other raptors. The move proved strategic. By the time the county's 2003 energy overlay zone took effect, the market for natural gas-fired plants had collapsed. Companies had canceled plans to build scores of new power plants in the region. The new promise, for Klickitat County and other rural Washington and Oregon counties on the broad Columbia Plateau beyond the Columbia Gorge—was blowing in the wind. A virtual forest of ethereal white wind towers rose on dry land wheat fields, marching across the landscape for as far as the eye could see. Green energy credits, both state and federal, drove a boom unimagined by rural communities five years earlier. The land, and rural economies, were transformed.

Defining Farm Land

At the other end of the gorge, fast-growing Clark County was embroiled in a spat with the Gorge Commission over whether a property zoned for agriculture could be sold for a home site. The controversy eventually got so heated that one county commissioner threatened to revoke the county's Scenic Area ordinance and turn over management to the Gorge Commission.

In February 2000, Sylvia Campbell applied to Clark County for a permit to build a one-story, 3,000-square-foot house and a 750-square-foot shop on 30 acres zoned for large-scale agriculture. Campbell and her late husband Don Campbell, former publisher of the *Columbian*, had bought the land in 1998 with plans to build a house there on a broad field with sweeping views of the Portland-Vancouver area, Washougal, and the Columbia River. Don Campbell died in December 1998. His widow decided to secure a permit allowing construction of a house on the land and then sell the property. She paid an architect $40,000 to design a one-story house that would be invisible from key viewing areas on the Oregon side. She paid another $20,000 for a well to ensure that the property would have a reliable water source.

Clark County approved the permit, but Friends of the Gorge appealed it, saying the county had failed to follow its own rule for determining whether a property zoned for agriculture could be profitably farmed. Under the rule, modeled on Oregon's strict land use law protecting high-value agricultural land, a nonfarm dwelling could be built on land zoned for agriculture only if the land was determined to be "nonsuitable for agriculture."

Those seeking to build a house on land zoned for agriculture were required to meet an income test showing the land could produce at least

$40,000 annually in gross income from farming. Friends said allowing the Campbell property to be converted without subjecting it to that test would set a damaging precedent.

Claire Puchy, the newly appointed executive director of the Gorge Commission, concurred. She faxed her letter denying the permit on August 17, the deadline for submitting written comments. But Clark County planners received it on August 18 and denied the Gorge Commission standing to file an appeal, a direct slap at its authority. County Prosecuting Attorney Bronson Potter said there was no reason to treat the commission differently from any citizen by granting it an extension. "We're not any more obligated to follow what they say (than) what someone else says," he remarked. Things heated up. Gorge Commission planner Allen Bell testified that the county had failed to conduct a cultural resource inventory or even to study whether the land was suitable for agriculture.

In December, county hearings examiner J. Richard Forester ruled that the Campbell property was unsuitable for farming because wetlands, buffers, and steep slopes covered all but eight acres of it. The only evidence of farming, he remarked, was that the owners had contracted to have the grass mowed and clippings had been fed to a neighbor's donkey.

Puchy then issued a formal notice alleging eleven violations of the Scenic Area Act, the Bistate Columbia Gorge Compact, and the county's own Scenic Area rules. But in early 2002, Clark County Commissioner Betty Sue Morris, a pro-growth advocate, upped the ante. She said she was ready to let the Gorge Commission take over all development reviews in the 6,000 acres of the county that lay within the scenic area.

"I'd be more than happy to suspend the (scenic area) ordinance and let the Gorge Commission take over," she said. Commissioners Judie Stanton and Craig Pridemore were less ready to rescind the county's year-old ordinance, at least until they got more direction from the Gorge Commission.

The real question, Morris said, was whether the county's Scenic Area ordinance conflicted with its comprehensive plan, which assumed that every legal lot was a buildable lot. "If you have a legal lot of record, you may build a residence" on it under the county plan, she said. But the Gorge Commission appeared to be imposing a new standard.

That standard was clear, said Gorge Commission Planner Brian Litt: On land zoned for large-scale agriculture, "you don't automatically have the right to build a home." That's because the Scenic Area Act was intended to protect farmland for farm use and prevent its conversion to other uses. He explained.

The concept that lands suitable for agriculture must be protected from conversion to residential development was settled law in Oregon, but not in Clark County, Washington, where farmland further and further from Vancouver was being gobbled up by developers. Friends of the Gorge warned that a decision by Clark County to rescind its ordinance would be unprecedented and would work against the county in the long run. Among other things, the county would become ineligible for grants dedicated to recreational development.

Michael Lang, Friends' conservation director, said the Campbells themselves had failed to back up their contention that they could profitably farm the property. "When the Campbells applied for the agricultural property tax assessment, they stated in writing that they would be producing over $40,000 in gross annual income from farming their property," he said. "The Campbells never even attempted to conduct farming on this scale but accepted the huge break in property taxes."

Richard Carson, Clark County's director of community development, complained that the Gorge Commission demanded too much of his busy planners and failed to adequately compensate the county for its work. "It's basically an unfunded mandate," he said. A detailed review like the one the Gorge Commission was demanding for the Campbell property would require hiring a lawyer. That single review would cost the county a thousand dollars, Carson said.

As for Sylvia Campbell, she believed that farming the property, perched atop a bluff 500 feet above the Steigerwald Lake National Wildlife Refuge, actually would damage the scenic beauty of the gorge. She felt caught in the middle of this grudge match. "This is not about my land," she said. "It's about this bitterness."

Chapter 9
Land Rush

For more than a decade after passage of the Scenic Area Act, money flowed steadily from Congress to the Forest Service, allowing managers to buy gorge property from willing sellers who could not develop their property under the new management plan. By 1999, the Forest Service had acquired about 30,000 acres, much of it through land trades with timber companies. Nearly two-thirds of the new public land was in Skamania County. But the breakneck pace of land purchases began to slow. By mid-1999, the Forest Service had spent just $3 million of its most recent $10 million appropriation, though there was no shortage of willing sellers.

The Forest Service's Washington, D.C. office dispatched a review team to the Northwest to identify the cause of the logjam. Senator Slade Gorton, a Washington Republican who chaired the Senate Appropriations subcommittee overseeing the Forest Service budget, had delivered the $10 million. Now he and other members of the delegation were calling for arbitration if necessary to get the process off center. "Senator Gorton's only goal is to break this logjam and try to facilitate a solution between the landowners and the Forest Service," said Cynthia Bergman, Gorton's press secretary. "He looks at the Interior budget every year, and when he sees money just sitting there, he wants to know why." Representative Earl Blumenauer, a Portland Democrat, grilled Northwest Regional Forester Robert Williams about why the National Scenic Area office had yet to spend the appropriated funds. "I am concerned this 'logjam' in spending the appropriated funds will hinder our efforts to protect critical lands in the National Scenic Area," he said. "The program has been a shining example of the foresight and vision of the act."

In fact, the stall was due to a complicated impasse over property appraisals. The impasse, rooted in language in the Scenic Area Act, was delaying a backlog of proposed land purchases in the Special Management

Areas. Willing sellers were running out of patience. Under the "hardship clause" in the act, the Forest Service was authorized to offer a price equal to the property's market value before passage of the law, at a time when development in the gorge was largely unrestricted.

For instance, if a property had been zoned for one-acre lots before 1987, the owner could sell it at the price it would have commanded if subdivided into one-acre lots back then, even though the law no longer allowed that. To arrive at a fair price under the law, the Forest Service had to complete two appraisals: one to establish the property's current market value in view of its limited potential for development; the other to set a price for the land pre-Scenic Area Act. The difference was the value of its development rights.

Once a property owner offered to sell, the Forest Service had three years to conduct its appraisals and decide whether to buy the property. If it chose to take a pass, there were consequences. The property would be reclassified as part of the General Management Area and far less restrictive rules on lot divisions would apply.

The hardship rule opened a deep rift between gorge property owners and Forest Service land appraisers over how to actually arrive at a pre-National Scenic Area appraisal value for individual properties under the law. Portland attorney Mike Neff represented several Skamania County landowners who were trying to sell. Their effort was further hampered, Neff said, by a 1970 county real estate law requiring that when the government buys private property, "it has to ignore the prospective value," whether as a freeway or as a garbage dump. "It cuts both ways. The problem in Skamania County is there is a disagreement over what is the fair market value if the act had not been passed," Neff said. "We have proposed a system of arbitration, but the Forest Service doesn't want that, they aren't interested in it at all."

In 2000, Senator Gorton broke the impasse—and effectively ended the Forest Service land acquisition program—when he won passage of a bill that required landowners to offer their gorge properties for sale by March 2001 and set a deadline for the Forest Service to make decisions on the purchase of those properties within three years after that. The bill put pressure on both landowners and the Forest Service. If landowners failed to make their offers by the deadline, they lost the opportunity to take advantage of the hardship clause. If the Forest Service failed to act on an offer within three years, the property would be downzoned.

Under an intense deadline, a team of Forest Service land officers fanned out across the Scenic Area, visiting eighty-four separate pieces of property that had been offered for sale. The team identified about fifty that met their guidelines for purchase. The agency had to take a pass on other scenic and ecological gems, including a property on the Washington side with valuable mature forests, for which the price tag was simply too high.

In fact, the Forest Service was stretched thin trying to manage the tens of thousands of acres it had already acquired. It had no money for signs or for trail development. Some Forest Service officials admitted that they had not proceeded strategically in their acquisition of land during the early years of the Scenic Area Act's implementation. The act had authorized the Forest Service to spend $40 million buying gorge properties from willing sellers who were unable to develop their land in the Special Management Areas. Gorge property owners had flooded the agency with offers to sell. But from the beginning, the Forest Service bought land on a first come, first-served basis from private landowners without any overall strategy.

In 1996, Forest Service land staff officer Ed Medina conceded publicly that the agency had purchased most of its gorge land without determining whether the acreage was worth buying. He estimated that one-third of the land the agency had acquired between 1987 and 1994 should not have been purchased. Some of those purchases were discontinuous patches of forest that could not readily be developed for recreation. Purchases had been made "on a first-come, first-served basis," Medina said. "If someone walked in the door, more than likely we were going to acquire it. That happens sometimes when you get an abundance of money."

The agency also spent years arranging a high-stakes land trade with SDS Lumber Co. and Broughton Lumber Co., the two major timber companies in the mid-gorge. Ultimately SDS Lumber agreed to exchange 945 acres in the National Scenic Area for 1,314 acres of the Gifford Pinchot National Forest outside the Scenic Area boundary. Broughton agreed to swap 1,837 acres within the Scenic Area for 705 acres of national forest land outside the Scenic Area. The Forest Service defended the exchange—2,332 acres of private property for 2,019 acres of federal forest land—saying it was based on appraisals that equalized the value of the timber land exchanged, and that the massive trade would not compromise habitat for the northern spotted owl.

At times, members of Congress intervened directly to make sure the federal government bought prized properties. Senator Mark Hatfield of Oregon, joined by Sen. Patty Murray of Washington, added language to a 1995 appropriations bill directing the Forest Service to acquire an old gravel quarry known as the Starr property near Lyle, at the mouth of the Klickitat River. The property was not on the Forest Service's list of high-priority sites.

Nonetheless, "it was a great acquisition," said Michael Lang of Friends of the Gorge. "It was an old quarry and junkyard, an eyesore. That decision certainly had its detractors at the time. But once the decision was made and the junk was hauled away, a lot of them changed their minds." The Starr property was cleaned up and became the Balfour-Klickitat day use area, which overlooks a popular winter sanctuary for bald eagles.

One-third of the money the Forest Service spent in the first two years—about $3.5 million—went toward buying land or development rights on 945 acres in the Mount Pleasant area, between Washougal and Cape Horn. Some people considered this area one of the most beautiful panoramas in the gorge as viewed from Crown Point on the Oregon side. The green quilt of fields and forests was dotted with small farms, but it was still sparsely developed. The fear was that it would not remain that way for long. By buying development rights, the Forest Service could block subdivisions and preserve rural farm use without buying the land outright.

Buying land in the gorge to save it from development was nothing new. For a century, wealthy philanthropists had made outright gifts of land to protect the most scenic, fragile, and ecologically valuable properties for public use. Land trusts, funded by investors to purchase and hold valuable lands until they could be purchased by government agencies or conservation agencies, gradually came to fulfill that role. One of the best-known was the Trust for Public Land. The San Francisco-based land trust began making strategic land purchases in the gorge in the 1970s to safeguard properties threatened with imminent development. This bridge funding was essential to acquiring and holding the Rizor property, Steigerwald Lake, and many other parcels.

But in December 1987, with passage of the Scenic Area Act, the Trust had announced that it was selling all its gorge holdings, worth a total of $11 million. It had held those properties five times longer than normal, paying interest, and other expenses while waiting for the Forest Service or some other agency to step up and purchase them for conservation purposes. In all, the Trust had conducted sixty-five transactions in the gorge that ultimately led to protection of nearly 17,000 acres as parks and open space.

Congress took that into account when it passed the Scenic Area Act by putting the Trust first in line for federal land acquisition dollars. It drew up a series of "special purchase areas" that included large chunks of Trust land. Appropriations to buy those lands began flowing, but not fast enough. "We couldn't hang on much longer," said Trust Vice President Harriet Burgess, who had taken a strong interest in buying land visible from key viewing areas in the Gorge.

In some cases, the Trust had made a profit on those purchases. For example, the Forest Service paid the Trust $1.2 million for the 1,900-acre Lauterback Ranch in Klickitat County, its first major land purchase. The Trust had paid $962,000 for the property. But the Trust lost money on St. Cloud Ranch, a historic farm along the shore of the Columbia River that eventually became a Forest Service day use area. The Trust had bought the ranch for $485,000; it sold it to the Forest Service for $335,000.

Nancy Russell was well aware of the urgency of buying key gorge properties to protect them before it was too late. She and her husband Bruce Russell began using their personal wealth to buy land in the gorge in 1980, when they purchased four acres above Memaloose State Park in the eastern gorge for $60,000. At the time the property was home to a dilapidated double-wide trailer, two outbuildings, and a collection of whirligigs. Russell called her new acquisition "Rancho Whirligig." She had the buildings removed and set about planting native lupine, balsam root, and Columbia River parsley on the slopes. The Russells eventually purchased 60,000 acres of sensitive land on both sides of the river, including bluff-top properties slated for upscale housing at Cape Horn. Russell was particularly determined to save the promontory, known as Pioneer Point, because it was Washington's premier gorge viewpoint.

Dave Cannard, one of the original Gorge Commissioners, also invested private funds in saving property at Pioneer Point—and waited years for the Forest Service to reimburse him. The campaign to save Pioneer Point and acquire it for public use was not initially supported by the Forest Service. It would take a full quarter-century of effort by the Russells, Friends of the Columbia Gorge and a local group, the Cape Horn Conservancy, to realize that dream.

Even before there was a National Scenic Area, The Nature Conservancy played a key role in the effort to protect one of the premier ecological treasures in the gorge. In 1978, with help from Oregon Gov. Tom McCall, the conservancy purchased 271 acres on the Rowena Plateau, a high basalt mesa just west of Rowena Crest near the Oregon town of Mosier. The preserve, a botanical jewel, is located in the transition zone between the moist, heavily forested west side of the Cascades and the drier bunch-grass prairies of the east.

The plateau is an artifact of the Ice Age floods, which unleashed more than 200 feet of floodwater over the plateau and stripped it of vegetation. Over the next 10,000 years, Cascade volcanoes covered the plateau with three to four feet of windblown ash, known as loess, which eventually eroded into mounds. These "biscuit mounds" bloom with wildflowers in spring.

In designing the Historic Columbia River Highway, architect Samuel Lancaster created the Rowena Crest Viewpoint to highlight the view of the mesa and the surrounding landscape. Here, the conservancy established the Tom McCall Nature Preserve, named for the Oregon governor whose name is synonymous with the state's conservation ethic. A one-mile trail crosses the plateau to spectacular cliff edges and a three-mile trail climbs a thousand feet to the summit of McCall Peak.

Until 2004, Friends of the Gorge was a passive player in the gorge land acquisition process. Friends could lobby the Forest Service to buy specific properties, but its modest budget of $650,000 did not allow the nonprofit organization to buy land on its own. Then, in early 2004, Norman Yeon, son of legendary Oregon lumber and real estate baron John B. Yeon, and brother to Columbia Gorge advocate John Yeon, died and left half his $8 million cash estate to the Friends, enabling the organization to establish its own land trust. The news, announced to members in March 2005, signaled a shift for Friends. Its arsenal now included not only lawsuits and appeals but direct purchase of land. Four million dollars was not enough to acquire all the land on Friends' wish list. But it was a start.

Friends directors were anxious to begin acquiring land. Executive Director Kevin Gorman said the land trust would look first at nearly 2,000 acres the Forest Service had been unable to buy even though the owners had offered to sell.

No one was happier at the news than Nancy Russell. "I've been scrambling around for twenty-five years to keep Friends of the Gorge in business," she told the *Oregonian*. "This group was the little engine that could. It's a small group, but it's capable of very big things."

Train passing orchards near Hood River, Oregon. Photo by Darryl Lloyd.

Chapter 10
Oregon Pushback

Martha Bennett was flipping through a newspaper in 2001 when she saw a notice that the Columbia River Gorge Commission was looking for a new executive director. Bennett had a graduate degree in public policy from the University of California at Berkeley. She had won a prestigious fellowship on Capitol Hill, working for U.S. Sen. Mark Hatfield on local government and environmental issues. Eventually she decided Washington, D.C., was not for her and moved home to Oregon, where she landed a job with the city of Albany, then went on to an administrative post with the city of Milwaukie, a Portland suburb that was trying to stabilize its economy.

She started reading up on the Gorge Commission. She read the National Scenic Area Act. "I thought, 'This agency seems cool,'" she said. She got an interview with the commission, then a second interview. "It was one of those moments in your career when every question they asked, I knew the answer to," she recalled. One of those questions was how she would deal with people who told lies about the commission. That told her the commission had a political problem.

Bennett landed the job and moved with her husband to Hood River. Though Claire Puchy, her predecessor, had made improvements, the Gorge Commission office still had the feel of a backwater agency, she said. "The phone system was dysfunctional. There was hand-me-down furniture. There were desks that didn't open." More critical, the Gorge Commission appeared to lack even the most basic operational rules. The directors who had preceded her—Richard Benner, Jonathan Doherty, and Puchy—had been occupied with setting up the commission and writing and enforcing the Scenic Area management plan. "There was no personnel policy, no policy for leaves of absence." Where to start?

That wasn't a theoretical question. The Washington Supreme Court had just ruled against the Gorge Commission in the Bea house case. "At the very top of the list was that Supreme Court ruling," she said. The court had made it clear that the Gorge Commission could not invalidate a permit granted by a county. "We had to figure out what that meant."

Legislative foes were turning up the heat. Oregon State Sen. Ted Ferrioli, a Republican whose district included the east end of the gorge, attached a note to the commission's 2001-03 state budget withholding part of its two-year operating appropriation. Ferrioli was hearing from disgruntled constituents about the Gorge Commission. He wanted their concerns addressed.

"Ferrioli viewed himself as a private property rights person," Bennett said. "He wanted oversight. He believed that the counties did not have sufficient leadership." The Oregon legislator also was hearing from conservative state legislators in Washington who opposed the Gorge Commission, and from Gorge Reality, which was rankled because the Gorge Commission was not bound by the federal Freedom of Information Act. The group had asked Oregon House Speaker Mark Simmons to convene the oversight hearings after Gorge Commission officials refused to release a draft document that Gorge Realty was trying to get its hands on.

Washington critics of the commission had pressed their case with conservative Republican U.S. Rep. Doc Hastings, who represented the eastern gorge. They had delivered petitions with 5,000 signatures requesting congressional oversight hearings on the commission's role and the 1986 law.

In March 2002, Ferrioli scheduled the first in a series of legislative oversight committee hearings on the Gorge Commission's role and accountability. He invited his Washington counterparts to join the proceedings. At issue, he said, was whether the states, under the bistate Columbia Gorge Compact, had any powers over the commission beyond the power to approve its budget and appoint half its members. Ferrioli already had a legal opinion from Oregon's Office of Legislative Counsel that concluded the states had more than just budget authority over the Gorge Commission.

It would fall to Bennett to defend the law and the commission's role. She was asked to discuss recent litigation, how the commission resolved conflicts, and its relationships with state and local governments and gorge residents.

The first oversight hearing was held in The Dalles. People from throughout the Gorge showed up to testify. A few defended the Gorge Commission, but most complained of inflexible development standards, high-handed bureaucrats, and endless delays. Several speakers described being put through what they considered unnecessary hoops by Gorge Commission planners. The hearing stretched for more than seven hours, well past 9 p.m.

Ferrioli, a former timber industry lobbyist, took pains not to present himself as a fire-breathing dragon. "What this is not, is an issue of whether we will have a Columbia Gorge Commission or a national scenic area," Ferrioli said. Congress had spoken on those issues. Instead, he said, he wanted to identify problems that state lawmakers might have the power to address, like the commission's need for a system to resolve conflicts with landowners outside the formal appeals process.

Michael Ferguson, Idaho's state economist, was a star witness. He said it had taken him nine months to get an answer when he tried to find out whether property he had bought near The Dalles lay within the scenic area. Gorge Commission planners made him pay for his own survey and then rejected it, he said. That issue, in part a result of sloppy boundary-drawing, had since been resolved.

Georgia Murray, a realtor in The Dalles, criticized the way the Forest Service appraised property offered for sale by her clients. "I believe they cheated people out of a fair value for their land," she said. Casey Heuker broke down describing how her family's house in the scenic area had burned to the ground fourteen months earlier and she was still waiting for a permit to rebuild on the original site. But under questioning, she admitted that the Gorge Commission had approved her permit; an appeal from Friends of the Columbia Gorge was holding it up. Norm Haight of Skamania County complained that he was not allowed to build a cluster development on his land near Washougal because it was zoned for large-scale agriculture under the management plan, yet neither did he have the option to sell the property to the Forest Service, either—a perceived unfairness written into the law. The Portland area had passed a $130 million bond measure to buy green space, Haight said, and that's how open space in the gorge should be protected, too.

Several speakers complained about the lack of effective investment in job creation in gorge communities. "It's clear that that the economic development aspect was oversold to residents of the gorge," Ferrioli said.

Congress had authorized $10 million for economic development projects, $5 million in each state, but most development that had occurred so far was "really recreation enhancement," said Jim Wilcox, a realtor in The Dalles.

Former Gorge Commissioner Sally Newell of Underwood responded with some history. In the early years, she said, the commission wanted to play an active role in economic development, but Washington state officials insisted on screening funding proposals through an investment council, relegating the commission to rubber-stamping its recommendations.

When it was her turn, Bennett pointed out that it was former Oregon Gov. Vic Atiyeh and former Washington Gov. Booth Gardner who had pressed Congress to give the states authority through the Bistate Compact so that the federal government would not have sole oversight of development in the gorge. "We are an invention of the states," she said.

As a result, she said, the Gorge Commission was neither a federal agency nor a state agency —"neither fish nor fowl," in Ferrioli's words—and was covered by neither state's laws but only by its own administrative rules.

Washington State Rep. Marc Boldt remarked that the only time the two states had worked together successfully on Scenic Area issues was in 1997, when the two legislatures had agreed to make deep cuts in the commission's budget. "It wasn't the best process, but it certainly got attention," he said.

Bennett presented a vigorous defense of the Scenic Area Act. It was working, she said, and she had the numbers to prove it. Despite a few headline-producing controversies, the commission had had to weigh in on only about forty of the 1,600 development applications submitted so far under its 1992 management plan.

Michael Lang of Friends of the Columbia Gorge backed Bennett up. Scenic Area rules were not stymieing development, he said. In fact, 600 houses had been built and 200 land divisions approved in the gorge under the 1992 plan. "Overwhelmingly, people who apply for development permits get what they want," he said.

At the end, armed with his legal opinion, Ferrioli said he wanted the oversight committee to identify proposed changes to the compact for the 2003 Oregon Legislature to consider. He acknowledged that any changes would have to comply with the 1986 law and be agreed to by both states. "There are a host of issues that the compact is silent on," Ferrioli said. "Maybe after fifteen years it is time to revisit this."

In late November, Ferrioli issued findings of fact resulting from the oversight hearings. They amounted to a ringing endorsement of the Scenic Area Act and a mild scolding of the Gorge Commission for the way it was implementing the law.

The committee found that citizens of the Mid-Columbia region overwhelmingly supported the objectives of the act, but were less supportive of the Gorge Commission "because of perceived issues of fairness, procedures/processes for appeal, and overall administration" of the law.

It recommended that a standing committee be established to conduct legislative oversight of the Gorge Commission and recommend changes to the Bistate Compact to resolve disputes. It also identified jurisdictional issues of concern. For example, disputes affecting landowners and property within Oregon had been heard by a Washington state court, a situation the committee called "unlawful." It called for changes to assure that appeals and litigation would originate and be fully adjudicated in the appropriate state court.

Ferrioli made it clear that he expected these issues to be addressed. Because the two legislatures controlled the commission's budget, they could make it next to impossible for the commission to do its job. Neither legislature followed up on the recommendations. But Gorge Commission foes continued to use the threat of funding cuts to keep the commission in line.

Bennett had passed her first test as an executive director of the Gorge Commission. Her political savvy worked to her advantage. And she insisted that the implied threat from Ferrioli's committee did not faze her. "I don't think the priorities of the legislators are that far away from those the commission itself has identified," she said. Gorge counties, she said, "now worked more closely with the Gorge Commission staff to enforce scenic area rules than ever before."

Meanwhile, back at the office in White Salmon, Bennett and the Gorge Commission had a more immediate crisis to deal with. An inspection of the agency's leased offices in July 2002 revealed dry rot, mold, loose wiring, poor ventilation, and exposed asbestos-containing insulation around a water pipe above the kitchen area. Gorge Commissioner Walt Loehrke, a licensed building contractor, agreed to perform the inspection at no cost because the Gorge Commission had no money in its budget to pay for it.

On advice from the Washington Industrial Safety and Health Agency, commission staff members vacated the office for three days in August while the state conducted its own inspection. It found two violations of state standards and fined the building's owner.

The commission already had asked the two legislatures for an additional $65,000 in the next budget cycle to cover the cost of relocating its offices to a newer building. But after commissioners learned they had an asbestos problem that threatened employees' health, they decided not to wait for the legislatures to act and risk a civil suit. A single asbestos exposure claim could cost the agency $300,000, Bennett pointed out. Instead, Bennett said, the Gorge Commission would find the money to make the move, even if it came out of program costs. Bennett herself was eight months pregnant. She'd recently noticed a peculiar smell in her office and moisture stains on the walls. It wasn't the first time the commission had asked for relocation money. Claire Puchy had requested help from the states in 2000, after it was discovered that the 1960s-vintage building was plagued by rats, a leaking roof, and contaminated drinking water. Her request went nowhere.

Complicating the issue was the fact that the commission had no insurance to cover legal liability if a court ordered it to pay damages in a civil suit. That hadn't been an issue until Brian and Jody Bea filed a $1 million claim for damages against the Gorge Commission for costs associated with their inability to complete and occupy their Skamania County house.

The two states had agreed to cover any costs resulting from the Bea claim, but Bennett had been unable to find a private insurer willing to provide liability insurance to cover future claims. Both states had initially refused to allow the commission into their state risk management pools. Washington later reconsidered and said the commission could join the pool if it paid a premium of $7,000. That expenditure was not in the Gorge Commission's budget.

At a meeting in July 2002, some commissioners appeared stunned when Bennett informed them that they were not insured against legal claims for decisions they made in their official capacity. In a memorable exchange, Kenn Adcock, the Gorge Commissioner from Klickitat County, asked, "Right at the moment we're not covered?"

"Right," Bennett said.

"At all?" Adcock asked.

"Right," Bennett said.

The commission eventually moved into newer offices in downtown White Salmon and found a liability insurance carrier. Just in time, too, as the impoverished agency tackled its next big challenge: amending its 1992 management plan.

Chapter 11
A Pile of Rocks

The rock mounds scattered among pines and oaks captured Susan Johnson's imagination when she first walked the five-acre property near Underwood in the mid-Columbia Gorge. Moss-covered and mysterious, they rose in piles up to six feet high and 20 feet across. Ferns and flowers grew up amid the boulders. One sprouted a large scrub oak. "I was just struck that they were such a unique feature," she said. "They were really, really beautiful. They felt very old."

Susan and Brett Johnson were living in Seattle in 1999 when their son Caden was born. They wanted to raise him in a rural community. They fell in love with the gorge property and bought it for $85,000. They would drive down from Seattle on weekends, spread a blanket on the ground, and uncork a bottle of wine as they planned their dream house in the woods. The Johnsons hired a Portland architect to design a house around the rock piles. They planned to leave them untouched, except for a three-foot by twelve-foot section of a low rock wall that lay in the driveway's path. They checked to make sure the property had the necessary permits and learned that the Gorge Commission had signed off on its development.

The Commission's charge—to protect cultural resources in the Scenic Area—is not limited to Native American artifacts. Relics associated with the early years of white settlement in the gorge—farming, logging, mining—though that power has seldom been tested.

As part of his review of the proposed Johnson house, a Forest Service archaeologist Thomas J. Turck had conducted a cultural resources survey in 1997. "The area was very rocky and there were several rock walls," Turck wrote. But he had found no cultural remains. Based on that finding, the Johnsons applied for a building permit and hired a contractor.

But just as construction was about to begin, regional Forest Service archaeologist Mike Boynton happened to be passing by on his way to survey another property and spotted the rock piles. He immediately recognized what he believed to be an archaeological treasure trove—a "culturally significant resource."

The resulting bureaucratic nightmare dashed the Johnsons' dream of living on this land—and ultimately resulted in the destruction of one of the most prominent rock piles, which would have filled the view from their living room window.

"Rock walls are relatively common, cairns are not unheard of, but the magnitude of these was unusual," Boynton told a reporter after his discovery. "I've never seen anything of that scale and extent." He notified Skamania County planners that there might be important cultural artifacts on the site and said all construction activity within 100 feet of the rock piles must stop at once.

In his follow-up report, he concluded that the piles might even be eligible for the National Register of Historic Places. He opined that they might be evidence of early settlers' efforts to clear land for apple orchards and build irrigation ditches. In fact, he noted, there had been an apple boom between 1905 and 1920 in the Underwood area.

"While they may appear to be prosaic piles of rock, they represent several obvious and possibly as-yet-undiscovered elements of land settlement, distribution, and utilization on Underwood Heights at about the turn of the twentieth century," Boynton wrote. Even bits of metal and broken glass found on the site might be significant, he said. He speculated that a survey might find a soldered condensed milk can, a milk pail, a plowshare, a grate, an ox shoe, or shards of amethyst-colored glass of a type that was not manufactured after 1928. Boynton waxed eloquent about the clearing of the land and the blasting of the rocks to make room for orchards. He recommended no disturbance of the rock piles during construction or, alternatively, that construction be delayed until detailed research, including physical examination of the actual rock piles, could be completed.

Under Scenic Area rules, the displacement of cultural resources during construction must be avoided unless avoidance isn't "practicable," defined as "able to be done, considering technology and cost," he pointed out.

The Washington State Historic Preservation Office lost Boynton's report. Five days before its deadline for responding, an official rubber-stamped it. The state did no on-the-ground survey of its own. But its concurrence set

Susan and Brett Johnson and their son Caden stand on the property near White Salmon where they hoped to build their dream house. Piles of rocks on the site that archaeologist deemed culturally significant doomed their plans. Photo by Janet L. Mathews of *The Columbian*.

in motion a process to consider whether the rock piles should be included on the National Historic Register.

The Johnsons were incredulous. In a letter to a Skamania County planner, Brett Johnson said he had found advertising circulars, plastic caulking tubes and other junk in and around the rock pile. "Our development of this property will end its use as a rural garbage dump, which was not one of the culturally significant activities pointed out by Mr. Boynton, but seems to be the real use of this land for the last eighty years or so," he quipped.

A contractor and construction crew were standing by. Options for moving the house to a different site on the property were severely limited by the fact that the Washington Department of Fish and Wildlife had designated four of its five acres as western grey squirrel habitat and placed that portion off-limits to development.

Yet the couple chose to cooperate. They offered to pay $6,000 to have the few rocks blocking the path of their driveway relocated to adjacent piles, under the supervision of archaeologists. "We thought we were home free," Susan Johnson said.

Not so, Boynton said. "They never submitted a mitigation plan. A document was never prepared or presented. We don't do anything on verbals."

On January 25, 2001, Susan Johnson called a county planner to confirm that excavation of the building site could proceed. Actually, she was told, there could be no mitigation because Boynton had used the term "culturally significant" in his report. The house would have to be redesigned to avoid the rock piles entirely.

She reached her husband via satellite phone in Alaska's Bering Strait, where he was overseeing pollock harvests for an Alaska fishing cooperative. "It's over," she said. The Johnsons were out $25,000 for architectural fees and other costs. They abandoned their plans and asked the previous owners to release them from the sale. The owners agreed, and joined the Johnsons in appealing the planning department's finding to the Skamania County Board of Adjustment, which hears and considers county land disputes.

The board met, took testimony, and ruled that the rock piles were not "significant," not "discovered," and could not be grounds for revoking the Johnsons' building permit. "It is unfair to burden or delay the current use and development of the subject property based on this late review of the piles of rocks by Mr. Boynton," they wrote. The Forest Service and Gorge Commission had had ample time to evaluate the property for cultural use during the process of approving its building permit, the board ruled. "That final decision cannot be negated now." The staff of the Gorge Commission and the Forest Service appealed that ruling to the full Gorge Commission.

In the meantime, the original owners saw the writing on the wall. They knew their property would lose significant value as a building lot if the Gorge Commission upheld the planning staff's decision. They consulted a lawyer. Then they called in the bulldozers.

The large rock pile at the north end of the property was leveled. Some of the rocks were scattered about the property. About ten truckloads were hauled away. At that point, "It was no longer a matter of discussing whether the rocks were significant or not,'" said Martha Bennett, executive director of the Gorge Commission. "We were now dealing with the issue that the rocks had been moved."

The Gorge Commission was scheduled to hear the appeal in May 2002. The Skamania County Board of Adjustment planned to argue that the Gorge Commission could not overturn a final land use decision in light of new information. It was the same argument Skamania County had used to persuade the Washington State Supreme Court to overturn the Gorge

Commission's ruling that Brian Bea must move his partially built house after obtaining a county building permit.

But on May 7, the item was yanked from the Gorge Commission's agenda following a day-long mediation session involving all the parties. The owners agreed to recognize the remaining rock piles as culturally significant, to pay up to $10,000 for an archaeological survey, and to donate $5,000 to an organization that worked for the preservation of cultural resources in the gorge. They had decided to cut their losses. They were out $11,000 in legal fees, and they knew it would cost them far more to pursue their case through the courts. "They wanted two pounds of flesh and we gave them a half-pound to get this over with," said property owner Jim Boaz.

The Johnsons moved on. They bought a half-acre lot within the urban area of White Salmon, where gorge protections do not apply, and built their house there. The view from their living room was stunning, but they found it hard to forgive and forget. "It's difficult to feel anything but violated," Brett Johnson said. "I wanted to protect those rocks and not let anyone touch them," Susan Johnson agreed. "If at any point in the process someone had come along and said, 'We think these rocks are significant and we will buy your property,' we would have done that. The whole purpose of the act is to protect the beauty of this area. The way the act is being enforced is forcing people to do things that are counter to the purpose of the act, just to protect their investments."

For Martha Bennett, it was a hard lesson learned about the need for open communication. In this case, she said, "the government agencies failed to communicate with each other and the Johnsons paid a high price for that failure."

Windsurfers, with the Columbia Gorge Hotel in the background, 2002. Photo by Darryl Lloyd.

Chapter 12
Time to Amend

At the end of 2002, a daunting new task loomed for Martha Bennett and the Gorge Commission. The Scenic Area Act required the commission to review the 1992 management plan after a decade and consider whether amendments were required. That process already was behind schedule. Amending the plan was no small thing. During its first decade, it had been subject to a volley of legal challenges. Some of its language was ambiguous. Any changes the Gorge Commission proposed would be subject to approval by the U.S. Secretary of Agriculture.

Some Gorge Commissioners felt the plan's visibility standard for new buildings needed tweaking in the wake of the Brian Bea and Gail Castle cases. Bennett agreed. The issue of whether to require developers to "minimize the visibility" of their houses was at the top of the list, she said, because it had generated the most appeals. It had also given the commission and its staff a reputation as stiff, unyielding, and bureaucratic. Critics said the commission's rules tied landowners in red tape and infringed on their property rights.

Friends of the Gorge, however, considered any change to the standard a major misstep.

"In its own 1998 monitoring report, the Gorge Commission said that requiring siting of new development to minimize visibility was the most valuable tool they had," Friends Conservation Director Michael Lang pointed out. "Now the staff has flip-flopped on that. What happened? We believe political pressure happened."

A major revamping of the management plan was premature, Lang argued, until the Gorge Commission had a clearer picture of how a decade of development had affected the Scenic Area. Approximately a thousand new buildings had been built there since the beginning of 1987. Friends pushed for the commission to analyze the cumulative effects of its decisions to approve those developments, identify where new buildings had marred scenic views, and hold those areas to a higher standard.

Gorge Commission Chair Anne Squier, a land use attorney, agreed that analyzing the cumulative impact of development would be useful. "It's clear we don't have as much baseline information as we need," Squier said. Unfortunately, she added, the commission lacked the resources to do the analysis.

Gorge Commission planners, working with the Forest Service and the six gorge counties, developed a list of proposed changes aimed at making the rules fairer to property owners, easier for county planners to administer and more effective in protecting scenic vistas, open space and natural resources in the gorge.

In January 2003, Bennett announced that the public soon would have its say on proposed changes. Her staff scheduled scores of briefings and public hearings on proposed changes, some minor and some far-reaching. In the "minor" category were issues such as whether to limit construction of sheds and garages on lots visible from key gorge viewpoints. In the "far-reaching" class were proposals to relax overall standards for new development. "We are trying to streamline the process and address areas of overregulation wherever possible," Bennett said. "Our goal is not to decrease resource protection as a result of that process."

She knew, however, that what was riding on the outcome of the political tug-of-war surrounding revision of the gorge protection rule book was nothing less than the political survival of the Scenic Area Act. She knew also that the future of threatened gorge landscapes could depend on addressing the legitimate concerns of those most affected by restrictions on development.

As expected, the most consequential debate came over whether to relax the rule requiring that property owners "minimize visibility" of new developments that were visible from key viewpoints.

In the Gail Castle case, gorge planners had interpreted that language to mean any new house built in the Special Management Area must be built on the property's least visible building site, even if that site had no view of the Columbia River. Some Gorge Commissioners already had concluded that this interpretation amounted to regulatory overkill. In fact, planners already had softened their stance by the time plan review began. A consensus was forming that property owners in the Scenic Area no longer would have to hide their houses from view, though new buildings still would be required to blend in with their surroundings.

Commissioners strengthened the standard in other ways. They agreed that developers no longer would be able to rely on trees alone to screen their houses from view. Instead, they would have to show that even if all the trees were cut down, existing topography would allow their houses to blend in with the landscape. In an effort to reach out to frustrated landowners, commissioners also authorized development of a handbook to guide property owners in choosing appropriate building materials and exterior colors. Under the new plan, buildings visible from key viewpoints would have to be painted in dark earth tones. By then, the Beas had long ago painted their nonconforming house black.

The plan amendment process was slow getting off the ground. "There was a level of detail that was slowing the process down," Bennett admits. "We were talking about mailboxes and flagpoles." Meanwhile, new issues kept popping up that made it clear the management plan needed clarification.

Tim and Casey Heuker lived on a family compound in Warrendale, Oregon, inside the National Scenic Area, that was also a fish-processing plant. On New Year's Day 2001, their sixty-year-old house in the National Scenic Area burned to the ground. The family filed for a permit to build a new house on the site. Multnomah County and the Gorge Commission granted the permit. But the question of what restrictions should be put on their replacement dwelling was a gnarly one that would eventually reach the Oregon Court of Appeals.

In early 2003, with the new house still under construction, Casey Heuker stood in the two-story main room and showed off her million-dollar view. It took in Bonneville Dam upstream and Hamilton Mountain and Beacon Rock directly across the river. A barge loaded with sawdust filled the window frame as it slid past on the Columbia River. A fierce east wind had whipped the river's surface into whitecaps and swept the clouds away.

Though the new house could be seen from the river and parts of the Beacon Rock trail, it was permitted because the Gorge Commission and Multnomah County had deemed it to be an "in-kind replacement"—a structure roughly the same size and occupying the same footprint as the house that had burned down.

The Heukers had scaled back plans to build a larger house in order to qualify for this loophole. But they had chosen a more contemporary design, with large windows and a deck facing the river. They still had to make their house "visually subordinate" to the surrounding landscape—in this case, a narrow strip of river frontage backed by steep forested slopes. They had agreed to paint it dark brown and use non-reflective roof shingles and windows and to plant trees on both sides of the house. But they drew the line at planting several large conifers between their house and the river, as demanded by Friends of the Gorge.

Casey Heuker said she did not take her million-dollar view for granted. "You do feel lucky you have it, and you don't want to take advantage of it, but you don't want it taken away either," she said. She and her husband argued that the only landscaping they should have to replace was that damaged by the fire.

Friends of the Gorge had originally objected to the design of the house. It was 50 percent larger than the previous house, with twice as much window surface facing the river. But Friends had agreed not to challenge the design, so that the Heukers could proceed with construction. The organization stood firm, however, on the landscaping issue, arguing that Scenic Area rules required replacement dwellings to be less visible than the houses they replaced. In June 2002 the Gorge Commission agreed that the visibility standard did apply to the Heuker house, but only to the extent it was "practicable" for the Heukers to comply.

Friends appealed, accusing the Gorge Commission of making up the rules as it went along. It pointed to photographs taken by the Forest Service from the Beacon Rock Trail in 1993 as evidence that the original Heuker house had enjoyed only a partial view of the river then, because large cottonwood trees lined the shore to the east and west. Those trees had since been cut down. The Heukers denied that they had logged the cottonwoods.

Joined by a private property rights group, Oregonians in Action, the Heukers appealed the Gorge Commission's "visually subordinate" rule. Casey Heuker said it would cost up to $30,000 to buy and plant fifteen to twenty trees 20 feet tall, as Friends was demanding. She also questioned whether the trees would survive the fierce east winds that buffeted the property.

Friends said it was asking only that the Heukers partially shield the view of their house from the river. "We're not asking them to replace the

100-foot cottonwoods that were there before," Lang said. "No one has said they have to completely lose their view."

For Friends, the objective was clear: No loss of scenic values. For Gorge Commissioners, confronted with real people facing government rules they found arbitrary, the balancing act was more difficult to pull off.

As it happened, the Heukers' fish processing business loomed as a larger issue as the Gorge Commission considered amendments to the 1992 management plan. The plan made no provision for non-treaty commercial fishing in the Scenic Area. The Heukers argued that the business was a legitimate pre-existing use that should have been grandfathered into the plan.

Tim Heuker was one of five brothers in the business that had been founded by their father Bernie Heuker. The Heukers fished mostly in Alaska, but also on the Columbia River when it was open to commercial fishing for sturgeon and spring and fall Chinook salmon. In late May, when the fish were running just offshore, the brothers would be on the river until 10 p.m. The next morning they would be cleaning and packing their catch for shipment to San Francisco's Asian markets. By June, they would be setting their nets for salmon in Alaska's Bristol Bay, but they would be back home in time for the late August fall Chinook run on the lower Columbia.

The Heukers stored and repaired their Columbia River boats and nets in a cavernous 5,000-square-foot warehouse set back from the river. They cleaned, iced, and packaged their catch in a 2,500-square-foot addition they had built onto a cluttered fishing shed. Their houses faced the river and their children had the run of the family compound. It was a way of life that had vanished elsewhere on the river, at least for non-Indians. And whether it would survive now rested with the Gorge Commission.

Fishing was not the issue. Fish processing was. What the Heukers did with their catch met the definition of an industrial use. And under the management plan, new industrial uses were specifically prohibited outside cities and towns.

The Heukers' lawyers had proposed amending the plan to allow fish processing in the National Scenic Area, but only for commercial fishermen with licenses that predated 1992. Because theirs was the only such operation, that would have left the Gorge Commission open to accusations of "spot zoning," setting a precedent that could come back to haunt it.

There was a further complication. The Heukers had built their new warehouse and addition, covering a total of 7,000 square feet, in the early 1990s, without seeking the necessary permits from Multnomah County or the Gorge Commission. The county had prohibited such commercial and industrial activities since 1962. The brothers claimed to be unaware of the prohibition. "No one informed us until 2001," Chris Heuker maintained. Though the new buildings were painted brown, they were clearly visible from the Columbia River and Beacon Rock, a clear violation of the Scenic Area Act.

Multnomah County had issued an enforcement order against the Heukers but stayed the order until the Gorge Commission decided what to do about the situation. At the commission's May 2003 meeting, Chris Heuker tried to argue that what he and his brothers did could fall under the definition of agriculture. "We filet and ice the fish. We are not canning, smoking, or brining fish. What we do is bring our own fish in and preserve them before distributing them to processing companies. We get them in a box and move them on."

Gorge Commission planner Allen Bell wasn't buying it. "We don't see how you can fit fishing into the definition of agriculture."

Chris Heuker also invoked cultural history, pointing out that the stretch of river just downstream from Bonneville Dam had been the site of numerous fish wheels from 1879 until 1926, when Oregon outlawed the wheels because they were depleting salmon runs. Strong currents and back eddies on the river had turned the huge log wheels. A large fish cannery had once stood on the Heuker property.

The Heukers began developing their fish-processing plant prior to the passage of the Scenic Area Act, which allowed activities legally established before 1986 to continue. Chris Heuker maintained that U.S. Sen. Mark Hatfield had assured him the family's pre-existing operations would be allowed to continue. But non-treaty commercial fishing was not addressed in the original management plan. "We were very surprised when we got a notice from Multnomah County that our activities were illegal," Heuker said.

At a hearing on the issue, commissioners peppered the Heukers with questions. Where did the fish processed at Warrendale come from? Were they truly Columbia River fish? Some were caught in the river just offshore from their property, Chris Heuker said. Others were harvested near Astoria and trucked up the gorge for freezing, a two-hour trip by road as opposed to a six-hour trip by boat. "We have a niche in the market," he said. "Our fish is the freshest in the area."

His concern, he said, was for the future. "It's a family enterprise. There are fourteen kids below us. Are we going to be able to expand?"

Gorge Commissioner Dave Robertson saw some middle ground if the Heukers were willing to make changes on the property to screen the processing and storage buildings from view. The family was "looking for a solution that will recognize this is a preexisiting use," he said. "It doesn't damage the river. It should be limited to places where fishing took place historically. It shouldn't be so broad that similar operations could pop up elsewhere."

The Gorge Commission ended up grandfathering the fish-processing plant into the plan as a permitted use. Years later, Bennett said she thought the issue had been handled appropriately—even though, in her opinion, the Heukers had always been of the attitude that "We don't need to get no stinkin' permit."

Not every plan amendment was complicated. Some recognized that protecting scenery could conflict with other legitimate goals. For instance, requiring homeowners to plant trees near their houses to screen them from view could increase the risk of damage from wildfire. The amended plan put fire prevention first. The commission also adopted a more pragmatic approach to permitting road and utility work in the Scenic Area, bowing to the reality that state and federal transportation agencies had limited patience with rules protecting scenery.

Bennett also wanted the plan to be forward-looking. By 2003, the gorge, long a magnet for hikers and wildflower lovers, and more recently a destination for windsurfers from all over the world, was also becoming a popular destination for upscale tourism. Visitors came for vineyard tours and weekend bed-and-breakfast getaways. Brides planned weddings at the historic Columbia Gorge Hotel.

Some property owners wanted the commission to amend the plan to allow new commercial activity in the rural gorge. They wanted to be able to host weddings on their property and open wine-tasting rooms at the vineyards that were blossoming in Hood River and Klickitat counties. Friends of the Gorge protested that opening a loophole for such activities would undermine the act's ban on commercial development outside designated urban areas.

The issue was on Bennett's radar going into the process. But there was no way she saw Geoff Thompson coming. Thompson, a flamboyant body-builder with a checkered past, and his partner Angelo Simione, a former actor, owned a historic inn near Corbett, Oregon, that they hoped to restore and operate as a restaurant and wedding venue. As the plan amendment process got underway, they applied to the Gorge Commission and Multnomah County for permission to open the inn as a commercial establishment.

The View Point Inn had a classy pedigree. A Tudor arts-and-crafts style teahouse, it perched on a bluff east of Corbett. Its long, elegant dining room featured a massive river rock fireplace and a west-facing alcove with French doors and windows that opened to views of Crown Point below. Designed by noted Portland architect Carl Linde in the 1920s, it was one of several roadhouses built to serve automobile tourists who ventured into the gorge on the newly completed historic Columbia River Highway. It was also on the National Register of Historic Places.

The inn closed after the completion of Interstate 84. But even after its closure, its proprietor, William Moessner, kept the tables set and the restaurant ready for business. Thompson bought it as an investment in 1997, paying $650,000, only to find a maze of regulatory roadblocks. For Thompson, it was the realization of a lifelong dream. He had grown up in a working-class Portland neighborhood, one of five sons of a divorced mother who struggled to support her boys. He told Multnomah County he planned to operate the elegant inn as a school for mentally disabled adults.

The county permitted Thompson to operate the View Point Inn as a vocational school and to offer limited restaurant service on weekends. Neighbors soon complained that he was operating the restaurant seven days a week and hosting banquets, weddings, and late-night concerts on the site. Thompson said he needed the revenue to support the program. But in April 1999 the county issued him a notice of violation.

Thompson had anger management issues. That same year, he was banned from Multnomah County office buildings because of "continued verbal abuse, use of profanity, displays of anger, and physical and verbal threats against county workers." Friends of the Gorge dug into his past and publicized his confrontations with the county and his Corbett neighbors.

Partners Geoff Thompson, foreground, and Angelo Simione savor victory in their fight to reopen the historic View Point Inn at the west end of the Columbia Gorge. A portion of the inn was later destroyed by fire after the owners let their insurance lapse. Photo by Janet L. Mathews of *The Columbian*.

Later that year, the Portland newspaper *Willamette Week* profiled Thompson in a story entitled "Buff Daddy," which detailed his bad behavior and also revealed that his past included work as a body builder and nude model.

In 2003 Thompson quit drinking. That same year he met Simione at a Gold's Gym in Hollywood. A former Broadway actor who had appeared in several musicals, Simione came to share Thompson's dream of restoring and reopening the View Point Inn. He also had the money to help make it happen, and a calm, reasonable demeanor that offset Thompson's rough edges.

In 2004, during plan review, Thompson and Simione applied to the Gorge Commission and Multnomah County for a permit to operate a restaurant and small hotel at the inn. Because it was in an area zoned for rural residential use, they needed a plan amendment in order to operate it as a commercial establishment. The two hired property rights attorney John Groen, who helped them navigate the bureaucratic maze.

Thompson and Simione made common cause with the private property rights group Columbia Gorge United. They chartered buses to deliver these supporters to Gorge Commission meetings and even provided sandwiches to stave off their hunger pangs during the long hearings. Thompson was passionate, Simione was cool and businesslike. The openly gay men became an unlikely cause célèbre for the property rights movement. But

Thompson's flamboyant style and his willingness to pull out all the stops to get the commission's stamp of approval left some people skeptical of his motives.

Bennett quickly realized that she was dealing with two publicity hounds. Thompson and Simione "were C-grade actors," she said. "They were going to make it a drama. They were the leading actors and they would not accept that someone else would play a starring role." At one point, she got a frantic call from an aide to Oregon Gov. Ted Kulongoski. The two had shown up at the governor's formal reception area and fallen to their knees, pleading for the state to intervene in their quest to reopen the View Point Inn. Bennett decided not to play that game.

The facts were clear. The inn had been left off the list of buildings on the Historic Register in the Scenic Area inadvertently. Thompson and Simione had a valid case. But she wasn't comfortable making an exception just for them. She stepped back and considered the policy implications of letting owners of historic buildings in the gorge use them as sources of income, in order to preserve them.

"What I was trying to do was separate the View Point Inn from the issue of old historic buildings," she said. "Those buildings eligible for the Historic Register needed to be saved."

Bennett ordered a survey of buildings more than fifty years old in the Scenic Area. The survey found four, including the View Point Inn, and fifty more that were eligible or potentially eligible. She argued that allowing weddings, catered events, art galleries, and other commercial uses of historic properties would offer an incentive for their owners to reinvest in them. They would have to demonstrate that offering such activities would allow them to restore the buildings. Events or services would have to be incidental to the main uses of the property.

Thompson and Simione's application for a zone change and plan amendment came before the Gorge Commission in October 2005. The hearing drew 100 property rights advocates, who packed the Rock Creek Center in Stevenson. The commission voted 7-4 in favor of the zone change, but it couldn't muster the required three votes from Oregon commissioners.

Friends opposed both permitting the inn to operate as a restaurant and also the broader policy, calling it "clearly inconsistent with the Scenic Area Act." But most of those who spoke at the hearing favored the inn's reopening, including the mayor of nearby Gresham.

Thompson warned that unless they were allowed to operate their home as an inn, they could not afford to continue heating and maintaining it over another winter. "We need a roof, we need a chimney," he said. "We need the revenue from the inn to do it, and we need a commitment from the Gorge Commission that they are going to support the View Point Inn before I can invest any more money in it."

He gave the commission a month to reconsider the application. "If the Gorge Commission doesn't do the right thing, we'll lead a revolution and march on with this property," he vowed. "We'll go all the way to Congress if we have to."

The following month, instead of approving a narrow plan amendment to allow the View Point Inn to operate a hotel and restaurant, the commission opened the door for the owners of all historic buildings in the gorge to use their properties for commercial purposes.

In January 2007, Thompson and Simione cleared their last hurdle when they obtained a building permit from Multnomah County to allow renovations of the inn. In his flamboyant style, Thompson had two boxes containing 850 letters of support delivered to the county.

The couple began remodeling the kitchen and other rooms to prepare the grand old roadhouse for its second debut. They invested a reported $1.2 million in landscaping the grounds, repairing a fountain, installing a state-of-the-art restaurant, remodeling an upstairs bathroom and installing cedar flooring in the dining room to match the original wood. They paid $50,000 for a new water heater and furnace and replaced radiators that had burst during a hard freeze.

They hired two young chefs, (one from a tony Portland bistro) as well as an events coordinator, an administrator, dishwashers, and waiters. They set to work finding local suppliers. They designed a menu featuring Northwest foods such as Dungeness crab cakes, Walla Walla sweet onion and saffron soup, and pan-roasted salmon.

"We are going to make everyone proud," Thompson said.

The inn quickly became a popular wedding venue. It was featured in the *Twilight* movie series. But Bennett had no illusions that Thompson and Simione would abide by the terms of their county permit over the long term. She was skeptical that this story would have a happy ending.

Sure enough, in 2011, both Simione and Thompson filed for personal bankruptcy to prevent a foreclosure auction of the inn. On July 10 of that

year, fire destroyed most of the inn's roof and damaged the hotel's second
floor and gracious dining room. As it turned out, the owners had stopped
making fire insurance payments on the building in April. Many brides-to-
be lost the hefty deposits they'd made on weddings at the View Point Inn.

Faced with another round of budget cuts, the Gorge Commission cut short
its plan review process in 2004, leaving key decisions on recreation and
development of agricultural land for another day. Friends of the Gorge
challenged the amended plan in both federal court and the Oregon courts
system. They argued that the changes weakened protection for scenic
landscapes, failed to establish adequate buffer zones to protect water
quality and salmon habitat, allowed new clearcutting even within Special
Management Areas, and failed to address the cumulative visual effects of
more than 600 new residences and thousands of new structures built in the
Scenic Area since its designation.

In 2009 and again in 2012, Friends won partially favorable rulings from
Oregon appellate courts. The courts ordered the Columbia Gorge Commission and the Forest Service to go back to the drawing board and write a
plan to protect natural and cultural resources from the cumulative effects
of development.

The View Point Inn, now a derelict building, stood open to the elements
with no sign of rescue. But amending the Scenic Area Management Plan
would continue to be a work in progress for years to come.

Part III

GREAT DEBATES

Lyle Point, May 2012. Photo by Darryl Lloyd.

Chapter 13
Showdown at Lyle Point

It's easy to fall in love with Lyle, Washington: its scattering of historic houses, its vintage hotel, its setting at the mouth of the Klickitat River in the rugged mid-gorge. Few visitors passing through are aware that in the early 1990s, a spit of land at Lyle became the site of one of a heated conflict over protection of cultural resources in the gorge—a conflict that pitted tribal fishermen and conservation groups against a property developer, wind surfers, conservationists, and elected officials in Klickitat County.

The cultural footprints of native people are all over Klickitat County: in the huckleberry fields near Mount Adams, where tribal members burned large swathes of forest to regenerate the fields of sweet huckleberries; in meadows and seeps where they gathered medicinal plants; along the banks of the Klickitat River, where they fished for salmon using traditional dip nets; and at Lyle Point, along the shore of the Columbia River.

Lyle itself is located along an ancient Indian route. For thousands of years Indians of the mid-Columbia fished at Lyle Point, a flat, windblown expanse of land that juts out into the Columbia River. Its Indian name means "place where the wind blows in both directions."

White settlement began in the 1880s, when Lyle became a sheep and wool-shipping center, but the town remained isolated until 1933, when tunnels along the state highway connected it with the rest of the Columbia River Gorge. In 1938, the construction of Bonneville Dam submerged the Indian village at Lyle Point. But tribal members never stopped fishing from the peninsula's edge.

Because Lyle Point is within the urban boundary of the town of Lyle, it is outside the jurisdiction of the Gorge Commission and the Forest Service. The drama that unfolded there in the early 1990s played out independently of the Scenic Area Act. Yet the saga of Lyle Point provides a textbook case of what can happen when treaty rights conflict with development schemes and a county's hunger for tax revenue.

For years, Lyle Point was an overlooked spot on the Washington shore. As beaches downstream overflowed with windsurfers, the town of Lyle, which huddles close to the river and climbs steep hills to the north, was largely untouched by growth. On the river side, between the last row of small houses and the windswept shore, the peninsula was covered with brush, grass, and clusters of pine amid basalt outcroppings. The BNSF Railway ran along the town side of the point. An overpass provided access.

The railroad owned the land, but Indians had fished there, at their usual and customary places along the river, for as long as anyone could remember. There was no development pressure and no conflict. Then in 1974 an organization called Treaty Indians of the Columbia listed Lyle Point as one of the sites it wanted the U.S. Army Corps of Engineers to develop as an "in lieu" site, in order to fulfill the government's obligation to protect traditional fishing areas that had been flooded by Bonneville Dam. With three-quarters of a mile of river frontage, terrain suitable for platform fishing, a boat-launching site, and good gillnet fishing just offshore, it was an obvious choice.

Peaceful coexistence at Lyle Point faded as the popular sport of windsurfing marched east. In 1991, the railroad sold the 40-acre point to Columbia Gorge Investors Limited Partnership, a Massachusetts company. Despite protests from the Yakama Nation and the Bureau of Indian Affairs, Klickitat County commissioners changed Lyle Point's land use designation to facilitate the point's development.

Hiram E. Olney, the BIA superintendent for the Yakama Nation, said from the outset that he feared conflicts between the new owners and tribal fishermen exercising their treaty rights. "We are opposed to any redesignation or future development which would impair access or lead to conflicts when Yakama fishermen exercise this right," he said.

Indians continued to fish at Lyle Point. But in 1993 county commissioners declared the point a place of "nonsignificance" environmentally and culturally, a finding required in order for the county to approve a subdivision at Lyle Point. The Yakama Tribe appealed.

William Yallup, manager of the Yakama Cultural Resources Program, told Klickitat County officials that the tribes and the Corps of Engineers had been talking to Henry Spencer, the new owner of Lyle Point, about buying part of the property for an in-lieu site. "One day Mr. Spencer is a willing seller and the next day he is not," Yallup said.

County commissioners eventually approved a thirty-three-unit gated housing development at Lyle Point. The development, called Klickitat Landing, would feature tennis courts, a swimming pool, a sailboard launch, and a sailboard speed course just offshore. Lots of up to 1.4 acres would sell for between $70,000 and $280,000. Spencer planned to close several primitive roads crossing the site. But he said tribal fishers could continue to use a 100-foot strip of beach, though they would have to share it with windsurfers and boaters. Soon after the county granted Spencer his permit, the heavy equipment arrived.

Margaret Saluskin was the wife of a fisherman who caught salmon at Lyle Point for use in Warm Springs tribal ceremonies. She thought at first that the land was simply being cleared of dry brush, and stayed away. But as the weeks passed workers began installing streets and utilities. "It became an issue and struggle for the Columbia River people because it interfered with our inherited fishing rights," Saluskin told journalist Roberta Ulrich, whose book *Empty Nets: Indians, Dams, and the Columbia River* chronicles the decades-long battle by Columbia Basin treaty tribes to win their in-lieu sites.

Tribal fishermen feared the planned road closures would eliminate their access to fishing sites and boat docks and that luxury houses would cover their sacred fishing grounds. Already, they were feeling friction from recreational boaters when they unloaded their salmon at boat launch sites. Non-Indians were annoyed by the sight of Indians cleaning their salmon and spreading their fish nets to dry on the beaches.

A dispute had erupted recently between tribal fishermen and sailboarders at a nearby federal fish hatchery. A sailboard tournament coincided with a special Indian fishing season at the hatchery, where a surplus of returning salmon had prompted fishery managers to invite tribal fishermen to harvest some of the returning fall Chinook salmon.

Neither group had been told about the other's event. The sailboarders sailed across the Indian fishing nets. Fishermen and sailboarders clashed on shore. Klickitat and Skamania county officials contributed to the heated rhetoric when they suggested that the Indian treaties were having an illegal impact on the counties' economy.

Saluskin determined to stop the new housing development. She enlisted the support of Yakama tribal leaders, the Columbia Gorge Audubon Society, and Greenpeace. Tribal fisherman Johnny Jackson of the Klickitat Band of the Yakama Nation pointed out that bald eagles, which were protected by the Endangered Species Act, had recently returned to Lyle Point. He predicted that a gated subdivision would drive the eagles away again.

Protesters set up a tepee village on the site, which was visible from the Columbia River and Oregon's Interstate 84. They staged demonstrations in Olympia in February 1993 and asked Washington Gov. Mike Lowry to intervene. He declined.

The Trust for Public Land made inquiries about purchasing Lyle Point. So did the Native American Rights Fund and the American Indian Movement. Columbia Gorge Audubon filed suit in state court challenging Klickitat County's right to close the primitive roads. Lyle Point quickly became a cause célèbre.

In 1994, the Yakama Nation filed its own federal lawsuit arguing that the upscale Klickitat Landing development would violate its treaty rights. The Warm Springs Tribal Council joined the suit. A federal judge threw out the challenge of the road closures but kept the rest of the tribes' lawsuit alive. Negotiations began between the tribes' attorneys and the developer. By then, paved roads and underground utilities were in place.

The stalemate continued to draw headlines across the Northwest. Nearly a year passed. A confrontation between protesters and the Klickitat County sheriff's office erupted when ten Indians and several dozen non-tribal protesters marched onto the Lyle Point property intending to stage a religious ceremony. Deputies tried to stop them. There was shouting. There were arrests. The next day, thirty sheriff's deputies and tribal police were on hand. More arrests ensued. The tepees stayed.

In July 1995 the tribes and the developer reached a settlement. Spencer agreed to sell two lots to the Corps of Engineers for an in-lieu fishing site and another five acres outside the proposed subdivision to the Yakama Nation. The company agreed not to construct the planned shoreline improvements for sailboarders, to establish boat-launching facilities for tribal fishermen, and to ensure tribal access to the shore.

In return, the Indians agreed not to camp on the site, not to occupy company land, and not to invite non-members of the Yakama and Warm Springs tribes to enter the property. The court order finally was issued in March 1996. The tribes celebrated the settlement. But the key issue remained unresolved. The sacred sites at Lyle Point still were without protection.

Development of the project appeared to be stalled. Gorge winds swept over the peninsula, now crossed by paved roads and pocked with utility boxes.

In 2000, the Trust for Public Land upped the ante when it announced that it had purchased twenty-seven of the lots from Spencer. Two years later it acquired the remaining four lots from another party. That same year, the Corps of Engineers completed its purchase of two lots at Lyle Point for the long-awaited in-lieu fishing site. Klickitat Landing was not to be.

The Trust's purchase of Lyle Point meant that the land, with most utilities already installed, never would sprout houses. County commissioners were furious. "Lyle is at risk of losing its tax base," declared Klickitat County Commissioner Joan Frey. "The Trust for Public Land is not concerned with the economic well-being of the community. My guess is that they are going to be diligent in trying to get it off the tax rolls."

County commissioners challenged the Trust's tax-exempt status before the state Board of Tax Appeals. The Trust appealed but lost in Superior Court and was ordered to pay the county $20,000 a year in property taxes. Trust officials had initially hoped to sell Lyle Point to the Forest Service. But the agency wasn't interested, because the land lay within Lyle's urban area and thus outside its jurisdiction.

Chris Beck, the Trust's project manager for Lyle Point, then proposed that the land become a community asset. He offered Klickitat County a one-time payment of $455,000 to set up an interest-bearing trust fund that could be used to help support Lyle-area schools and local services. He also offered to build a children's playground at Lyle Point. In exchange, he asked the commission to repeal the ordinance requiring the Trust to pay property taxes. County commissioners rebuffed the offer. Instead, they passed an ordinance prohibiting the use of Lyle Point for park purposes.

Pitching Expansion

In 2003, in a politically charged move, the commissioners hired a Portland lawyer and a Lake Oswego development consultant to try to make the case that Lyle needed more room to accommodate future growth. They planned to petition the Gorge Commission to expand the town's urban boundary, allowing development in areas that were at the time off-limits. If the county could not get Klickitat Landing back, it wanted Lyle's urban boundary expanded acre for acre to make up for land it could no longer develop at Lyle Point.

The request, the first of its kind to come before the Gorge Commission, was not backed by any evidence that Lyle was about to run out of land. It was an act of pure revenge. At the time, the unincorporated town had a population of about 530. It had a single grocery store, a couple of gas stations, a historic hotel that operated only sporadically, two bars, and a cafe. Realtors said the demand for real estate was sluggish at best. Options for expansion, aired at a community hearing in late July 2003, were limited by topography and by the Columbia River itself. About the only direction the town could expand was to the north. But that steep hillside was visible from viewpoints across the river in Oregon, including the Historic Columbia River Highway. The county was prepared to argue that Lyle had suffered a severe loss in 2000 when the Trust paid nearly $1.9 million to save the windswept point. County officials said the loss had reduced Lyle's taxable land base by 30 percent and deprived it of a potential $120,000 in annual tax revenue, a figure TPL disputed. Beck noted that the property could still leave the tax rolls if the Trust sold it to the state, the federal government, or an Indian tribe.

The fate of Lyle Point remained unresolved until May 2007, when the Trust and Yakama tribal leaders announced that Lyle Point would return to the tribe. The Trust had agreed to sell the land to the Yakama for $2.4 million. The transfer would end the tribe's decades-long effort to regain ownership of the point and it would adjoin the recently completed in-lieu fishing site.

"The younger generation will continue to exercise their Creator-given right to our very important salmon," tribal official Lavina Washines told the Yakima *Herald Republic.* "All Yakamas will benefit with this accomplishment by the current tribal council officials." Washines, the first woman to head the Yakama tribal Government, died four years later. Klickitat Chief Wilbur Slockish said the purchase ensured that Lyle Point would remain unscathed by development and that the ancestors buried there would continue to rest peacefully. "To me, it means that the spirits there will be spared any development, and there won't be any houses put on top of them."

The trust had offered Yakama tribal leaders various options for protecting and conserving the site in exchange for a lower sales price. But in the end, the sales agreement was silent on how the property would be managed.

Attorney Bowen Blair, former executive director of Friends of the Gorge, led negotiations with the Yakama. Tribal leaders were adamant, he said, that decisions about the future of Lyle Point would be theirs to make.

"Our goal was always to protect it for the Indians," Blair said. "When we offered it for sale, we proposed a conservation easement to make sure it wasn't developed inappropriately. The tribal leaders flatly rejected that, even though they were offered $1 million for development rights. They said, 'This is our land and no one tells us what to do with it. We decide.'"

The tribe could theoretically build a casino or hotel on the property, Blair said. But he believed that was unlikely. "Lyle Point is sacred to them. They think of it as a graveyard. They would like to remove the roads. They believe the spirits of ancestors can't breathe, can't get out. As long as Johnny Jackson and Wilbur Slockish are there, they won't let anything happen to Lyle Point."

Chapter 14
A Destination Resort

The view from a granite outcrop above the 60-acre Broughton Lumber Company mill site near Underwood takes in several derelict mill buildings, a world-famous windsurfing beach and the town of Hood River, Oregon, with Mount Hood looming beyond. It's a good vantage point for taking in the history of logging in the Columbia Gorge, the industrial engine that drove the gorge economy for most of the twentieth century

From 1923 to 1987, logs from private, state, and federal forests in Southwest Washington were cut into sections and sent on a fast ride down this mountainside via a nine-mile log flume to a planing mill along the railroad tracks near the mouth of the Little White Salmon River. Remnants of that historic flume remain visible from spots along Highway 14, although a 2006 fire destroyed most of the flume and with it, a vivid reminder of the heyday of logging in Skamania and Klickitat counties.

Standing on the promontory on a November day in 2006, Broughton Lumber Company President Jason Spadaro described his company's vision for this piece of land: A high-end destination resort, built to serve the windsurfers who converge on the gorge each summer to ride its legendary gusts. It took a leap of imagination to envision the shuttered mill buildings and rusting wigwam burner transformed into an upscale resort. But the proposal soon would confront the Columbia River Gorge Commission with one of its most controversial decisions yet: Whether to allow a large resort in the rural gorge that could become its own town, with year-round residents, and retail stores.

On its face, the proposed Broughton Landing Project seemed an outright violation of the 1986 Scenic Area Act. But the issue was not black and white. Because the Broughton mill property had been an active industrial site in 1986, when Congress passed the National Scenic Area Act, its owners were allowed to redevelop it for limited commercial recreation use. The

Broughton property was the only piece of land in the Scenic Area that qualified for the exemption.

Broughton's owners had applied for a permit to redevelop the site as a resort back in 1989, but they had later withdrawn that original application after doing the math and concluding it would not be profitable. Among other restrictions, the management plan limited the number of lodging units on the site to thirty-five. Now Broughton's owners they were back, with a far more ambitious proposal. The Broughton family wanted a legacy, and was willing to pull political strings to get it.

Broughton Lumber had been a major landowner and key power player in the gorge for most of a century. Its history was intertwined with that of SDS Lumber Company, an aggressive timber company with a highly competitive profile. The two companies had dominated the development of the timber industry since the 1920s. In 1923, members of the Stevenson and Broughton families built a mill in Willard, a remote outpost near the south boundary of the Gifford Pinchot National Forest. They also bought an unfinished flume designed to carry logs down the mountain on water diverted from the Little White Salmon River. The flume was completed and used for seventy years to bring raw material to market.

The rough-sawn log sections, called cants, made the trip down to the planing mill on the river in fifty-five minutes. The finished lumber traveled by rail to customers in the gorge and in the fast-growing Portland-Vancouver area. Broughton Lumber quickly became a major source of jobs in the small timber towns that grew up along the river.

After World War II, new players arrived on the scene. In 1946, brothers Wally and Bruce Stevenson formed a partnership with Frank Daubenspeck, the longtime foreman at Broughton, and bought a bankrupt mill on the Columbia River at Bingen, in western Klickitat County. They incorporated as SDS Lumber Company. Two years later, the mill burned to the ground, but a portable sawmill at the site was soon up and running.

Broughton Lumber and SDS Lumber thrived during the boom times of logging in the Northwest. The towns of Stevenson, Carson, Home Valley, Cook, and Bingen were built on timber from the forests of Southwest Washington and Oregon's Hood River Valley. By 1960, Skamania County ranked fourth in timber production among Washington counties, with 345 million board feet logged annually. Timber jobs supported the local economy and revenue from state and federal timber sales paid for roads and schools.

In 1978, government regulation reared its head. The state of Washington began requiring environmental review of logging operations and temporarily suspended timber sales on state land. Officials from SDS, never shy about lobbying legislators and members of Congress, testified against the new logging reviews before the Washington Legislature.

SDS was quick to adapt new technologies. It built a steam plant to supply its lumber and veneer dryers and plywood presses, with surplus steam converted to electricity. In 1984, it launched a marine division with a tugboat that hauled wood chips downriver to pulp mills. Twenty years later, the company operated a fleet of five tugs.

In 1980 a deep recession brought on by high interest rates in the housing market flattened the Northwest timber industry. SDS Lumber laid off 280 of its 480 workers. Desperate for raw material, the company contracted with the Forest Service to salvage $709,000 worth of timber blown down in the 1980 eruption of Mount St. Helens. In 1982, SDS filed a lawsuit challenging a state law that allowed timber companies to default on their state logging contracts. The law was meant to help companies struggling to weather the recession by releasing them from costly contracts. But SDS officials said Skamania County would lose $586,000 over six years if companies were allowed to default and the standing timber was not cut.

In 1986, as Congress was debating the National Scenic Area Act, Broughton Lumber closed its sawmill in Willard and partially dismantled its wood flume. It was struggling with a shortage of raw material and an outdated mill. At about the same time, SDS Lumber designed and built a modern, computer-controlled stud mill at Bingen to process high-quality Douglas fir and white fir.

During congressional debate on the Scenic Area Act, SDS and Broughton were at the table from the beginning. They successfully fought language that would impose special restrictions on private-land logging in the gorge. In the end, in most of the Scenic Area, the act merely required commercial timber companies to comply with the states' forest practices rules.

The companies later negotiated land exchanges with the Forest Service allowing them to swap their own timbered property in the Scenic Area for Forest Service land outside the Scenic Area boundary. Those deals did not stop Broughton and SDS companies from joining a lawsuit challenging the Scenic Area Act's constitutionality—one of sixty-three suits filed to overturn the law. The act survived every challenge.

SDS had another stake in the legislation. The Scenic Area Act designated a 40-mile section of the White Salmon River as part of the federal Wild and Scenic Rivers system. The company owned land in the corridor. But the protection provided by the act was ephemeral at best; the company had no obligation to protect its private land in the river corridor, and the Forest Service could only try to acquire it through purchase or trade.

Friends of the White Salmon, a grass-roots group that had been fighting proposed dams and diversions on the White Salmon since the 1970s, stepped in. It sued to stop SDS from logging centuries-old trees along a stretch of the river corridor between Husum and BZ Corner that was popular with white-water rafters.

A federal judge refused to block the logging and in October 1988, Friends of the White Salmon organized a road blockade and tried to halt operations on another SDS property in the watershed. It was an early volley in the new timber wars. But it was quickly eclipsed the following year, when federal courts blocked most logging on federal forests west of the Cascades to protect habitat for the northern spotted owl.

The court ruling sent tremors across the rural Northwest. Three hundred loggers and timber industry supporters descended on White Salmon in March 1989 to protest the appearance of Oregon forest activist Lou Gold at a gathering of environmentalists. In May 1989, SDS Lumber gave its workers the day off without pay so they could attend another massive timber industry rally protesting the federal injunctions. It was in this charged political atmosphere, in 1990, that Jason Spadaro went to work for SDS Lumber as a staff forester.

President Bill Clinton's 1994 Northwest Forest Plan made permanent court-ordered changes in federal logging practices, dramatically reducing the volume of timber that could be cut from westside forests in Oregon and Washington. Across the Northwest, timber companies were forced to search for new sources of timber if they hoped to stay afloat. Many shifted to smaller-dimension logs on private and state land and built new computerized mills to turn this lower-grade timber into plywood and two-by-fours.

In 1997, SDS President Bruce Stevenson died of a heart attack and Spadaro succeeded him. The Broughton family still had significant timber holdings in Skamania County and also bought logs from other private sources. Broughton and SDS had board members in common. By 2004, the two companies were looking for new ways to make money. Spadaro, now president of both companies, led the search for ways to keep them vibrant. It was the Broughton family that proposed building a new destination resort to tell the story of how the company had built the timber industry in the small communities in the gorge.

But Broughton Landing would not be a museum. The company also hoped to capitalize on the windsurfing boom by developing its own private windsurfing beach directly across Highway 14 from the mill site. Three other nearby beaches, including one adjacent to the Spring Creek Federal Fish Hatchery, already attracted boarders from all over the world.

The project would incorporate the rusting wigwam burner, used to burn wood waste in the days before the Clean Air Act; several of the cavernous mill buildings, including a 19,000-square-foot structure that would house the resort's main lodge; and many of the massive timbers from other structures that would be demolished to build the resort.

Initially, Broughton officials envisioned nine condo units, 154 recreational vehicle sites, a 30-unit motel, a restaurant, and 100,000 square feet of retail space on 68 acres directly across from the hatchery and the windsurfing beach. Spadaro knew that a project of this size in the rural gorge would require an amendment to the Scenic Area Management Plan. He also knew that the Gorge Commission, its staff stretched thin, had recently placed a twelve-month moratorium on new plan amendments.

Spadaro also knew that a resort of the size the company had in mind would face a steep, if not insurmountable, challenge in winning approval from the Gorge Commission. He turned to Skamania County's elected officials for political backup. In April 2005, county commissioners sent letters to two congressmen with a stake in the gorge: U.S. Rep. Doc Hastings, a conservative eastern Washington Republican whose district included the Broughton site, and U.S. Rep. Brian Baird, a moderate Democrat from Vancouver who represented the west end of the Scenic Area. Baird and Hastings were asked whether they would consider introducing legislation to create a special "destination resort" zone in the gorge near Underwood. Such a zoning rule would let Broughton Landing bypass the Gorge Commission and trump the Scenic Area Act.

Jason Spadaro (right), general manager of Broughton Lumber Co., leads a tour of the old planing mill near Underwood that the company hoped to transform into a destination resort for windsurfers. Photo by Dave Olsen of *The Columbian.*

Former Skamania County Prosecuting Attorney Bradley Andersen, an attorney for Broughton, helped draft proposed legislation. But members of Congress were noncommittal. "It makes a lot of sense to me that something be done to use that site in a way that is more economically productive," Baird said. "Ideally this is something that people should work through the Gorge Commission."

Andersen also approached Martha Bennett, executive director of the Gorge Commission. The mill site was an eyesore, he argued; the new resort would be an improvement. "There is no reason not to convert this to something that would offer recreation and provide jobs." Bennett did not reject the idea out of hand. Instead, she suggested the company seek a plan amendment to allow a destination resort at the site.

"We got a sense from them that they might be able to tweak the current land use regulations, but they weren't willing to create a whole new zone," Andersen recalled.

Without some incentive, he told Bennett, Broughton had no motive to do anything with the property. "The Gorge Commission's current regulations don't allow for the type of development that is needed for this site. We think congressional action is necessary to make this thing happen."

In fact, he argued that Broughton Landing was exactly what Congress had envisioned when it passed the Scenic Area Act—a project that would protect scenery, develop a recreation resource, and boost the economy of gorge communities. But when he asked Bennett directly whether the resort was something she could support and take to the Gorge Commission, she said no.

His client, he told her, "was not willing to present something that is going to be dead on arrival."

Bennett doubted Congress would agree to override the Scenic Area Act. Still, she saw an alarming precedent in any effort to get Congress to designate a new urban area in the rural gorge. She felt she couldn't take that chance. After giving it some thought, she decided she had to step in.

Spadaro had not given her many specifics about the size and scope of the proposed resort. "We would like to see a development there, too," she said. "But we can't have a discussion about something no one is willing to air." She also warned that a resort of the size the company seemed to envision would be larger than many gorge towns. It would, she said, be "extraordinarily controversial."

Again, she urged Broughton officials to apply to the Gorge Commission for a plan amendment. Again, they insisted that unless they could get full support from the commission in advance, "they wouldn't bother" to apply.

At that point, Bennett talked realpolitik with Spadaro. "I told Jason that, A, the chances of getting something through Congress were remote, and B, the chances of getting it the way you want it will involve a deal. The deal could be no private logging. Why would you want to take that chance?" She vowed that she herself would go to sympathetic members of Congress and point out that Broughton Lumber had not even tried to work through the system to get the resort approved.

Friends of the Columbia Gorge was the other key player in the destination resort scheme. The organization did not dismiss the idea outright. Executive Director Kevin Gorman was open to discussing the idea with Broughton and the Gorge Commission. In fact, Friends recommended that Spadaro hire Mike Usen, a highly regarded development consultant, to lead the project.

Usen was enthusiastic. "My company does resorts all over the world, and this is one of the most spectacular sites we've ever seen," he told the Gorge Commission during hearings the following year. But those early negotiations broke down after Spadaro asked Friends' board of directors whether it could support the company's plan. The board's unanimous verdict: No. The project's size and scope were incompatible with the purposes of the Scenic Area Act, which limited commercial development to urban areas.

"Jason really wanted 'yes,'" and we couldn't go there," recalled Friends Conservation Director Michael Lang. "We would have been happy to continue with the discussion, but what we heard from Jason was, 'We are done.'"

Ultimately, Spadaro and Broughton's board of directors decided to take Bennett's advice and apply for an amendment to the Scenic Area Management Plan, a lengthy and expensive process. On an April morning in 2006, Spadaro took the wraps off a bold proposal to transform the site into a world-class windsurfing resort. He led Gorge Commissioners, members of Friends of the Gorge, local officials, and the press on a walking tour of the old mill site. In the afternoon, he made his formal presentation to the Gorge Commission.

Spadaro and Usen described a high-end resort with 255 residential units, including small cottages and cabins, four-plexes and townhouses, all laced together by roads and paths and a footbridge connecting the property to a private windsurfing beach on the other side of the BNSF Railway tracks. Spadaro also envisioned a network of trails climbing the bluff behind the mill site, following the route of the historic wood flume. The company, he said, had its sights set on a resort to compete with Black Butte Ranch in the Oregon Cascades, a place that would attract visitors from far and wide.

It was a bold, even brazen proposal. Allowing such a massive redevelopment outside an urban area would require major changes to the management plan. Under the zoning in place at the time, the company was limited to building thirty-five units of overnight lodging, a campground with up to fifty sites and a small restaurant.

Bennett was on her way out as executive director of the Gorge Commission by the time Broughton Landing landed in the commission's lap. She had accepted a job as city administrator of Ashland, Oregon, and had given notice. She wanted the Gorge Commission to try to find middle ground if that was even possible. She advised commissioners to focus not on the Broughton proposal but on the Scenic Area as a whole—to look at the big-picture policy issues. The company had, after all, scaled down its earlier proposal for a 550-unit resort and a large retail component, in the face of opposition from businesses in nearby Underwood, White Salmon, and Bingen.

But Spadaro said the project still had to succeed financially. Anything less than 250 units would be "marginally viable." He questioned whether other gorge landmarks, including Multnomah Falls Lodge and Vista House, ever would have been built if the Scenic Area restrictions had been in place at the time.

Proponents and opponents lined up quickly. Officials from Skamania and Klickitat counties were enthusiastic. The *Columbian* newspaper in Vancouver, Washington, editorialized in favor of keeping an open mind.

One sticking point was the plan to sell 30 percent of the units to private owners as fulltime residences and the rest under arrangements that would require the owners to share occupancy or make them available in a rental pool. That underscored Bennett's warning that the resort could become a new gorge town.

Sally Newell, a former Gorge Commissioner and a resident of Under-wood, opposed allowing units that would not be short-term rentals. She also spoke out against building trails on the bluff. "The bluff is a wild place," she said. "There are animals on that bluff that you don't see anyplace else." On the other hand, Gorge Commissioner Joe Palena of Vancouver called the proposed destination resort "a gift" that the commission should embrace.

After a search for Bennett's replacement, the Gorge Commission hired Jill Arens, an experienced administrator and a native of Hood River. Arens' impressive resume included an extensive background in higher education and health care policy. But she had no land use experience. Tom Ascher, a Gorge Commission planner, advised her that the intent of any plan amend-ment should be to help bring a "visually discordant industrial complex" into conformance with the purposes and standards of the Scenic Area Act.

The commission could not legally amend the plan for the benefit of a single company, but this was all about Broughton Landing. As the com-mission's staff slowly geared up to deal with the lengthy plan amendment

process, Spadaro and Usen made the rounds of local governments and so-
licited endorsements from state agencies and elected officials. Washington
State Parks and Recreation Commission, which operated a state park at
the Spring Creek Hatchery, endorsed "the concept of an environmentally
sensitive, recreation-oriented resort with destination accommodations and
associated facilities."

Refinement of the proposed plan amendment continued for a year and
a half. At one point, the Gorge Commission suggested a 210-unit resort
might be acceptable. Spadaro said he wouldn't proceed unless the commission allowed at least 240 units, along with thirty-six campsites.

In November 2007, as the date for a decision neared, Friends of the
Gorge released an economic feasibility study suggesting that a recreational
vehicle park on the site could be profitable—and would also fill a need for
more campsites on the Washington side of the gorge. Spadaro scoffed at the
study. An RV park was not what Broughton had in mind.

In March 2008, Gorge Commissioners Jim Middaugh and Honna
Sheffield, both recent appointees, threw a new issue into the mix. They
called on the Washington Department of Ecology to launch an immediate
investigation of possible industrial contamination at the former Broughton
mill property. The letter, written at the behest of Friends of the Gorge,
backfired and opened a schism on the commission. The two newcomers
had failed to notify Executive Director Arens or their fellow commissioners
before sending it.

Spadaro was indignant. "They are trying to generate controversy where
none exists," he said. He noted that under the proposed plan amendment,
the company would be required "to remove all vestiges of past industrial
use."

The Department of Ecology vowed to conduct an investigation, but the
issue quickly faded as the Gorge Commission prepared to take its final vote
on the plan amendment. On April 8, 2008, the commission approved the
amendment on a 10-2 vote. Middaugh and Sheffield voted no.

Under the plan amendment, Broughton got most of what it wanted. If
its proposal cleared a long series of regulatory hoops, the company would
be allowed to develop a total of 245 condos, townhouses and cottages, a
large lodge, some retail shops, hillside trails, and a private beach.

The vote followed a three-hour debate on the key issue of how to limit
occupancy of resort units by their owners to avoid creating a new town

that would compete with existing communities and businesses. The amendment stated that all units should be designed for short-term occupancy "to ensure the resort protects and supports the economies of urban areas." But it included only loose limits on how long owners of the units would be allowed to live in their condos and townhouses each year. And it kicked the responsibility for enforcement of those limits to Skamania County.

Commission Chairman Jeff Condit, a Portland attorney, proposed language that would allow owners to stay in their units for no more than thirty days at a time and a total of sixty days per calendar year. But the majority of the commission latched onto a compromise proposed by Commissioner Harold Abbe of Camas that would allow owners to occupy their units for no more than forty-five consecutive days in every ninety-day period. Abbe said the stricter limit proposed by Condit could leave the resort vacant during winter months, when gorge tourists were few and far between.

Spadaro called the forty-five/ninety rule a reasonable compromise. "Thirty-day occupancy would put us in competition with local hotels and motels," he said, and wouldn't provide the up-front capital the company needed for the $70 million redevelopment.

After debating various formulas, the commission in the end punted, in effect signing off on a high-end private enclave. Middaugh and Sheffield dissented. "I can't see how six months out of a year equates to short-term occupancy," Middaugh said. The commission also defeated Sheffield's amendment restoring language that would limit the average size of individual units to 1,000 square feet. Smaller units were more in keeping with short-term visits, she argued. The adopted plan instead limited individual units to 1,600 square feet and two-and-a-half stories. "At every step of the way we're chipping away at our legal obligation to protect existing urban areas," a frustrated Middaugh exclaimed. "In the end, we've failed in our charge to pursue other options that might be more consistent with the Scenic Area Act."

Michael Lang of Friends of the Gorge called the vote illegal and immediately vowed to appeal.

"The Gorge Commission has given up the responsibility to enforce the Scenic Area Act," Lang fumed. The plan amendment would violate the act by creating a new urban area in the gorge, he declared.

Spadaro was relieved, but not ready to pop the champagne corks. He predicted that appeals and litigation would delay the effective date of the plan amendment for up to three years. The Secretary of Agriculture would have to sign off on the plan amendment. It would have to survive a legal appeal. Then Skamania County would have to incorporate the plan amendment into its own Scenic Area ordinance. And once those issues were resolved, Broughton would still be required to submit a detailed master plan to the county, a plan that would also be subject to review by the Gorge Commission.

After two-and-a-half years of hearings and debate, most commissioners were ready to be done with the issue. Gorge Commissioner Doug Crow pointed out that the Broughton property had been available for redevelopment for twenty years, but no other plan had moved forward.

In late 2008, as the mortgage loan meltdown plunged the homebuilding industry into deep recession, SDS was forced to lay off workers and reduce production. The timber industry was on the ropes. As middle-class families scrambled to pay for the basics, a $70 million luxury resort in the gorge began to seem like a dicey investment.

As late as 2012, Broughton Lumber Co. had taken no steps to advance its destination resort proposal. Broughton Landing remained an unfulfilled legacy.

Chapter 15
Rails to Trails

A curtain of cold rain descended west of the Cascades on a November day in 2002. But in the rain shadow east of the mountains, sunlight pierced the clouds and lit up hillsides blanketed with Oregon white oak in fall foliage of deep burnt orange. It was a good day for a hike on the Klickitat Trail. It was also the last day this trail would be open to the public for a while. On the following day, Washington State Parks Director Rex Derr would announce that he was closing most of the trail in an effort to ease tensions between hikers and property owners along the old rail bed. Birdwatchers and naturalists who hiked a section of the trail along Swale Creek that day were treated to views of a soaring golden eagle, deer loping along the canyon ridge, and scores of tiny goldfinches bursting from a clump of willows. Where the trail entered Swale Creek Canyon, green mosses and orange lichens covered the canyon walls. Hikers also encountered beaten-down stream banks and cow pies where cattle had access to the creek.

At its opposite end, the trail begins at Lyle and follows the Klickitat River, crossing from the east bank to the west on an old railway bridge two miles upstream from the river's mouth. It passes by a Native American treaty fishing site where spawning salmon leap through a narrow canyon as the river flows north between steep walls. Further north, it passes through the tiny communities of Pitt, Klickitat, and Wahkiakus.

Bob Hansen and the other local volunteers who had organized this hike were fighting what appeared to be a last-ditch effort to keep the right-of-way in public ownership. Some were inspired by the Critical Mass urban cycling movement. Their goal: to keep hiking and occupying the old railbed while introducing it to new hikers to build a base of support.

A handful of angry property owners along the railroad right-of-way had fought the trail, harassing hikers and even state workers. Forest Service employees had recently been threatened with a shotgun and forced to turn back. A hiker's dog had been shot and killed.

The campaign to build a 31-mile trail connecting the rugged lower Klickitat River with the stark canyons of south-central Washington began in 1992. It began shortly after the federal government transferred title to the railroad right-of-way to the Rails-to-Trails Conservancy, a national organization dedicated to converting abandoned rail lines to recreational hiking trails. The idea had obvious appeal to hikers and trail advocates, and also to the Forest Service, which was charged with expanding recreation opportunities in the gorge. But local ranchers were adamantly opposed. Many opponents of the trail belonged to a national property rights group that was committed to repealing the federal Rails to Trails legislation. Though vocal, they appeared to represent only a minority of ranchers and others living long the rail right-of-way.

A group of committed volunteers had their hopes set on converting the abandoned rail bed to a popular trail that would follow the Klickitat River north from its mouth through a steep-walled canyon, through gentler forested terrain, then east into drier country, providing access to a little-visited transition zone of Klickitat County range land.

The former rail corridor had once transported sheep and lumber from Goldendale and the ranches and forests of south-central Washington to Lyle, at the mouth of the Klickitat. But the Burlington Northern Railway (which later became known as BNSF) had abandoned the line in 1992. Some years earlier, the Forest Service had begun writing a plan to restore the trail and improve its safety. But the agency misjudged the intensity of opposition from local ranchers and other landowners along the right-of-way. Eventually it backed down in the face of this opposition. So did the Washington State Parks Commission, which held title to the east end of the right-of-way.

Parks Secretary Derr proposed to close the trail for at least two months, after which the parks commission would decide whether to terminate the state's ownership of the railbed. Parks officials said they had no money to develop the trail and that holding title to the rail corridor had cost the state hundreds of thousands of dollars over the previous eight years. If the state relinquished title, the rail bed would revert to the nonprofit Rails-to-Trails Conservancy, the national organization that had conveyed it to the parks commission in 1994. The Conservancy would have to find another agency to develop the trail.

The late fall closure was the latest skirmish in a battle that had raged for ten years. It angered gorge advocates, who hoped to see the Klickitat designated a national recreation trail. "In the past few months you have had local citizens out there organizing hikes, doing stewardship projects, urging people to get their food and gas in Klickitat," said Kevin Gorman, executive director of Friends of the Columbia Gorge. For state officials to buckle now, he said, was "just disgraceful."

But the hardy volunteers refused to take no for an answer. They mobilized, they organized, they pressured the State Parks Department to reconsider. Leading the anti-trail campaign were Tracy and Lori Zoller, who operated a fishing guide service along the Klickitat River. The Zollers had found allies in Klickitat County Commissioner Joan Frey and state Sen. Jim Honeyford. In late October 2002, they summoned Derr to a meeting in Goldendale that was also attended by several state and county officials. Trail supporters were not invited.

Lori Zoller argued that the state was legally required to establish ownership of each parcel along the railroad easement and negotiate with individual property owners who would be affected by public use of the trail. In some cases, she said, landowners could be entitled to compensation for "take" of their land at the time the railroad relinquished it.

A federal appeals court had disagreed with this argument in 1996, dismissing a lawsuit filed by the Zollers and seven other landowners seeking compensation for the loss of land along the rail corridor. Under the 1983 National Trails System Act, a railroad may contract with an agency to use an out-of-service rail corridor as a trail until it is needed again for rail service. The law specifies that unused rail corridors may be sold, leased or donated to a trail manager without reverting to the adjacent landowners. The appeals court ruled that the federal government had acted legally in 1991 when it transferred title to the Rails-to-Trails Conservancy, a process called "railbanking." In 1994, after removing the rails and ties, the conservancy had given the land to the Forest Service and the parks commission for development of a public trail. Private property rights groups across the country had unsuccessfully challenged the constitutionality of the railbanking provision all the way to the U.S. Supreme Court.

The federal government had originally deeded large sections of the Lyle-to-Goldendale rail corridor to Burlington Northern in the late nineteenth century. Over the years the line was used to haul sheep, deliver logs to a mill in Klickitat, and pick up grain in Goldendale. The railroad abandoned the rail line in 1992 and sold the conservancy its rights to the Lyle-to-Warwick section the following year. In 2000, trail supporters canvassed the communities of Lyle and Klickitat and found that 80 percent supported the trail. Community councils in Lyle and Klickitat had passed resolutions calling for development of the trail. "I think it would help all of the businesses in Klickitat," said Marsha Martell, owner of the Chevron gas station and convenience store in Klickitat and a third-generation resident of the small community. "It would be wonderful for our community, for our children to walk on, for our grandkids."

Most of the trail was in good shape. A Forest Service environmental assessment that had been gathering dust since 1995 called for decking railroad trestles, repairing a few washed-out areas, and building restrooms and parking areas at access points. It also proposed steps to reduce conflicts between hikers and cattle on open range adjacent to the trail by requiring hikers' dogs to be leashed.

The Forest Service met with landowners and members of the Klickitat Band of the Yakama Tribe, which held treaty rights to a fishing site near the mouth of the river. The agency wrote a draft environmental assessment. But property owners and county politicians put pressure on then-Northwest Regional Forester Bob Williams not to release the environmental assessment. "A handful of property owners absolutely refused to accept that the state now held the title and it was a public right of way," said Forest Service spokesman Mike Ferris.

The most recent showdown over use of the unimproved trail had come to a boil in May 2002, when Sean Stroup, a University of Oregon architecture student, rode his mountain bike on the trail while researching the conversion of the old railbed to a public trail for a college project. A Klickitat County sheriff's deputy cited Stroup for criminal trespass. County prosecuting attorney Tim O'Neill dropped the charges only after Deputy Washington Attorney General Barbara Herman sent him a scathing letter chastising him for the citation. "I am not sure how I could have been clearer in communicating that State Parks owns the trail and permits public use of that trail," Herman wrote. Property owners in Klickitat County "should stop interfering with and intimidating trail users. If they do not like the law, they should go to Congress and attempt to change it." Parks followed up with a letter to O'Neill stressing that the state had jurisdiction over the rail corridor and that hikers did not need landowners' permission to be on the property.

Things escalated from there. Trail proponents organized several hikes to publicize the trail's attractions and establish their right to be there. In response, some landowners erected illegal gates and posted "no trespassing" signs. Hikers were threatened and even forced to leave the trail. State parks workers trying to get access to a fish habitat project on the Klickitat River were confronted with an illegal six-foot-high barricade of barbed wire and hog wire erected across the trail. They returned a few days later to find another illegal gate, which they replaced with a hinged rancher gate, padlocked to keep vehicles out but let hikers in. They notified the sheriff, but no citations were issued.

After the meeting in Goldendale, parks officials backpedaled on whether the trail was in fact open to public access. Parks spokeswoman Virginia Painter said hikers who used the trail during the closure would not be cited for trespassing but would use it at their own risk. The Parks Commission was actually a minor player in the controversy, she said. "We own it but we are only holding it until the Forest Service develops it."

Lori Zoller maintained that state law required the state to conduct title searches and negotiate with individual affected landowners before establishing a recreation trail along their property line. "Each one of these people has a right to say, 'This is not going to work for me,'" she said. Whether or not her argument had legal merit, the Zollers now had the state's attention.

Hike organizer Bob Hansen was trying to keep his eye on the prize. "We really want a long-term solution," he said. "Hostility is not a long-term solution."

Trail advocates said they were more than willing to make accommodations to address property owners' concerns about encounters between dogs and livestock, sanitation and other issues. They packed a November 2002 public meeting in Lyle and a park commission meeting the following month. They wrote 135 letters urging the state to retain ownership.

About thirty trail supporters, nearly all residents of western Klickitat County, came together to form the Klickitat Trail Conservancy. They set ambitious goals: Raise $5,000 by June to reimburse the state for costs associated with the trail, enlist volunteers, and raise money to upgrade a railroad trestle over the Klickitat River with decking and handrails. The Forest Service, for its part, agreed to take its 1997 environmental assessment off the shelf and update it to evaluate the impacts of developing the rail corridor as a national recreation trail.

Derr was the roadblock. He recommended that the trail remain closed to hikers through the coming spring and summer unless the Forest Service or trail supporters came forward to cover the state's costs of managing it. He also recommended that the commission transfer ownership of the rail corridor back to the Conservancy unless the state could reach a trail management agreement with the Forest Service or a nonprofit group by September of 2003. The commission had spent $320,000 responding to legal challenges and ongoing management issues since it acquired the right-of-way, and $315,000 in federal money repairing damage to the trail after the 1996 floods.

But in February, the State Parks and Recreation Commission voted to overrule Derr and retain state ownership of the former railroad right-of-way while working with other parties to develop it as an improved recreation trail. Parks commissioners were swayed by the fact that so many people were willing to donate money, time, and labor to develop the trail. They lifted the temporary trail closure. They authorized Derr to work with the Forest Service on developing a cooperative agreement with a nonprofit organization for trail maintenance and support services.

Trail advocates were jubilant. So was the Forest Service. "It will allow us to step up and fulfill the commitment we made in 1997," Mike Ferris said. "We're going to start right away."

Initially the Forest Service planned to protect only the lower two miles of the rail right-of-way, from the river's mouth to the National Scenic Area boundary. Trail proponents persuaded the agency to go another six miles to Pitt, the north end of the Wild and Scenic River segment designated in the Scenic Area Act. Eventually the Forest Service agreed to extend the trail all the way to the town of Klickitat, a timber-dependent community that strongly supported the trail.

In August 2003, the Forest Service released a plan that proposed to develop a 15-mile hard-surfaced trail along the river between Lyle and Klickitat at a cost of $5 million. It proposed to pave some of the widest and most accessible sections for the use of cyclists, local residents, and people in wheelchairs. The new trail would fill a demand for more hiking trails on the Washington side of the gorge. Another 16 miles of rail bed

Klickitat Trail hikers. Photo by Darryl Lloyd.

between Klickitat and Warwick, which crossed rangeland and open terrain east of the mountains, would be left undeveloped. The agency estimated that 38,500 hikers annually would use the shorter section. "It produces a low-elevation trail for mountain bikers and hikers," recreation manager Stan Hinatsu said. "Families will be able to walk side by side by a beautiful river."

Nonetheless, trail supporters said they would continue to press for designation of the entire 31 miles as a national recreation trail, a designation only the Forest Service Regional Forester could make.

"The push for us is still going to be the entire 31 miles," said Klickitat Trail Conservancy board member Cheryl Steindorf. "Developing the entire length will offer hikers a variety of terrains and give them an opportunity to hike through more isolated areas far from the river and highways. I think people will travel further to see it."

Bob Hansen of the Conservancy praised the Forest Service proposal as "a big step forward," adding, "Now we'll work with state parks to help manage the rest."

In June 2005, a half-dozen Klickitat County landowners once again sued the Forest Service to halt the trail project. The last-ditch lawsuit threatened a $240,000 federal grant Congress had approved for trail improvements. The agency had planned to deck the railroad trestles, add handrails and build parking areas and restrooms along a 15-mile section of the trail that year. It put those plans on hold.

Scenic Area Manager Dan Harkenrider said he wouldn't move forward until the federal Surface Transportation Board acted on the legal challenge. "It would be taking an incredible risk" to commit the money, he said, because if it was not spent by June 30, it would have to be appropriated anew by Congress in 2006.

The landowners had used a technicality to petition the board to reconsider its finding that BNSF had abandoned the rail right-of-way. In order for an abandoned railroad right-of-way to be railbanked and included in the rails-to-trails system, it had to be part of a continuous corridor in railroad ownership that could be reconnected to a main rail line if needed. Opponents argued that the railroad had severed the link in 2003 and again in 2004. A BNSF lawyer maintained that the railroad continued to own a continuous corridor. The lawsuit failed, and in February 2006 the Forest Service formally signed a cooperative agreement with the Washington State Parks Commission committing itself to manage the lower trail.

Converting an old railbed to a safe riverbank trail would be an expensive endeavor. Trestles would have to be decked and equipped with handrails for user safety. Flood damage along some sections would have to be repaired. Trailheads with parking would be needed at Lyle, Pitt, and Klickitat. Development of the eastern half of the trail would require rerouting it in three flood-damaged locations and developing three additional trailheads.

The Conservancy immediately took up the challenge. In the first year, members installed three portable toilets and contributed $2,500 toward the cost of placing signs along the trail. Three dozen active members continued to organize hikes to familiarize people with the trail. In August they celebrated the one-year anniversary of their effort.

But opposition from the Klickitat Band of the Yakama Nation, which maintained a traditional dipnet fishery on the lower river, remained unresolved. Tribal leaders warned that increased public access would disturb cultural artifacts near the river, including a cemetery, village sites, and ancient petroglyphs and pictographs. The fishing site had been vandalized in the past, Tribal Council Vice Chair Jerry Meninick said. He accused the Forest Service of failing to adequately consult with the tribe regarding the new trail alignment.

Meninick's concern reflected growing tension between the tribes and Forest Service recreation planners. Recreation use in the Columbia Gorge was increasingly encroaching on Native American treaty sites, Meninick said. For example, tribal fishermen often found themselves crowded out by windsurfers at Doug's Beach, a popular windsurfing site.

"This is what is going to happen to the Klickitat Falls fishery," Meninick predicted. "Sooner or later we are going to be found to be in the way of a tourist attraction. We will be requested to move our fishery, or decrease the days we fish, in the interest of 'the economy.'"

The Forest Service attempted to hold government-to-government meetings with the Yakama Tribal Council over the trail right-of-way, but those meetings were "deferred or delayed" by tribal leaders, Hinatsu said. The agency was willing to consider erecting visual barriers along the trail to protect the tribal fishing site and even closing the trail during the tribe's annual First Foods ceremony.

No agreement was reached. In the end, the entire 31-mile rail Klickitat Trail was opened to public access. The first 17 miles follow a congressionally designated Wild and Scenic River section of the Klickitat River. The trail then heads east through Swale Creek Canyon, a rugged, remote canyon that draws mountain bikers as well as hikers to its secluded narrow gorges, its rolling hillsides forested with oak and pine, and its columnar basalt cliffs, visible from the trail near Wahkiakus. In spring, the canyon blooms with spectacular wildflower displays and offers amazing birding opportunities. In winter it offers solitude and cross-country skiing.

It's a classic transition zone, said Andy Kallinen, who oversees the trail as a state parks manager. In just a few miles, hikers can pass from a westside Douglas fir forest to open stands of oak and pine to shrub-steppe prairie.

Today, thousands of hikers use the Klickitat Trail every year, taking advantage of their hard-won access to rare landscapes that reveal the amazing diversity of the Columbia River Gorge.

The Zollers now list the Klickitat Trail as an amenity their clients can take advantage of while they're in the area. And Klickitat County promotes hiking the trail as a way to promote fitness, said Jim Denton, a member of the Conservancy. "It's a real satisfying thing" he said, "to see the opposition drop away."

Chapter 16
The Haze Curtain

It's the nation's only National Scenic Area, which makes the irony even more profound. Haze blurs views of stunning landscapes in the Columbia River Gorge year-round. The visual pollution is made worse by the gorge's geography and weather patterns. The walls of the gorge create an 85-mile-long funnel, trapping pollutants from cars, trucks, locomotives, tugboats and fossil fuel-burning power plants, and from countless urban and rural sources both west and east of the National Scenic Area. Haze lingers in the gorge both summer and winter, obscuring the very vistas the National Scenic Area was established to protect. Haze-producing sulfur dioxide and nitrogen oxide also threaten natural and cultural resources, including sensitive lichens that serve as canaries in the coal mine by detecting haze-producing pollutants.

Twenty years of studies by the Forest Service and university-based air quality specialists, beginning in the early 1990s, thoroughly documented the air quality problem in the gorge and began to hint at the complex sources of persistent gorge smog. In 2000, the Columbia River Gorge Commission and the Forest Service launched a well-intentioned effort to draw attention to the problem and develop solutions. But the commission proved impotent at navigating the scientific, political, and regulatory challenges involved in cleaning up gorge air. It took mountains of scientific studies, litigation, and belated enforcement actions by Oregon's Department of Environmental Quality to begin addressing two of the major sources of gorge haze: Oregon's only coal-fired plant and a huge dairy feed lot, both east of the Scenic Area boundary.

The lesson learned: Despite the high-minded goals set forth in the Scenic Area Act, there's no substitute for well-crafted and aggressively enforced regulation by the states and other regulatory agencies.

The federal Clean Air Act amendments of 1990 addressed visual pollution in national parks and other special areas through a Regional Haze Rule. Under the rule, which the U.S. Environmental Protection Agency did not formally adopt until 1999, it was up to each state to decide on its own how to clean up air pollution in parks and wilderness areas within its borders. States were supposed to show steady progress in reducing the haze that affects the nation's most pristine natural areas, with the goal of eliminating it by 2064. But because haze occurs at levels much lower than those affecting human health, addressing it seldom became a top federal or state priority.

The 1992 Scenic Area Management Plan called for a study to determine whether the Gorge National Scenic Area should be classified as a federal Class 1 air shed, placing it in the same category as pristine national parks and wilderness areas. But it was clear that the gorge, with its growing load of industry and commerce, could not meet that standard.

Air monitoring by the Forest Service began in 1993 at Wishram, near the east end of the gorge, and in 1997 at Mount Zion, near the west end. It revealed that haze was noticeable in the gorge 90 percent of the time and severe 15 percent of the time. A 1999 Forest Service study ranked the National Scenic Area sixth-worst in "light extinction" or visible air pollution among all national parks, monuments, and other natural areas in the West. Only a handful of natural areas near cities, including Mount Rainier National Park in Washington, ranked worse.

Sulfur and nitrogen, both ingredients in the acid rain emitted by fossil-fuel burning industries, cars, and trucks, contributed to the haze. The humid climate in the west end of the gorge made matters worse, scattering light and obscuring scenery more dramatically than in the dry east end. Yet some of the poorest visibility in the gorge occurred in fall and winter, when winds typically blow from the east. Scientists initially could not explain this.

In May 2000, the Gorge Commission, under executive director Claire Puchy, amended the Scenic Area Management Plan to address the air pollution threat. Jurgen Hess of the Forest Service wrote the new language, which declared that "air quality shall be protected and enhanced" in the Special Management Areas, and called for continued monitoring, analysis and annual progress reports. But the commission had neither the money nor the staff expertise to get a handle on the many complex sources of

Haze in the Gorge, viewed from Dog Mountain. Photo by Darryl Lloyd.

gorge haze—or to determine what to do about them. Instead, it called on the states to step up.

Commissioners asked the states to expand monitoring of air pollution and visibility in the gorge, analyze the data to identify "all sources, both inside and outside the Scenic Area, that significantly contribute to air pollution," and, based on that data, develop and implement a regional air quality strategy for the gorge. It was a tall order for the Oregon Department of Environmental Quality and the Washington Department of Ecology. About the only baseline data available at the time on sources of gorge pollution was from the two Forest Service monitoring stations. The technology to do the monitoring was expensive, and interpreting the data gathered over such a large and varied landscape posed a huge challenge.

Bob Bachman, a meteorologist in the Forest Service's regional office, was an outspoken advocate for improved gorge air quality. He saw a train wreck coming in the form of a boom in applications to build new natural gas-fired generators in the region. In 2000 and 2001, the region's energy picture was in disarray. Faced with projections of a looming West Coast energy shortage, the Bonneville Power Administration was besieged with proposals for development of nearly thirty new natural gas-fired plants along its power grid in and near the gorge. Bachman warned that permitting more natural gas plants would make gorge air quality worse. The Bonneville Power Administration agreed. Its own 2001 study predicted significant deterioration of visibility in the gorge if all the gas-fired plants on the drawing board actually were built.

Bachman's warnings did not sit well with Klickitat County, which was preparing to put out the welcome mat for energy developers. Under its vision, much of the sparsely populated county would fall within a vast "energy overlay zone" where new facilities would be fast-tracked to approval with scant environmental review. The county predicted the new zoning would spur the development of up to four 25-megawatt natural gas and biomass plants. County officials saw this new focus on air quality concerns as just one more roadblock.

As Bachman sounded the alarm about the impact of a slew of new natural gas plants, Linda Geiser, a Forest Service lichenologist, was completing a six-year study of sensitive lichens on public forest land in western Oregon and Southwest Washington. Lichens have the capacity to soak up pollutants such as nitrogen oxide in the air and in rainfall and in fog water. Some lichen species gradually stop growing or disappear altogether in heavily polluted areas. Others thrive in polluted, high-nitrogen environments. Geiser discovered that nitrogen-loving species usually found in urban and industrial areas were thriving in the gorge west of Hood River. But nitrogen-sensitive species like *Lobaria oregana*, usually abundant in pristine forested areas, were extremely scarce. The lichens she collected in the gorge contained the highest levels of nitrogen and sulfur of any she tested. Geiser's study also was the first to suggest that acid deposition in the gorge, in the form of rain or fog, might be causing ancient rock to deteriorate, threatening petroglyphs and pictographs carved by Columbia Basin tribes.

Those findings alarmed the Yakama Tribe, which eventually joined with other Columbia Basin treaty tribes to commission their own air quality study.

Bachman called the information from the lichen studies compelling. "It shows a clear and significant air pollution signature," he said.

The news about the gorge's murky air should not have come as a surprise. The gorge is a heavily traveled corridor. Pollution from the Portland metropolitan area and beyond flows in on west winds in spring and summer;

emissions from power plants and agriculture funnel into the east end in fall and winter. Even pollutants from Asia, carried across the Pacific on prevailing winds, contribute to the stew.

As the Gorge Commission prepared to tackle the air quality issue, interest groups lined up. Portland environmentalists supported the new focus on cleaning up the gorge air shed. Representatives of rural communities packed commission meetings to protest that new air quality rules could quash economic development. Klickitat County hired its own air quality consultant to make that case. The process quickly bogged down over arguments about the size and makeup of an advisory committee that was to be charged with devising a gorge air quality strategy, and about what role the states would play. In the fall of 2003, three years after the commission took on the issue, the Forest Service finally installed equipment to begin conducting additional monitoring of air quality at three sites in the gorge. But the path to arriving at a strategy remained far from clear.

Then, the financially strapped Washington Department of Ecology threw a monkey wrench into the process by announcing that it was eliminating its entire visibility program, including its involvement in the gorge air quality study. The Oregon Department of Environmental Quality soon followed suit, announcing that it would reduce its own funding for the program. Southwest Washington Clean Air, a small regional agency based in Vancouver, offered to step up and fill the gap. It won a federal grant to develop models for air monitoring and tried to salvage what was quickly threatening to become a futile effort.

With sharply curtailed funding, the Gorge Commission decided the thirty-two-member advisory committee that was supposed to convene soon to begin working on the air quality strategy would not meet until 2005 at the earliest. Air quality officials in both states said they had no money to staff the unwieldy committee, which had been expanded to give every possible interest group a seat at the table. The committee's charge was nebulous. In fact, it never was formed and never met.

With the clock ticking, Gorge Commission Executive Director Martha Bennett appealed to Washington Gov. Gary Locke. Since the Washington Department of Ecology had ended its participation in July 2003, she said, Southwest Clean Air had led technical elements of the project, but beginning in 2007, the public process for designing a strategy would begin, and the states' involvement was crucial. "No long-term solution can be created without the support of all of the agencies responsible for air quality in the gorge," she wrote. Her appeal fell on deaf ears.

Bachman was disgusted. "What we have seen in the past three years is a compromise between science and politics," he said. "There hasn't been a single ounce of air pollution reduced." In a last-ditch effort, he called for recruitment of a committee of "well-connected people" to raise funds for a more complete air quality study, promote voluntary efforts to curtail pollution, and raise public awareness.

But Dana Peck, Klickitat County director of development, opposed allowing the Forest Service to pursue such a "unilateral approach." He warned commissioners not to tamper with the air study work plan, which he said had been developed over months. "Klickitat County strongly objects to having the Forest Service come in at the end of the process with its own proposal and ignoring the coordinated interjurisdictional process that has taken place to date," he said.

Martha Bennett, who had inherited this mess, pointed out the obvious: The work plan Peck was defending left unresolved what the end product would be. "I don't know what the strategy will have in it or specifically what the public process and the decision-making process will be," Bennett said. "Right now that is the weakest part of the plan."

The Gorge Commission had reached a dead end. But Bachman wasn't about to let the haze problem fade away. He had made no secret of his impatience with the states' slow progress. If the commission refused to build broad public support for reducing gorge haze, he would act on his own. Bachman contracted with ecologists Mark Fenn and Timothy Blubaugh of the Forest Service's Riverside, California, research station to conduct a new $50,000 study of acid deposition in the gorge. In August 2005, the Forest Service released the study's headline-grabbing conclusion: The gorge experienced acid rain and acid fog as severe as in some industrial areas on the East Coast. Rain samples collected at eleven gorge sites between October 2003 and February 2004 were as caustic as those measured in the industrial city of Pittsburg, and twenty to thirty times more acidic than normal rain in the Northwest, the scientists said. Air funneling west through the gorge in winter seeded gorge clouds with exhaust from cars, trucks, and trains, emissions from a large coal-fired power plant in Boardman, and ammonia from an enormous cattle feedlot nearby.

Gorge artifacts were at risk, the scientists warned. Acid fog could erode Native American petroglyphs and pictographs. The Forest Service had recently identified ammonia in the Snake River Canyon between Oregon and Idaho as the likely cause of eroding petroglyphs on rock surfaces there. "We can't say when the trees will start to show detrimental effects, but definitely the soil chemistry is changing, and the effects are beginning," Fenn wrote. As it happened, the two major contributors to the acid deposition problem had largely escaped regulation by the Oregon DEQ. Both operated legally, both were located east of the Scenic Area boundary, and both were exempt from modern air quality rules.

Portland General Electric's Boardman plant was Oregon's only coal-fired plant. Prevailing east-to-west winds in winter drove its emissions into the gorge, contributing to a toxic mix of ammonia, coal residue, vehicle exhaust from freeway traffic, and other pollutants. The aging plant had gone on line in 1975 with pollution controls that would become obsolete within weeks. The timing of its startup won the plant a federal exemption from sweeping new amendments to the 1970 federal Clean Air Act. As a result, the Boardman plant was among the dirtiest in the region, lacking even the pollutant-removing scrubbers that were standard equipment in other power plants of that era.

The EPA later admitted that the 1975 exemption was a mistake and that the state had provided no documentation to support it. An investigation by the *Oregonian* revealed that in 1977, state DEQ officials admitted they had little technical information about pollution from coal plants, and asked PGE to take them on a tour of other coal plants in the country, which the utility did, all expenses paid.

The nearby dairy feedlot, Threemile Canyon Farms, had expanded rapidly between 2000 and 2005. At the time of the acid deposition study, 52,300 cows produced a ton of manure per minute. The decomposing manure emitted more ammonia than the combined amount released by all regulated sources in Oregon. Yet the feedlot was exempt from Oregon state air regulations because it was classified as an agricultural enterprise. Department of Environmental Quality air quality specialist Andrew Ginsburg admitted the agency lacked the tools it would normally wield to regulate the huge dairy.

The farm had not obtained a federal Title 5 permit under the Clean Air Act. Oregon law exempted agricultural sources from the Title 5 permit process. But in this case, the EPA had approved the exemption for the dairy based in part on a letter from the Oregon attorney general stating errone-ously that the state had no agricultural sources that rose to the level of re-quiring a Title 5 permit. Environmentalists noted that California had found ways to regulate its own giant feed lots by capping the size of operations eligible for the agricultural enterprise exemption. The Fenn study found that clear days had become rarer in the east end of the gorge since 2000 as ammonia from the dairy combined with fossil fuel and exhaust from the coal-fired plant to form acid smog.

The new Forest Service study at last got the public's attention—and drew criticism of DEQ's enforcement record from environmentalists. "Air quality in the region continues to get worse and new sources of pollution continue to be added, yet the agencies have made no real progress toward addressing the problem," said Michael Lang of Friends of the Gorge. "The large amounts of pollution being emitted by Threemile Canyon Farms would not have happened had Oregon DEQ addressed the situation proactively."

Lang called on the Gorge Commission to contact the governors of Wash-ington and Oregon and top state environmental officials and insist that they make reducing gorge air pollution a priority. "I am asking the Gorge Commission to reinvigorate this process," he said. "We have hard evidence that we have an air quality problem."

The Yakama Tribe agreed. "Air quality is a big issue for us," said Rebec-ca Elwood, environmental program manager for the Confederated Tribes and Bands of the Yakama Indian Nation. "For approximately five years the Yakama Tribe has been asking for a strategy to be developed. The vision of the management plan is for stewardship of this land. We know economic development is important, but without stewardship we will defeat the purpose of the Gorge Scenic Area."

In 2006, another study of gorge air made headlines. Mark Green, an air quality specialist with the Nevada-based Desert Research Institute, analyzed 600 days of air sampling in the gorge conducted by the Forest Service over two winters and one summer between 2003 and 2005. Green's conclusion: Air in the gorge was cleaner than in downtown Las Vegas, but dirtier than in Texas' Big Bend National Park along the Rio Grande. It was loaded with soot, dust, auto exhaust, smoke from wood stoves and forest fires, diesel emissions from trains and tugboats, sulfur emissions from the

Camas paper mill, haze-producing nitrogen and sulfur compounds from the Boardman plant, ammonia from the dairy feedlot, and urban pollution from as far away as the Tri-Cities and as close as the Portland-Vancouver metro area.

On summer days, slugs of murky air from the metro area traveled east into the heart of the gorge—to Stevenson, Cascade Locks, Hood River, and The Dalles. But haze was even worse in winter, when prevailing winds blew dust and emissions from the east. Most pollution that affected visibility in the gorge originated outside the National Scenic Area, Green concluded. But rainfall did clean the air, washing away the microscopic particles that scatter light and producing a sharper view. Air quality in the gorge was a "medium problem," he said, not the worst he'd seen, but hardly pristine.

As the studies piled up, the Yakama Tribe joined with other Columbia Basin treaty tribes under the banner Sacred Breath to conduct yet another. The tribes hired Dan Jaffe, an air quality specialist at the University of Washington, to analyze twelve years of air samples from the Wishram site at the east end of the gorge on the Washington side. Jaffe's working hypothesis was that sources in the Portland metro area and in the east gorge/Boardman region were primarily responsible for pollution on the worst air quality days. He focused on the fifty worst days recorded at the Wishram site over the previous dozen years—specifically those days with the highest levels of particulates.

His conclusion: Sources at the east end of the gorge were largely responsible for impaired visibility on at least fifteen and possibly as many as nineteen of the fifty "worst days" studied. "While the west end of the Columbia River Gorge is probably responsible for elevated (particulate matter) on some days, sources in the eastern end of the gorge clearly dominate the worst air quality days," he said.

Jaffe's report, released by the Yakama Tribe in March 2008, confirmed that the Boardman plant was a major source of nitrogen and acid fog. When east winds pushed the pollutants downstream along the Columbia River, the plant contributed 55.5 percent of the nitrogen measured at Wishram. The worst visual pollution occurred in fall, Jaffe found. October and November accounted for poor air quality on twenty-four of the fifty worst days. November was by far the worst month, with eighteen days of high particulate levels. Spring had the clearest skies.

On days when the wind blew from the east, nitrogen concentrations were significantly elevated compared to all other days. That finding clearly implicated the large sources of ammonia and nitrogen oxide emitted by the Threemile Canyon Farms and the Boardman plant. By now, state regulators in Oregon were paying attention.

In August 2008, the Oregon DEQ released a draft plan requiring PGE to clean up its emissions at the Boardman plant at a cost of at least $424 million over ten years.

Andrew Ginsburg of DEQ said the plan would eventually reduce total emissions from the plant by 80 percent, or 21,000 pounds per year. "The result would be an improvement in visibility three times as great as the minimum level the human eye can detect," he told the *Oregonian*. If adopted, he said, the rule would be one of the strongest actions taken in the western United States to reduce air pollution from an older power plant.

Under the DEQ proposal, between 2011 and 2014 the company would be required to install new burners and other equipment that would allow the plant to burn coal more efficiently, reducing nitrogen oxide emissions by 46 percent.

Those reductions weren't optional, Ginsburg said; the Regional Haze Rule required them. It turned out that the job of improving air quality in natural areas, passed off to the states, did have teeth, if the states chose to use them.

Moreover, by 2014, the company would be required to install a "semi-dry scrubber" to reduce sulfur dioxide emissions by 80 percent—an expensive piece of equipment that required a complicated engineering design. And between 2016 and 2018, PGE would be required to install additional equipment to reduce nitrogen oxide emissions. "That's a Cadillac technology that meets today's standards," Ginsburg said. "We're requiring something more stringent than most states would require."

Portland General Electric submitted its own proposal for a series of retrofits to the coal plant that would cost about $300 million in 2007 dollars. Spokesman Steve Corson said those emission controls would meet the Clean Air Act requirement that existing power plants use the Best Available Retrofit Technology. He was noncommittal on the DEQ plan, saying the company would study its effects on its energy portfolio before making a decision.

The Department of Environmental Quality's new hard line came as a Sierra Club-led campaign to close the Northwest's two coal-fired electrical plants was gaining momentum. The plants were by far the major contributors of carbon dioxide in their respective states.

In Washington, conservationists had fought for years to close a Centralia coal-fired plant owned by the Canadian company TransAlta. The Centralia plant generated twice as much electricity as PGE's 600-megawatt Boardman plant. But because it had installed scrubbers to remove sulfur from its emissions, by 2003 the TransAlta plant was emitting 35 percent less sulfur dioxide than the PGE plant. In 2011, Washington Gov. Chris Gregoire signed an agreement with TransAlta under which the company agreed to phase out its coal-burning operations at the Centralia plant beginning in 2025.

Conservation groups had not been willing to wait for Oregon to negotiate a similar agreement with PGE. Instead, in 2008, six groups, including a high-powered public interest law firm, launched their own campaign to clean up emissions at the Boardman plant with a lawsuit filed in federal court. The conservationist' case was strengthened when the EPA issued a notice of violation against PGE. With the lawsuit underway and PGE facing potentially hundreds of millions of dollars in pollution control costs and millions of dollars in penalties, the utility bowed to the inevitable.

In July 2011, conservationists and PGE officials announced that they had reached agreement on an enforceable consent decree that would require the Boardman plant to invest in interim pollution controls as required by the DEQ and to stop burning coal no later than 2020. The investor-owned utility also agreed to establish a $2.5 million fund for environmental restoration projects and clean energy projects and to reduce acid depositions from the Boardman plant significantly.

"It means that over the next ten years, air quality will improve in the Columbia Gorge and Gorge residents can breathe cleaner air," Michael Lang said. "Also, PGE will agree to pay to restore damage from thirty years of emissions."

Conservationists, scientists, tribal leaders, state regulators, and lawyers had been able to accomplish what the Gorge Commission could not, through the straightforward process of documenting the major sources of air pollution in the gorge and enforcing the Clean Air Act. Yet despite this victory, Forest Service Scenic Area Manager Dan Harkenrider, in one of his last acts before retiring, inexplicably eliminated air quality from the list of natural resources protected by the Scenic Area Act. And in an acknowledgment that the Gorge Commission had no actual power to protect air quality, the two states formally reported to the commission in September 2011 that the Regional Haze Rule remained their best tool for monitoring and reducing the miasma of haze that would continue to plague the Columbia River Gorge for decades to come.

It was not a perfect tool, they acknowledged. "Due to the mix of urban and rural activities in the gorge, long-term visibility improvements cannot be expected to reach 'natural conditions' such as those in pristine wilderness areas," they said.

But the gorge, sandwiched between the Mount Hood and Mount Adams wilderness areas, would continue to reap benefits from the states' efforts to improve air quality around the Cascade peaks. It was a start.

Chapter 17
Logging Loopholes

In 2003, lifelong Skamania County resident Roy Ostroski decided to take advantage of an ambiguity in the Scenic Area Management Plan regarding logging. Six months earlier, Ostroski had bought a wooded 40-acre parcel with plans to cut and sell most of the trees and convert the land to winter pasture for his small herd of nine cows. At the time, his cows spent most of the year grazing land he owned on higher ground. But because 30 acres of Ostroski's property lay within the National Scenic Area, Friends of the Gorge saw an alarming precedent in his conversion plan. The group went to court immediately to challenge what it saw as a huge loophole in rules governing gorge logging.

The forty-eight-year-old logger cut trees fast and furiously for twenty-seven hours in early July before Friends obtained a stop-work order from Thurston County Superior Court that silenced his chain saw. The court ruled that the Washington Department of Natural Resources had erred when it approved the project after the Forest Service signed off on it.

Ostroski said he was well aware of the conversion provision before he bought the property near Cape Horn. He also knew the Forest Service planned to tighten it soon. "I applied for the permit because the Forest Service was going to change the rules," he said. "The rules right now are black and white." He obtained the necessary signoffs and permit, punched in about 2,700 feet of skid roads, and cut trees for two-and- a-half days before the stop-work order came down. The value of the trees he sold just about covered his legal costs of $13,000.

Ostroski was philosophical as well as pragmatic. He said he would not likely appeal the Superior Court ruling. In fact, he was considering starting over and applying for a more restrictive logging permit. Ostroski was also stockpiling ammunition for a possible 2006 Skamania County commission race. He downplayed the impact of the logging. When he logged, he said,

Roy Ostroski logged his property near Cape Horn for two and a half days in 2003 before a court order halted the logging. Ostroski, who said he wanted to convert forest land to pasture, was also testing the National Scenic Area Management Plan. His ploy prompted efforts to close a loophole in the plan that allowed conversion of forests even in highly visible areas of the Gorge. Photo by Janet L. Mathews of *The Columbian*.

he left some trees standing to protect views at the east end of his property, which looks out over the Columbia River. "I would challenge anyone to go on the other side and try to see this little patch."

Following this episode, the Forest Service decided it needed clearer standards for approving conversions of forest land to agricultural uses. Though the 1992 management plan allowed such conversions, Ostroski was the first person ever to apply for one. In 2004, the agency held a public hearing in Hood River to seek public comment on the larger issue of how forest land was being managed in the National Scenic Area. It proposed plugging—or at least modifying—the loophole Ostroski had taken advantage of, which allowed property owners to log their land if the purpose was to convert it from forest to agricultural use.

Scenic Area Manager Dan Harkenrider agreed that the agency did need to adopt some standards for allowing such conversions. But the advocacy group Friends of the Gorge took a harder line. Friends contended that all such conversions were illegal unless accomplished through formal zone changes approved by the Gorge Commission—a much more onerous process.

Underlying this disagreement was a longstanding failure by Congress, the Gorge Commission and the Forest Service to deal squarely with the issue of logging in the most scenic areas of the gorge. The issue had been there from the beginning. Major timberland owners, seeing the writing on the wall, had cut their own deals to protect their interests by negotiating massive land exchanges with the Forest Service after the bill became law. Congress had dealt with the issue by stating that on private lands, logging would be limited only by applicable state forest practices laws. The original Gorge Commission had taken a different tack in its first management plan, restricting logging on some private lands.

The 1992 management plan provided for a system of zoning on GMA lands. On certain highly visible forested sites zoned as Open Space or Small Woodlands, it imposed restrictions on logging and an outright ban on clearcutting. Because the language raised the issue of a regulatory "taking" of private property rights, Executive Director Richard Benner ran it by the two state attorneys general; Oregon signed off, but Washington did not. The two contradictory interpretations were bound to clash; it was just a matter of time.

Harkenrider's approach to cleaning up the ambiguities leaned toward accommodating timberland owners. As he considered adopting new conversion standards, Harkenrider also proposed to allow limited logging on GMA land zoned as Open Space—arguably the most contested real estate in the gorge—if it would promote forest health or improve fish and wildlife habitat. Landowners would be required to develop stewardship plans to protect scenic views. Under the 1992 plan, only minimal logging was allowed on land zoned as Open Space.

Harkenrider also said he would consider opening the door to some logging for forest health purposes in the Special Management Areas, where openings in the forest canopy were limited to 15 acres. That limit was critical to protecting scenic views near Beacon Rock, Table Mountain, Dog Mountain, and Wind Mountain on the Washington side, and Multnomah Falls on the Oregon side. Past Forest Service scenic area managers had recommended an outright ban on clearcutting in the SMAs.

Friends of the Gorge took sharp exception to loosening the conversion standard, saying Harkenrider's approach would set a precedent that would allow forests to be converted to agricultural use even in the most sensitive parts of the Scenic Area, where there were fewer safeguards to protect scenic views from logging.

"The GMA is really being hammered by big huge clearcuts," Michael Lang said. He estimated that the conversion loophole could open as much as 90,000 forested acres in the gorge to logging.

Jurgen Hess, the National Scenic Area's director of landscape planning for sixteen years before his retirement in 2002, argued that the Scenic Area Act required formal amendments to the management plan before land could be converted from forest to agriculture. "To me, it was quite clear what Congress intended," he said.

Harkenrider's interpretation was especially objectionable, Hess said, because no special restrictions applied on private forest land within the 150,000-acre GMA. Logging in the GMA on the Washington side had scarred Table Mountain, Underwood Mountain, and land near the Little White Salmon River.

Not only were Harkenrider's proposals controversial. He also drew scathing criticism from Hess and from many gorge residents for failing to allow adequate public comment on the changes. He originally released his draft plan October 31 and set a November 17 deadline for public comment. Under pressure from members of Congress he extended the deadline to December 8, but he refused to schedule any public hearings.

The proposed changes came as the Forest Service and Gorge Commission were wrapping up nearly three years of work on revising the Scenic Area management plan, during which extensive public involvement had been invited.

Hess pointedly asked Harkenrider why he had not provided more opportunity for public comment on what he called "these major and far-reaching changes." He also asked in an October 25 letter why Harkenrider had not proposed strengthening protection for forests as past Scenic Area managers had.

Harkenrider denied that he was promoting commercial logging in the gorge. "The mission of the National Scenic Area is not to log," he insisted. "Our mission is to protect and conserve the gorge."

Loopholes that permitted logging in highly visual areas would continue to be a thorny issue for the Forest Service, the Gorge Commission and owners of private timberland. The reluctance of both the Forest Service and the Gorge Commission to enforce the management plan when it came to logging made zoning an imperfect tool for protecting gorge views from the chainsaw. The issue would explode under a new executive director, Darren Nichols, who, just weeks into office, approved the notorious Mosier Bluff clearcut of 2012, a scar visible for miles in one of the most scenic areas of the gorge.

As with most issues, there were political and legal considerations. If strictly enforced, zoning that prohibited timber companies from deriving any economic use from their land could invite takings lawsuits from property owners. Over the years, the Forest Service in particular walked a careful line, trying to avert legal showdowns with timber companies by buying valuable timber land to preserve it.

The states were a different matter. Oregon had a well-established forest practices act, and most of its forested land in the National Scenic Area was in public ownership, But in the early years after the Scenic Area Act became law, the Washington Department of Natural Resources, which approves logging permits on state and private land in Washington, seemed not even to recognize the new logging restrictions.

In June 1995, Gorge Commission Executive Director Jonathan Doherty wrote to the DNR's regional forest practices coordinator to explain the rules of the game. The state had approved an application by Skamania County resident Peggy Bradford to log 75 acres of her property. The lower section was zoned as Small Woodlands; the upper portion was designated Open Space to protect scenic views.

"Commercial forest practices are prohibited on lands designated Open Space by both the Management Plan and the county ordinance," Doherty wrote. The Gorge Commission had approved a four-lot subdivision on the portion land zoned for Small Woodlands in 1992; no development of the property had followed.

Now Bradford wanted to log. But Doherty said the proposed harvest would violate rules requiring him to screen the site from key viewpoints and retain buffers around springs and streams. He reminded DNR officials that "state agencies are required to carry out their respective functions and responsibilities" in accordance with federal law, the Bistate Compact, the Gorge Management Plan, and county ordinances.

Skamania County Planning Director Harpreet Sandhu contested Doherty's reading of the law. Both the Scenic Area Act and the county ordinance "specifically exempt forest practices activities occurring on land located within a General Management Area," she wrote.

Another area of conflict was the Pacific Crest Trail, the 2,650-mile trail that extends from the Mexican border to the Canadian border, spanning the length of three states and crossing federal, state and private lands. The trail bisects the National Scenic Area, winding through the Mount Hood National Forest and down to Cascade Locks, where it crosses the Columbia River at the Bridge of the Gods. From the Washington trailhead west of Stevenson, it climbs through a patchwork of state and private land, skirting Table Mountain, a regional landmark, before it enters the Gifford Pinchot National Forest north of the Scenic Area boundary.

Surprisingly, logging is not banned on the Pacific Crest Trail. Since 1991 the Washington DNR had permitted numerous clearcuts on state land along the trail. In 2003, the DNR proposed a thinning sale along the trail that called for cutting trees on 288 acres scattered across twelve separate units. During active logging, logs would be skidded across the trail in some places and loggers would pile slash along the trail, forcing its temporary closure. "You can reach out from the trail and touch the trees that are marked for cutting," remarked Jim Hutchison, a retired Oregon Fish and Wildlife biologist who lived near the Washougal River. The state agency had no plan to leave buffers.

The easement the state of Washington had granted to the Forest Service for the trail right-of-way allowed the DNR to continue to log as it saw fit, raising revenue for counties, schools, and universities. Long-distance hikers might not expect to see active logging, but the Scenic Area Act gave the trail right-of-way no special protection.

In 1991, the Washington Legislature did step into protect the uniqueness of a high-elevation gorge wildland near Table Mountain. The state bought the 2,197-acre parcel of state land from the DNR to protect it from logging and established the Table Mountain Natural Resources Conservation Area to protect stands of old growth noble fir and western red cedar. The area is home to mountain lions, bears, deer, peregrine falcons, osprey, and bald eagle, as well as the finest known population of the rare Howell's daisy, which grows only in the gorge and is considered a species of concern under the state's Endangered Species Act.

In 1997 the state bought an additional 600 acres, increasing the size of the preserve to 2,800 acres. The Pacific Crest Trail crosses the western part

Rock Cove and Table Mountain, Skamania County, Washington. Photo by Darryl Lloyd.

of the reserve, and Beacon Rock State Park borders it on the southwest. Nearly the entire area lies within the National Scenic Area—and is now off-limits to commercial logging.

Chapter 18
The Casino Deal

By the late 1990s, the Confederated Tribes of Warm Springs, based on a 644,000-acre reservation in Central Oregon, had been struggling for years to revive its economic base. Tribal leaders first turned their eyes toward Hood River County as the site for a new casino in 1998. The tribe's remote Kah-Nee-Ta High Desert Resort and Casino had opened in 1995 at a site 10 miles from the nearest major highway. Three years later it was producing just $1 million in revenue annually. The tribe needed a new revenue source to make up for the downturn in profits from its timber and hydroelectric operations. Without that boost, the tribal government faced cuts in social, education, and health care services. At the time, about 4,000 enrolled tribal members lived on the reservation. Unemployment stood at 60 percent. Tribal leaders faced the prospect that more and more young people, unable to find jobs, would leave the reservation.

The Warm Springs had an asset in the gorge that offered a brighter future: Forty acres on a high cliff, facing the Washington shore, held in trust for the tribes by the federal Bureau of Indian Affairs since the 1920s. Nearby, just east of the thriving tourist and recreational town of Hood River, a restored section of the Historic Columbia River Highway had recently been dedicated as a state park and national trail.

Thus two worthy goals—helping Oregon's largest Native American tribe chart a course to economic prosperity while protecting scenic views in the gorge as required under the 1986 National Scenic Area Act—came to clash in a long-running saga that tested the wills of two Oregon governors and challenged the federal government.

The Confederated Tribes of Warm Springs and their Central Oregon reservation were both creations of the 1855 treaty the U.S. Government signed with the Warm Springs, Wasco, and Paiute tribes. These were people with deep roots in the Columbia Basin, where for millennia their people and their culture had been sustained by the great Columbia River salmon runs. In the 1855 treaty, tribal chiefs had ceded 10 million acres of their traditional territory to the U.S. government. But they had retained the right to fish, hunt and gather roots and berries in the ceded areas—their usual and customary places.

Warm Springs tribal leaders argued that they needed no one's permission to develop their 40 acres as a casino under the 1988 Indian Gaming Regulatory Act. But their plan to site their casino on the steep ground met with stiff opposition from both the city of Hood River and Hood River County. A group of gorge residents mobilized to stop the casino. Not only would it be visible from both sides of the river; it was adjacent to the recently completed Mark O. Hatfield State Park and a stretch of the Historic Columbia River Highway that had been restored and converted to a hiking and cycling trail with funding authorized by the National Scenic Area Act.

Hood River County argued that a casino on the site would damage its culture and identity. A survey returned by nearly 6,500 county residents in late 1998 revealed that nearly three-quarters opposed the site. Tribal leaders were unmoved. "We are making this decision for our well-being and survival, that's the bottom line," Rudy Clements, the tribes' casino liaison, said in announcing the decision to build on the Hood River site. Though the trust land was within the National Scenic Area, like all tribal lands it was exempt from regulations restricting development under the Scenic Area Act. Opponents looked for a legal or administrative hook to challenge the project.

A local group, No Casino, argued that the project might be subject to federal environmental review and that the tribe would have to receive a permit from the Oregon Department of Transportation to build a highway access ramp to the site. The Forest Service Scenic Area Office noted that access to the 40-acre trust property would require development of non-tribal lands within the National Scenic Area and that those lands—unlike the trust lands—would be subject to county and Gorge Commission review.

Tribal leaders took strong exception to these arguments. "We have a legitimate and lawful right to use our tribal land and we are going to defend it," declared Joe Moses, a member of the Warm Springs Tribal Council.

The concept of siting a large casino anywhere in the gorge was immediately controversial. It was also widely regarded as politically untenable while

Oregon Gov. John Kitzhaber, a staunch opponent of off-reservation casinos, remained in office from 1995 to 2003 during his first tenure as governor. Oregon already had nine tribal casinos, all on reservation land. Kitzhaber saw no need for more, and no need to expand tribal gaming to land outside reservations. He had made that position clear throughout his long career.

In 1999, as opposition to the Hood River site heated up, the tribal council proposed another option: Government Rock, a 32-acre former quarry owned by the Port of Cascade Locks. Kitzhaber rejected the proposal out of hand, citing his authority under the Indian Gaming Regulatory Act.

Government Rock was newly acquired by the tribe. Under the act, only parcels purchased before 1988 had sovereign status and were eligible for casino development. Exceptions required a governor's finding that the alternative site would better meet the tribes' economic needs and that the casino would not be detrimental to the host community.

Disregarding Kitzhaber's objection, in the spring of 2001, the Warm Springs Tribal Council announced that it would purchase Government Island and 175 acres east of Hood River and formally apply to the Bureau of Indian Affairs to take both parcels into trust. Trust status would exempt the new properties from state tax and land use laws as well as from Scenic Area Act rules, the tribal council contended. If state or federal agencies tried to block the proposal, Clements warned, the tribes would build a multistory casino on their 40 acres and use the newly acquired land for a hotel and other support facilities. The tribal council was prepared to invest $150 million on building the casino complex and installing a sewer system, gas stations, stores, and restaurants.

The Bureau of Indian Affairs sent letters to Hood River County, the Forest Service's National Scenic Area office, and the Gorge Commission seeking their opinions on the proposal. The City of Hood River immediately issued a letter of protest to the BIA stating that a gambling operation adjacent to the city limits would destroy the city's character and economic development plans. "A casino is enormously in conflict with the lot we cast for ourselves," wrote city councilman Chuck Haynie. "People come here for windsurfing and other natural activities, and that will be trashed by an operation which is not even subject to regulatory supervision."

The Forest Service's National Scenic Area office asked for more time to prepare a response. Agency officials wanted to see an environmental assessment on the proposal before they issued an opinion.

No Casino hired Perkins Coie, a law firm with roots in Seattle known for its success in helping communities fight tribal gaming facilities. Attorney Guy Martin urged local property owners to unite in their stance against the Hood River project and not to wait for the tribes to act.

The city of Hood River asked Hood River County to take the lead in organizing a political and legal battle against the casino because it was the county, not the city, that had jurisdiction over property bordering the tribes' trust land. The county agreed to join Cascade Locks in lobbying Kitzhaber to reverse his decision on the use of Government Rock as a less objectionable alternative. But the governor again refused.

In August 2001, the Warm Springs Tribal Council announced that it had bought 160 acres adjacent to its 40-acre parcel east of Hood River and had asked the BIA to exempt the property from state and local land use laws. The Gorge Commission, the state of Oregon, the Forest Service, and Hood River County scrambled to respond to this latest announcement.

Converting the land to trust status would transfer it to tribal jurisdiction and exempt it not only from local zoning rules but from the National Scenic Area Act. The Bush administration's Interior Secretary, Gale Norton, would make the final call. "Right now, you have 160 acres that could become hotels, restaurants, RV parks, gas stations," warned Kevin Gorman, the recently hired executive director of Friends of the Gorge. "It has the potential to become a casino village up there."

Engineering and architectural plans called for carving out a bluff to form a semicircle around the casino and an adjoining eight-story parking garage. The casino itself would be located about a half-mile inside the west end of the historic state highway, which had been reopened to hikers and cyclists in 2000 after completion of the $20 million restoration project.

The Gorge Commission had no power to stop the casino, but development on nontrust land surrounding the proposed casino would be subject to review by the Gorge Commission at some future date. "It's a tough place for the Gorge Commission to be," said Executive Director Martha Bennett. She predicted that some commissioners would not want to weigh in on the topic of Indian gaming.

In fact, at an August Gorge Commission hearing in Stevenson, more than a dozen speakers, most of them from Hood River, urged the commission to oppose trust status for the 160 acres. In testimony by turns impassioned, tearful, and emphatic, speakers said allowing the tribes to convert the land to trust status would strike at the heart of the National Scenic Area. "It is profoundly demoralizing to think that 200 acres that abuts my property can be removed from the National Scenic Area," said Hood River pear orchardist North Cheatham. "Nothing threatens the character of the gorge more than this issue," testified Hood River nature photographer Darryl Lloyd.

Many residents of White Salmon and Bingen, Washington, joined in opposing a casino on the site, which would be clearly visible directly across the Columbia River. Several speakers warned that if the land conversion was approved, it could be just the beginning, setting a precedent for other tribes to take gorge land into trust.

The Gorge Commission took a middle ground, voting unanimously to send a letter to the BIA urging it to take no action on the tribes' application until the Forest Service had analyzed its potential impact on the Scenic Area.

But Warm Springs leaders insisted they would build on land they controlled in Hood River, despite objections. They said they had given up on Cascade Locks. "Everybody thinks we're bluffing, but we're going to build a casino on our Hood River trust property," Clements vowed.

Sure enough, tribal leaders hired consultants to begin geotechnical studies of the Hood River site. They released a conceptual drawing of a wood structure with a full northern glass face and an 11,600-square-foot deck, set into a terraced slope screening six to eight lower floors of parking covering 70,800 square feet. The casino itself would cover 50,000 square feet with an additional 63,400 square feet for a restaurant and other amenities. Such a complex would destroy the forested slope east of Hood River and totally dominate the view for miles around.

Faced with this prospect, the city of Hood River softened its position. City officials agreed that if there was going to be a tribal casino in the gorge, it should be at Cascade Locks, and they agreed to remain neutral on that proposal. In a letter to county commissioners, the council said it "did not wish to appear to oppose the legitimate desires of the city of Cascade Locks to address its own employment and economic development issues."

The city then mailed the BIA a sixty-nine-page comment letter with forty-seven attached exhibits detailing the "devastating effects" of placing a casino on the slope east of Hood River. "It's the equivalent of putting a casino right in the middle of Yosemite or Yellowstone," said casino foe Toni Vakos.

In October, the Forest Service weighed in. National Scenic Area Manage Dan Harkenrider notified the BIA that conversion of the tribes' newly acquired land to trust status would be inconsistent with the Scenic Area Act because it would remove the land from the law's protection.

"It's about the Scenic Act and whether it's okay to withdraw land from the protection of the act," Martha Bennett stressed.

Warm Springs Tribal Council Chairman Olney Patt Jr. dissented. In a letter to BIA Regional Director Stanley Speaks, he insisted that the Scenic Area Act clearly allowed land within the Scenic Area to be purchased and held in trust for the tribes.

With all the angst and legal maneuvering surrounding the Hood River site, in January 2002 Warm Springs tribal officials unveiled a new plan: They proposed to build their casino within an industrial park east of Cascade Locks owned by the Cascade Locks Port Commission.

Tribal spokesman Greg Leo told the *Hood River News* the port site would work well with a destination resort on Government Island, which the tribe had purchased in 1999 and was still seeking to have taken into trust. In exchange, he said, the Warm Springs Tribes would agree not to develop the 200 acres it now owned east of Hood River.

The reason for the tribes' shift became clearer in March, when BIA headquarters released a sharply critical review of the tribes' draft development plan for converting the Hood River property to trust status. George Skibine, director of the BIA's Office of Indian Gaming Management, called the measures the tribes had proposed to reduce the environmental impacts of developing the site "mere vague statements of good intention."

"The BIA cannot rely on them to reduce any significant impacts to a level of insignificance," Skibine wrote. "The mitigation measures proposed with regard to the many threatened and endangered species and species of concern...are inadequate and unacceptable." The Warm Springs, he wrote, must respond in detail to issues such as how they would dispose of wastewater, control stormwater runoff, provide access to the steep property, and manage traffic.

In May 2002, still unready to show its cards, the Warm Springs Tribal Council formally voted 724-210 to finance, build, and operate a casino in the Columbia River Gorge, without specifying a site. Compromise was in the wind, but Kitzhaber said he still had "significant concerns" about siting a casino anywhere in the gorge, in part because of the precedent it would set.

In November 2002, the political climate abruptly changed. Ted Kulongoski, a Democrat and a former Oregon attorney general, won the race for governor, succeeding Kitzhaber. As attorney general, Kulongoski had once opposed the proliferation of tribal gaming establishments in Oregon. But as governor-elect, he said he had an open mind on the Warm Springs proposal.

Kitzhaber's staff, meanwhile, had begun meeting with Warm Springs tribal leaders to discuss their gaming future. The tribe was about to renegotiate its gambling compact with the state. Kitzhaber stood firm on his position that he would not allow a casino in Cascade Locks. He believed tribes should be limited to building on land they had owned before passage of the 1988 Indian Gaming Regulatory Act. But he said he would not block his successor if Kulongoski moved to approve the casino.

In a letter to state Sen. Rick Metsger, who represented Cascade Locks, Kitzhaber said he would respect the wishes of his successor and help negotiate that plan if requested to during the remaining two months of his term. Metsger then called on Kulongoski to break his silence. The election is over. We need to start moving forward on this issue."

The *Oregonian* editorialized for no casino in Cascade Locks or anywhere else in the National Scenic Area. "The prospect of a bright, noisy, crowded casino in the heart of the Columbia River Gorge National Scenic Area ought to alarm anyone concerned about preserving that precious natural resource," the editors wrote. "And even though Northwest tribes and small towns need and deserve economic help, legalized gambling is a shaky foundation on which to build any sort of stable, lasting business environment."

Local booster Chuck Daughtry, manager of the Port of Cascade Locks, defended the Cascade Locks site. In an op-ed piece, he noted that one of the two specific purposes of the Scenic Area Act was to protect and support the economies of gorge communities. To that end, he said, the tribes had budgeted more than $250 million in an initial cash outlay for their new casino.

For Cascade Locks, the economic stakes were indeed critical. The town had languished in a protracted economic recession for more than twenty years. An estimated 17 percent of its families, including 60 percent of those with young children, lived in poverty, double the statewide average.

The casino alone would create 1,000 new jobs with an average income of $31,500, more than double the town's median per capita income. "We need this to happen to have a chance to stop the economic death spiral that is strangling the Columbia River Gorge," Daughtry wrote.

In December, as negotiations continued, Kevin Gorman of Friends of the Gorge argued in the *Oregonian* that the Warm Springs had no automatic right to build a casino on the Hood River site, because building there would violate the governor's compact with the tribes. Because the Hood River site appeared to be off the table, Gorman was in a sense fighting the last war. But he was also laying the groundwork for a challenge of the Cascade Locks proposal.

The compact stated that moving a casino to an off-reservation site required renegotiation of the compact, approval by the governor, and the concurrence of the U.S. Secretary of Interior. And that concurrence, Gorman said, was by no means a sure thing. President George W. Bush's Interior Department had soured on off-reservation casinos. Interior Secretary Gale Norton had recently written to New York Gov. George Pataki of her concerns about the proliferation of off-reservation gaming proposals. "I believe that (the Indian Gaming Regulatory Act) does not envision that off-reservation gaming would become pervasive," Norton wrote. "I am extremely concerned that the principles underlying the enactment of IGRA are being stretched in ways Congress never imagined."

Gorman also argued that the Hood River site failed a key legal test, because at no time since its acquisition had the Warm Springs tribal government exercised governmental power over the property. "The 40-acre Hood River parcel is an isolated, undeveloped and uninhabited piece of land more than 50 miles from the 640,000-acre reservation," he wrote.

In December, Friends released a poll saying the majority of Oregonians opposed a tribal casino in the gorge and that residents of the gorge were sharply split. The new poll said that of 400 voters polled in Cascade Locks, Bridal Veil, and Corbett (but not Hood River), 47 percent were in favor, 45 percent opposed. A separate statewide telephone poll of 500 Oregon residents found 53 percent opposed the casino.

Cascade Locks city administrator Bob Willoughby disputed the poll's findings, saying the city's own past polling and recent election results showed overwhelming support locally for a casino that would bring a thousand jobs and lift the depressed town from its economic doldrums. "I am a small-town administrator and I know how people here feel about the casino," Willoughby said. "If half of this community opposed the casino, I wouldn't still be here."

In January 2003, Kulongoski was sworn in as governor of Oregon. Two years of negotiations between the governor and Warms Springs tribal leaders ensued.

Cascade Locks officials, meanwhile, entered into formal discussions with tribal leaders about locating their casino in the industrial park, a flat expanse of riverbank composed of fill material from construction of the second Bonneville Dam powerhouse.

The Warm Springs Tribal Council announced that it had been forced to cut $1.1 million from its budget to deal with reductions in timber revenue. Tribal officials now predicted that their new casino would bring in up to $15.5 million in annual profits.

Friends of the Gorge sharpened its own opposition, arguing that a tribal casino drawing a projected 8,200 visitors a day would dramatically increase traffic congestion and air pollution, both already severe problems in the gorge. It predicted that siting a large casino and resort in Cascade Locks would cause "an explosion of unplanned growth," leading to pressure to expand the town's urban growth boundary. Friends also predicted that the casino's approval would result in an expansion of Indian gaming statewide, even potentially more casinos in the gorge.

Undeterred, the Warm Springs Tribal Council hired an experienced team of architects from Albuquerque and Minneapolis to begin designing its casino. The council also retained Portland consultants to write the environmental impact statement for the casino and handle the press.

In December, the *Oregonian* reported that the tribes and the governor wanted a deal on the Cascade Locks site before the legislature convened. "Tribal leaders have been meeting furiously in recent months with Gov. Ted Kulongoski's staff on a casino deal that both sides say they want to close before the legislature convenes January 10," the newspaper reported. The governor's office confirmed that negotiations were underway to assure that the Hood River site would be protected from large-scale development.

On December 10, the *Oregonian* editorial board reversed itself and editorialized in favor of negotiations between the governor and the tribes for a casino at Cascade Locks. "This is a unique situation: The tribes have a casino-ready site in one of the state's most treasured natural areas," the newspaper declared. "As in every case of a tribal casino, Oregon must play the hand it's dealt."

In February 2005, smelling an imminent deal between Kulongoski and the Warm Springs tribes, Friends of the Gorge ran a half-page color ad featuring a spectacular rainbow over the Columbia River at Crown Point. The headline read, "Governor, Don't Gamble Away the Gorge."

The local group Cascade Locks No Casino put out a statement vowing to keep the community from becoming the gorge's first casino town. Kulongoski "does not have the authority to approve off-reservation casinos," a spokesman said, and moreover, "the tribes have yet to begin the long, uphill federal process required before any casino can be approved."

"If you believe everything you read, it seems as though everyone in Cascade Locks is welcoming this mega-casino with open arms and that the casino is a done deal," said local resident Richard Randall. "We represent a significant number of residents who are very concerned about the negative impacts a casino would bring to this town, which would destroy our quality of life and forever change Cascade Locks as we know and love it."

Local officials bent on siting the casino in Cascade Locks actually were driving away jobs and economic development, Randall said. For example, he said, one lumber company had been forced to leave town because the port would not extend its lease. Instead, city leaders were betting everything on the casino and the low-wage jobs it would bring.

The Oregonians for Gambling Awareness Organization weighed in regarding gambling addiction. "Think about the families in your area that will be affected, the jobs that will be lost, the wage and work time that will be lost, and crimes that will happen," wrote Ronda Hatefi, who said she had lost her brother to gambling debts. "Think about what you will lose if Cascade Locks is taken over by outside gambling interests. The money that will come into the area is not worth the loss of control of your town and lives that will be ruined."

But negotiations were too far along for the parties to turn back now.

On the *Oregonian's* op-ed pages, all sides weighed in. Tom Kloster of North Portland accused the Warm Springs of blackmail. "The tribes are clearly aware that their steep, poorly situated site in Hood River is not buildable, and are only using it to leverage a better location, off tribal lands," he wrote. Kloster also contested the town's argument that it needed the casino to bolster its depressed economy. "Cascade Locks has an unparalleled location that most rural towns would envy, and can do better than a casino." Rob Brostoff, a Cascade Locks city councilor, said the city had worked with the Warm Springs leaders for many years "and find them to be a proud, generous, and honorable people." "The facility they want to build would fit harmoniously into the gorge and not stand out like other big-box casinos," he wrote. "It would express the tribes' love of the river and salmon." Bernt A. Hansen of McMinnville argued that the impoverished people of the Warm Springs deserved the same benefits that the Spirit Mountain Casino had delivered for the Confederated Tribes of the Grand Ronde. "The (Grand Ronde) tribes now have better education, housing, and health benefits than the surrounding cities," he wrote,

In April 2004, the tribes released two design options, one for each casino site. Hood River County Commissioner Carol York presented them at a meeting of gorge county officials in Stevenson.

For Cascade Locks, the tribes proposed what she described as "a low-rise, earth-tone casino," and for Hood River, "an eight-story, stone-and-glass building." The Cascade Locks casino would incorporate basalt rock and wood planks in an artist's modeling of a Native American fishing village. Both casino options lacked the Las Vegas glitz of neon and water fountains spouting from concrete ponds.

In May, a dozen former Gorge Commissioners issued a statement asking Kulongoski to approve "the relocation of the proposed Warm Springs casino from Hood River, a community that is vehemently opposed to it, to Cascade Locks, a community that welcomes it." "We believe that the Cascade Locks site serves the spirit, intent, and purpose of the Scenic Area legislation in a way that the Hood River site does not," they wrote. The law created "a special relationship with, and responsibility to, the four listed treaty tribes," they said. Among the signatories was Kristine Olson Rogers, a former Gorge Commissioner, former U.S. Attorney for Oregon, and an expert in Indian cultural law.

April 6, 2005, was a day of celebration for the Confederated Tribes of Warm Springs and the Columbia Gorge town of Cascade Locks. Warm Springs tribal leaders, about a hundred enrolled tribal members, and Oregon Gov.

Bridge of the Gods, Photo by Darryl Lloyd.

Ted Kulongoski traveled to the historic marina along the river to announce that the state and tribal leaders had reached agreement on a compact that would allow the tribe to build a casino in the heart of the gorge. In an emotional ceremony, Kulongoski and Warm Springs Tribal Chair Ron Suppah took the wraps off the agreement they had reached.

The Court Street Drummers and Singers leaned into a circle, singing in high-pitched voices, and pounding ceremonial drums. The Cascade Locks High School Band played the overture from *Lord of the Rings*. Wasco Chief Nelson Wallulatum shook a rattle and offered a prayer in the Wasco language. The mayor of Cascade Lock got flustered and abandoned his speech. Governor Kulongoski briefly sported a "Casino Yes!" cap at the historic signing ceremony, which marked a milestone in the tribes' campaign to build a gaming casino in the Columbia Gorge.

The 500,000-square-foot casino complex would rise on land owned by the Port of Cascade Locks, just upstream from the iconic Bridge of the Gods. The project promised to draw three million visitors a year and bring more than 1,000 new jobs to the struggling town.

Oregon Gov. Ted Kulongoski, left, shares a chuckle with Rudy Clements, right, top gaming official for the Confederated Tribes of the Warm Springs, as they celebrate a newly signed compact that would have allowed the Warm Springs to build a large casino complex at Cascade Locks, Oregon. Photo by Dave Olson of *The Columbian.*

The tribes had "a very strong argument" for building a casino on their property east of Hood River, Kulongoski said. Yet they had agreed to permanently preserve that property for public use if they could develop the Cascade Locks site. They had also agreed to turn over $17 million of their annual profits from a Cascade Locks casino to the state for conservation, education, and economic development projects, including an $850,000 fund benefiting Oregon students.

The new governor was ebullient as he declared, "This represents the best of Oregon, it represents the best of this community—we are all Oregon, we are all one people."

For Cascade Locks, a former timber town without a year-round industry, the casino promised economic salvation of a sort. The town had lost its high school and most of its civic infrastructure. It was holding on by a thread. Signs went up all over town saying "Welcome Warm Springs Casino."

But the April celebration, attended by Warm Springs chiefs in full traditional regalia, was premature. Before the tribes could build on the Cascade Locks site, they faced several hurdles. They would have to petition the Interior Department to take the property into trust, prepare an environmental impact statement, and analyze how the project would affect local communities in the gorge and how many jobs it would provide for tribal members.

As if those hurdles weren't daunting enough, a new opponent immediately emerged; the Confederated Tribes of the Grand Ronde, which owned Spirit Mountain Casino in Oregon's Coast Range, ninety minutes from Portland. The Grand Ronde Tribes were quick to grasp that a rival casino a mere forty-minute freeway commute from Portland would pose an immediate threat to Spirit Mountain, the state's most popular tourist attraction. Friends of the Gorge joined the well-heeled tribal government in launching a campaign to defeat the Cascade Locks casino.

The Grand Ronde had earned net proceeds of $76 million from Spirit Mountain in 2001. Under their compact with the state, they shared a percentage of those proceeds with local communities, building a reservoir of good will. Grand Ronde tribal leaders mounted a lobbying campaign targeting elected state and federal officials, editorial boards, and the BIA. Tribal spokesman Justin Martin said the Grand Ronde Tribal Council was trying to prevent a gaming free-for-all under which Oregon's nine federally recognized tribes would all compete to build casinos close to metropolitan Portland.

Meanwhile, in faraway Washington, D.C., the Department of the Interior was taking a fresh look at a surge of applications it had received from tribes seeking to build off-reservation casinos. In January 2008, George Skibine, director of the BIA's Office of Indian Gaming, issued new guidance on taking off-reservation land into trust for gaming purposes.

Skibine announced that such proposals must now clear a higher bar. They must address the length of the commute tribal members would have to make from their reservations to work at the new casinos. Applicant tribes must also document the support for new off-reservation casinos—or lack of it—expressed by surrounding communities. At the time, the Interior Department was scrambling to evaluate thirty pending applications from tribes that viewed off-reservation casinos as a form of economic salvation. "Many of the applications involve land that is a considerable distance from the reservation of the applicant tribe; one involves land that is 1,400 miles from the tribe's reservation," Skibine said. "Processing these applications is time-consuming and resource-intensive" for an agency constrained by a large backlog and limited resources.

Decisions by the federal government on whether to take land into trust for treaty tribes—whether on or off reservations—rested with the Interior Secretary under the 1934 Indian Reorganization Act. That law did not address Indian gaming, but it did contain two provisions of particular relevance: the Interior Secretary must give "greater scrutiny to the tribe's justification of anticipated benefits" and must give "greater weight to concerns raised by state and local governments."

Among other issues, state, county, and local governments were entitled to have their say about how taking these lands into trust for distant tribes would affect their ability to enforce regulations, collect property taxes, and impose special assessments.

The 1934 law was primarily intended to redress the effects of the discredited federal policy of allotment, which sought to divide up the tribal land base among individual Indians and non-Indians and to destroy tribal governments and tribal identity. Its purpose was to consolidate allotments and ensure a tribal land base on which tribal communities governed by tribal governments could exist and flourish.

For that reason, Skibine said, the Interior Department would be more inclined, going forward, to take lands into trust that were within or near existing reservations. If gaming was to occur on off-reservation lands, Skibine said, those must be trust lands "over which an Indian tribe exercises governmental power."

In the case of proposed off-reservation casinos, Interior reviewers would question whether they were within a reasonable 'commutable distance,'" Skibine said. The further the casino from the reservation, the greater the potential for "significant negative consequences on reservation life."

A distant gaming establishment might produce more revenue, but Indian gaming also was supposed to provide job training and employment for tribal members. That opportunity diminished as the distance between reservation and workplace increased. Tribal members living on the reservation might have to move away in order to take casino jobs. "The departure of a significant number of reservation residents and their families could have serious and far-reaching implications for the remaining tribal community and its continuity as a community," Skibine said. Tribes also would be required to analyze whether a proposed gaming facility was compatible with nearby land uses. Incompatible uses would include national parks, monuments, wildlife refuges, and federally designated conservation areas.

The Skibine memo clearly posed new challenges for the Warm Springs Tribes. Nonetheless, the Department of Interior later that year released a draft environmental impact statement that analyzed the overall effect of placing a 600,000-square-foot casino on the river at Cascade Locks. It also reviewed the Hood River site and a location along U.S. Highway 26 on reservation land. It concluded that the Cascade Locks site was the preferred alternative.

The tribes' proposal languished in the Department of the Interior as the months ticked away. In November 2008, the political landscape shifted again when Barack Obama was elected president. He appointed U.S. Sen. Ken Salazar, a Colorado Democrat, as his Secretary of the Interior. Salazar soon announced that he was putting off all decisions on acquiring land in trust for tribal casinos until at least the following spring.

In November 2010, the political landscape shifted yet again. Oregon voters recast the Warm Springs casino debate overnight when they elected former Oregon Gov. John Kitzhaber to an unprecedented third term as governor.

Kitzhaber had not softened his attitude toward off-reservation casinos. To the contrary, he had campaigned against a casino in the gorge, telling a meeting of newspaper publishers in July, "I am opposed to it, period."

In January, when Kitzhaber was sworn in, the tribes' hopes, and those of Cascade Locks, were dashed. The following month, the Warm Springs Tribal Council announced that it would close its existing casino and build a temporary gaming establishment in the town of Warm Springs on heavily traveled U.S. Highway 26, which runs through the reservation, connecting Portland with Central Oregon.

The council had not given up on building a casino in the gorge, said Jody Calica, the council's secretary-treasurer. Its decision, he said, was intended to boost short-term revenues and help the tribes pursue the goal of a permanent casino at Cascade Locks. He stressed that the relocated casino would not solve the tribes' "long-term dire financial needs." Its long-term goal was still "a permanent Warm Springs casino location at Cascade Locks."

Friends of the Gorge praised the tribes' decision to build a temporary on-reservation casino as "a step in the right direction." "It would protect the gorge and keep large casino sites out of the gorge," said Friends of the Gorge Conservation Director Michael Lang. "It would increase revenue for the tribes, and it would provide more jobs for tribal members. Those benefits are clear."

The new casino opened in February 2012 next to the Warm Springs Museum in the heart of the reservation. In January, the Port of Cascade Locks had quietly let its lease with the Warm Springs Tribes lapse. The lease, originally set to expire in 2011, had been extended twice, but port commissioners decided not to extend it a third time.

After fourteen years of public debate, the issue appeared to be resolved. At least for the foreseeable future, the gorge would not become the site of a large tribal casino.

Cascade Locks cast about for a Plan B. It arrived, eventually, in the form of an international bottling company's offer to tap the town's pure spring-fed drinking water in a complicated exchange involving water supplied to a local fish hatchery. Port Director Chuck Daughtry said the bottling plant alone would be worth more than the assessed value of the entire town of Cascade Locks. That triggered a new debate by conservationists, who opposed selling the town's water supply to be distributed in plastic bottles worldwide.

In the meantime, the port built a new sailboat moorage and spruced up its riverfront. Cascade Locks remains a charming historic gorge community that is still searching for its future.

Chapter 19
Whistling Ridge

To Jason Spadaro, the president of Broughton Lumber Company, the idea seemed like a natural winner. It was 2007, and state and federal "green energy" tax credits were fueling an astonishing boom in wind farm development across the Columbia Plateau. Wind turbines were sprouting immediately east of the Columbia River Gorge National Scenic Area in both Oregon and Washington. Ranks of the ethereal white towers with their slowly rotating blades marched along the crest of the Columbia Hills in Klickitat County. On the Oregon side, they stretched across the dry plateaus beyond the Deschutes River as far as the eye could see.

From the beginning of the wind energy boom, developers had recognized the Columbia Plateau as an obvious choice for harnessing wind to meet the burgeoning demand for renewable energy in Washington, Oregon, and California. Gorge gusts were strong and the wind blew year-round, typically from the east in winter and from the west in summer. The landscape was sparsely populated and the topography was ideal, particularly in the Columbia Hills, which paralleled the Columbia River for 32 miles, from Maryhill State Park to John Day Dam. As an industrial use, wind farms were not allowed in the Columbia River Gorge National Scenic Area. But the giant installations were encroaching from the east, and many more projects were on the drawing boards.

Klickitat County Commissioners had seen the wind power boom coming and had taken early action to attract developers. In 2004, they had adopted an energy overlay zone to attract natural gas-fired plants, also invited wind farms virtually anywhere in the county outside the Scenic Area boundary. The new zoning also allowed wind farms on leased land virtually anywhere in the county outside the Scenic Area boundary. It succeeded beyond their wildest dreams.

Jason Spadaro, president of SDS Lumber Co., stands on the logged-over ridge where his company hoped to develop a wind farm just north of the National Scenic Area boundary. The state of Washington eventually approved a scaled-down project, but the shifting economics of wind energy left the future of the project in doubt. Photo by Ben Campbell of *The Columbian*.

Between 2006 and 2010, energy companies erected 624 turbines along the crest of the Columbia Hills and across the wheat fields that blanketed the dry ridges to the south and east. Each was the height of a forty-one-story building as measured from the ground to the top of the highest turbine blade.

Friends of the Gorge had few tools to halt the march of wind turbines over lands bordering the Scenic Area. But it tried. The group appealed the proposed Windy Flats project, a massive wind project that would skirt the north boundary of the Scenic Area for seven miles and be visible from across the river at Celilo Village. Now the village's few dozen remaining residents would look past The Dalles Dam, which had flooded their fishing grounds at Celilo Falls in the 1950s, to a landscape-transforming twenty-first-century energy project. Friends contended that Windy Flats would cause significant mortality to birds and visual impacts to the National Scenic Area, nearby Columbia Hills State Park, and a National Audubon Society Important Bird Area that was home to thousands of bats and raptors, including hawks and golden eagles.

To the east of Windy Flats, a project called Windy Point would stretch 11 miles southeast of Goldendale and east of Highway 97, covering nearly

15,000 acres, with up to ninety-seven turbines generating a maximum of 250 megawatts of power.

Bonneville Power Administration was building new transmission lines and power stations as fast as it could to accommodate the wind energy boom. With red strobe lights atop their towers, many individual turbines in the Windy Flats and Windy Point projects would be highly visible from within the Scenic Area both day and night. Yet opposition toward the new green energy was largely muted. "Wherever there's a BPA line, we're going to have these wind farms just outside the scenic area, up and down the gorge," said Dennis White, the co-founder of Friends of the White Salmon. He called for a regional dialogue on the proliferation of wind farms.

Spadaro had taken note of the wind energy boom as early as 2002. In 2007, after five years of collecting wind data and conducting bird surveys, he went public with a proposal for a wind energy project on the company's industrial timberlands in the hills of Skamania County. Saddleback Mountain, as the project was first named, would be located just 400 feet outside the north boundary of the Scenic Area on a north-south ridge, at an elevation of 2,000 to 2,200 feet. The logged-over site was between Underwood Mountain and Whistling Ridge, an actual geographic feature east of the historic timber town of Willard.

In April 2007, Spadaro met with residents of Willard and nearby Mill A to let them know the company's plans. Residents raised concerns about how the wind turbines would affect hawks, eagles, and other raptors, about the noise of the turbines, and about the possible health effects of living near them. "The most controversial aspect is the lights," Sally Newell, an Underwood resident and a former Gorge Commissioner, told the *White Salmon Enterprise*. "These towers would be on a ridgetop, so for aviation safety they would have to have red strobe lights on every tower." The prospect of flashing red lights penetrating the night sky gave others pause as well. Spadaro pointed to the financial benefits for Skamania County, which would see a boost in its tax base, and for Mill A and Willard, which would get a new fire protection district funded entirely by revenue from the wind farm.

The initial proposal was for a string of forty-four wind turbines running roughly north to south, skirting Scenic Area boundary. Spadaro knew the visibility of the turbines could be decisive. Already, a wind project across the river in Oregon's Wasco County had generated heated controversy. UPC Wind Partners of Massachusetts had proposed to build the Cascade Wind

Project on an east-west ridge near Mosier, just outside the Scenic Area boundary. The turbines would have been clearly visible from Interstate 84, Washington's Highway 14, Riverfront Park in The Dalles, and the Nature Conservancy's Tom McCall Reserve.

The Oregon project had drawn fierce opposition from gorge residents. In 2007 it was put on hold pending the company's response to numerous questions posed by the Oregon Department of Energy. The company later backed out of the project.

Saddleback Mountain would be smaller, less visible, and distant from houses and towns. But Spadaro's key argument from the beginning was that the National Scenic Area Act made no provision for a buffer zone outside its boundary. The authority of the Gorge Commission and the Forest Service stopped at the Scenic Area boundary, he said. This was a crucial point, because there was no way to hide the towering turbines.

The Cook-Underwood Road climbs a series of steep switchbacks to a narrow saddle, with views of the Columbia River and the town of Hood River to the right and the valley of the Little White Salmon River to the left. Tower sections and turbine blades would have to travel this road to the site. The ridgeline where the turbines would rise was logged-over timberland, crisscrossed by rough logging roads and BPA high-voltage transmission lines overhead.

During an October 2007 tour of the site, Spadaro brought along a laptop computer loaded with digital simulations to illustrate his argument that the project would not significantly affect gorge scenery. He turned on his computer and showed a series of three-dimensional images intended to simulate the view of the turbines from various viewpoints. The southernmost seven of the forty-four turbines would be visible from the Hood River Valley, he said. Some would be visible to drivers eastbound on the freeway between Hood River and Mosier. Seven would be visible from the Cook-Underwood Road, Willard, and Mill A. From the heart of Underwood, no one would be able to see any of them.

Spadaro was proud of his proposal to harness wind from the companies' commercial forest lands, an idea he had first broached with Broughton directors in 2002. "It was my idea to prospect our land," he said. He liked the look of the white turbines arrayed along the ridgelines to the east in Klickitat County. "Myself, I don't think they are ugly," he said. "I'll be proud to bring my kids up here and show them that we are doing something about global climate change. Here's an opportunity for a project that wouldn't add to gorge pollution. It's all commercial forest land that is actively managed. For us to be able to capture the wind above the land, it's a win-win."

The wind project would rise on 200 acres of SDS and Broughton land. In all, the turbines would stretch for about two miles along high ridges in the back country. "Where there are no trees, where the ground is flat, that is where the wind power companies go," Spadaro said. Now the idea was ready for prime time.

Wind energy development in Washington gained momentum in 2006, when voters approved an initiative that required most Washington utilities to get 15 percent of their energy from renewable sources by 2020. The Broughton location was strategic, as the company quickly realized: the generator powered by the turbines would hook up to the BPA's 230,000-volt regional transmission line, one of four such lines crossing Underwood Mountain.

Puget Sound Energy initially agreed to partner with SDS and Broughton to develop a $70 million project that would feed up to 70 megawatts of power into the BPA grid. That translated to 20 megawatts of constant energy, enough to power 14,500 homes—all the houses in Skamania County, with power to spare. But Puget Sound Energy backed out.

Saddleback Mountain was expected to generate about $500,000 in annual taxes to Skamania County, roughly as much as the proposed Broughton Landing destination resort down the mountain.

The wind farm would create an estimated one hundred jobs during construction and six to eight jobs when operating, Spadaro said. It would benefit the Skamania County Public Utility District by providing it with a reliable energy source within its own boundaries.

There were a few hurdles to overcome. One was the project's proximity to the Scenic Area boundary. Though the act did not protect land outside the boundary, the project would be visible from various points inside the Scenic Area. Saddleback would be a first—the first wind project built on commercial timber land that was being actively logged. The potential impact on birds and wildlife was largely unknown. Transporting the gleaming white tower sections and blades up into the hills on narrow, twisting logging roads would pose another challenge. It would require widening some sections of company roads inside the Scenic Area. That would mean getting a permit from Skamania County, which could bring the Gorge Commission into the process. There would also be interruptions of traffic on county roads leading to the project during four to six months of construction.

The wind itself was a known quantity by the time Spadaro went public with the plan. Two meteorological towers had measured wind velocity over time. In order to prove out, the system had to be capable of generating energy 30 percent of the time every year. It had passed that test.

Studies of bird and bat activity in the area had produced no indications of potential high bird mortality so far, and the land would never again grow a mature forest. After construction, trees would have to be trimmed so they wouldn't interfere with the rotation of the turbine blades. Still, many questions about bird and bat mortality remained unanswered.

The proposed wind farm drew 125 people to a meeting of the Underwood Community Council in October 2006, one of the biggest turnouts in memory. Gorge residents raised concerns about the project's impacts on property values, scenic views, noise, and human health. Spadaro downplayed those impacts. The nearest house was 2,600 feet away, he said, too far away for neighbors to hear the turbines. As for visual impacts, he dismissed them. "The million-dollar views are to the south and west," he said. "These turbines are to the north."

The Yakama Tribe had an open mind about wind power. "It's better than hydro power because that kills all our salmon," one tribal leader said.

Friends of the Gorge was still trying to figure out if it had legal standing to challenge the project and did not immediately take a position.

SDS and Broughton hoped to apply for the necessary permits from Skamania County by the end of 2007. They needed a conditional use permit, permission from the county to use its roads, and permission from the BPA to connect to its grid.

In 2008, as debate over the project continued, Spadaro approached the Washington Department of Natural Resources, which owned state timberland immediately to the north of the Saddleback Mountain site.

He proposed eventually doubling the size of the wind project by leasing 2,560 acres of adjacent state trust land in western Klickitat County. Klickitat, of course, already had a zoning ordinance that fast-tracked the siting of wind farms. The expansion could allow an additional forty towers and turbines at some point in the future.

Wind turbines, Centerville, Washington, with Mt. Adams in the background. Photo by Darryl Lloyd.

The Department of Natural Resources already was actively leasing land elsewhere in the state for wind projects. By August 2009, the agency had twenty-four active wind power leases in various stages and five projects already generating energy on state trust land. The leases produced $670,000 a year for state schools. But the DNR had no system in place for reviewing those projects to determine whether the turbines might harm threatened or endangered birds.

As it happened, the state trust land Spadaro had his eye on was in an area of scattered old growth and second-growth forest occupied by at least one northern spotted owl. The state was required to manage the area as a "spotted owl emphasis area" for the threatened bird under its federally approved habitat conservation plan. That could sharply limit logging.

Department of Natural Resources officials initially concluded that a decision to lease the land would have little or no environmental impact on the owl. They said that if they approved the lease, it would still be subject to a full environmental review by Klickitat County

But environmentalists insisted that the entire project should be vetted upfront, not on a piecemeal basis, to make sure environmental concerns were known and incorporated into the layout, construction, and operation of the project. Finally, they had a hook.

"Leasing this out for wind projects is incompatible with protecting spotted owl habitat," said Michael Lang of Friends of the Gorge. "The DNR is trying to escape environmental review, giving up the state's ability to enforce its own regulations and its own laws, and turning that responsibility over to Klickitat County."

The Department of Natural Resources had a new boss, elected State Lands Commissioner Peter Goldmark. Greener than his predecessor, Goldmark decided to review the department's entire wind energy leasing program statewide.

The review came after a consortium of energy companies proposed building a wind project on the Washington coast, near the mouth of the Naselle River. The Radar Ridge site, once an active radar installation, was now the heart of the most valuable habitat in the state for the threatened marbled murrelet, a small seabird that nests in old-growth conifers near the ocean.

In August 2009, Goldmark announced that because of issues with endangered species, DNR was no longer considering leasing state trust land to SDS and Broughton for possible expansion of their wind project. He went further, ordering a statewide review of DNR wind leases to learn whether they posed threats to protected birds and bats.

At about the same time, SDS and Broughton abandoned their attempt to get the project permitted under Skamania County's own new wind power-friendly zoning ordinance. Instead, they turned to the state for a permit—specifically Washington's Energy Facility Site and Evaluation Council. That decision came after a county land use hearings officer ruled that the project would require a full environmental impact statement, something the county was not prepared to undertake.

Skamania County commissioners themselves urged Spadaro to kick the project upstairs to the state. He followed that advice, though he acknowledged that the state review would be more rigorous. "It's a statewide issue now, but we're not afraid of the additional review," Spadaro said. "We think it's warranted."

Friends of the Gorge applauded the change of venue. "There is going to be a high level of scrutiny and review of this project, and there should be," said Michael Lang. "Frankly, I'm hard-pressed to think of a worse site for this to be proposed." Even the Klickitat County Energy Overlay Zone recognized that avian mortality was highest on forested ridgelines, he said.

With the new state application, the project also got a new name. It became the Whistling Ridge Energy Project, named for the actual ridge where the turbines would rise. And it grew in size, from forty-four turbines to fifty, with a maximum generating capacity of 75 megawatts of electricity. Whistling Ridge immediately ran into stiff headwinds.

The Forest Service recommended that the most visible turbines be removed from the project. "The National Scenic Area is a nationally known and protected landscape of high quality and high sensitivity," Scenic Area Manager Dan Harkenrider wrote in comments to the Energy Facility Site and Evaluation Council. He warned of "the risk of significant impacts to protected scenic resources if the proposed energy project is built as currently planned."

That drew an objection from U.S. Rep. Brian Baird, whose congressional district included the western gorge. Baird wrote to Northwest Regional Forester Mary Wagner admonishing Harkenrider for comments that "could have detrimental impacts on the project." Harkenrider was out of line, Baird said, in suggesting that some of the turbines be eliminated, because Harkenrider had no authority over what happened outside the National Scenic Area.

Harkenrider defended his comments. "I'm not asserting an authority," he said, "but we suggested strongly that they look at the scenic impacts inside the Scenic Area. I absolutely believe it's my responsibility to do that." Harkenrider also questioned the company's computer simulations, which indicated the tops of the turbines would be visible from only a few places in the gorge. The Forest Service's own analysis showed they would be visible from many more key viewpoints.

The SDS simulations "did not disclose the height used for the turbines or whether the software placed and sized the turbines or whether this was done in PhotoShop or as an arts project," he wrote with barely concealed sarcasm. The company's simulations also failed to show how night lighting of the turbines would affect the Scenic Area, he said.

Friends of the Gorge addressed the issue of buffers. "The National Scenic Area doesn't authorize buffers, but state law can require them," Lang said. He noted that Oregon's Wasco County had imposed its own buffers outside the Scenic Area boundary, where development was regulated.

A new player also weighed in. The Skamania County Agri-Tourism Association, a recently formed coalition of twelve wineries and farms based in Underwood, called on SDS to drop the seven southern-most turbines to preserve the bucolic setting of the Underwood area.

Those towers "would loom over one of the country's premier wine-making regions and the most valuable agri-tourism land in Skamania County," board member John Crumpacker testified. He warned that the giant rotating blades would intrude on the experience of visitors who came to tour wineries.

Spadaro denied that there had to be a conflict. "In Walla Walla, they offer wind and wine tours, where the wind energy industry has joined forces with the wineries," he said. SDS would be a willing a partner in a similar marketing strategy.

Wineries versus wind turbines in rugged Klickitat County? Something new was indeed blowing in the wind.

Meanwhile, BPA, which had to sign off on connecting the project to its grid, was awash in new wind energy proposals. In fact, the wind boom was presenting some tricky technical issues as the agency attempted to deal with highly variable surges of wind-generated energy during periods when its hydroelectric dams also were generating excess power to the grid.

"BPA is a strong proponent of getting renewables into the grid, but people are really scrambling to find ways to absorb it and manage it," BPA spokesman Michael Milstein explained in a May 2009 statement. "It's turning out to be extremely variable and unpredictable. Literally in the course of a couple of hours, you can have the equivalent of a couple of power plants turning on and off. You have to constantly have some source of backup power that can fill in, depending on what the wind is doing."

Whistling Ridge was now in the state's hands. Applicants were required to prepare a massive, detailed environmental impact statement. Once it was completed, Energy Facility Site and Evaluation Council was required to hold a hearing within sixty days. It held two.

On May 6, 2009, about eighty people showed up in Stevenson; thirty testified. Many were supportive. Their biggest concern was the visibility of the project from within the boundaries of the National Scenic Area. A second hearing the next day at the Underwood Community Center drew sixty people. Opinion there, closer to the project, was sharply divided. The applicant and the county both testified that the project was consistent with the county's existing land use plan. Friends of the Gorge and Save Our Scenic Area, a local group, insisted it was not.

Both Skamania and Klickitat counties had been designated as part of the Columbia Gorge Bi-State Renewable Energy Zone, created by five counties in the east end of the gorge to promote green energy development. During the environmental review, state wildlife biologist Michael Ritter warned that the wind project could result in high wildlife mortality. Surveys of the site showed the logged-over ridge was heavily used by bats, raptors, and other birds, Ritter said. Those included the barred owl, a competitor with the northern spotted owl for prey and habitat. And he estimated that as many as 7,000 bats annually could be killed by the spinning turbines.

He called for additional surveys of the area, but added, "It is unlikely that the additional data…will alleviate the concerns we have with potential impacts to birds and bats with this energy project." Comparisons with existing wind projects in Washington were all but meaningless, he said, because Whistling Ridge would be the first such project in a westside conifer forest. All others in the region were in open areas of shrub-steppe vegetation or on agricultural land. He urged the state agency to proceed cautiously "and slow down the incentivized green energy freight train that is barreling through the state of Washington."

Members of the Energy Facility Site and Evaluation Council board, which was chaired by former Gorge Commissioner Jim Luce, toured the site and met with local residents. Two years of review ensued.

At a meeting in Stevenson, in November 2011, the board approved the project—with an important proviso: Fifteen of the fifty turbines must be removed to minimize the impact on views inside the Scenic Area.

It was a de facto recognition by the state panel that a visual buffer was warranted to protect views within the Scenic Area from new development outside its boundary. Sixty days later, Washington Gov. Chris Gregoire approved the scaled-down project. She said her support reflected a "balanced approach" that would benefit both the state's environmental and economic goals.

"A modified project with thirty-five wind turbines would help meet our need for clean energy and bring needed jobs and revenue to Skamania County, while preserving the esthetic and recreational benefits of the gorge," Gregoire said in a statement. The governor's approval gave the applicants a permit to start construction of Whistling Ridge within five years.

But Spadaro was not celebrating. The project was not dead, he told the *Columbian* newspaper, but it would not be economically viable in its scaled-back form.

By then, state and federal officials were taking a critical look at the tax credits that had spurred the wind energy boom. A federal tax credit for wind energy development was due to expire at the end of 2012. The window for projects like Whistling Ridge was closing. Low energy prices and uncertainty surrounding the availability of tax credits would halt the project for now, he said.

"I don't think either party can say that they're happy in this case," Spadaro told the *Columbian*. Even in a downsized configuration, he said, the governor's approval was better than an outright denial. But limiting development on private land outside the Gorge Scenic Area boundary set a "dangerous precedent," he warned.

Friends of the Gorge vowed to challenge the approval of the project in any form. "Some places should be off limits to industrial wind development," Friends staff attorney Nathan Baker said. "And we believe that the Columbia River Gorge National Scenic Area is one of those places."

In April 2012, Friends of the Gorge and a local group, Save our Scenic Area, kept their promise, filing a petition for judicial review in Thurston County Circuit Court. They focused on the visibility of the scaled-back project—the flashing lights, the spinning blades, even traffic impacts in rural Underwood.

"Icons of the Northwest, like the Columbia River Gorge, Mount Rainier, and the Olympic Mountains should be off-limits to development," said Friends Executive Director Kevin Gorman. "We can combat global warming without having to sacrifice our special places and our core values."

Part IV

RESTORING A LEGACY

Oneonta Falls. Photo by Darryl Lloyd.

Chapter 20
Rebuilding a Historic Route

Few Pacific Northwest legacies are more treasured than Sam Lancaster's historic Columbia River Highway. Yet "progress" began nibbling away at the 73-mile-long route between Troutdale and The Dalles barely more than a decade after the scenic roadway was completed in 1922. In 1933 the Army Corps of Engineers began construction of Bonneville Dam on the Lower Columbia. When completed, the dam raised the level of the river upstream to a mile east of The Dalles, And when The Dalles Dam was completed in 1957, it submerged Celilo Falls, obliterating the most important Indian fishery on the river, and flooded hundreds of tribal artifacts. The raising of the river level also required a realignment of the highway between the dam and Cascade Locks.

By the late 1940s, the postwar economic boom was driving increased demand for a faster, wider, and more modern highway to connect Portland to The Dalles and points east. By 1949, construction of a new water-level highway by the Oregon Department of Transportation was underway. Alas, the road builders of the postwar period had little respect for the craft and artistry that had gone into construction of the nation's first scenic highway. The historic Columbia River Highway had been hailed as one of the engineering marvels of the age. Its soaring loops and its leisurely route, designed to showcase the most spectacular views from the Oregon side, remained wildly popular. Local boosters called it "The King of Roads."

But the trucks and cars of the postwar period were larger and faster, making travel on the narrow, winding road more difficult, even dangerous. State highway engineers deemed it ill-equipped to handle the growing commerce. A highway more muscular and utilitarian was required. What would happen to the beloved historic highway? Little consideration was given to that question at the time.

By the summer of 1949, a section of the new highway from Troutdale to Dodson, initially named U.S. 80, was completed. By 1954, the new highway reached The Dalles. Its construction inflicted significant damage on the original highway. Nearly 26 miles of the old highway between Dodson and Hood River were destroyed or abandoned.

In 1966, the world-famous Mitchell Point Tunnel, west of Hood River, was dynamited to allow for widening a section of the new highway from two lanes to four. Its guardrails, modeled on the Axenstrasse Tunnel in Switzerland, were demolished, breaking promises politicians had made to preserve them. Many of the original bridges, stone guardrails, and obser-vatories, including Vista House at Crown Point, fell into disrepair. Towns and businesses bypassed by the new highway suffered decline.

Many of the wealthy benefactors who had donated land along the Co-lumbia Highway were distressed to see the fine handiwork of the Italian stonemasons destroyed. "Lancaster would have been heartbroken had he lived to see the result," Marilyn Wheeler, a reporter for the Associated Press, wrote in 1988. "Parts of the scenic highway were bypassed, but other features—including six bridges and the distinctive Mitchell Point Tunnel—were blasted away."

"To bureaucrats, the Columbia River Highway was just another road," Wheeler wrote. "Once the new freeway was complete, the state vacated its right of way and part of the old highway reverted to local ownership. In Hood River County, the highway was used for a garbage dump, gravel pits, and a public firing range. By 1980, only one-third of the highway remained intact. The rest had been abandoned or destroyed." By then, however, sup-port was building for a restoration project to save what could be saved and restore what could still be redeemed.

In 1980, the National Park Service undertook a survey of the historic highway in connection with its study of threats facing the Columbia River Gorge. In 1983, as Congress was debating federal protection for the gorge, the Oregon Department of Transportation nominated the surviving high-way sections for listing on the National Register of Historic Places. The Historic Preservation League of Oregon led the effort to create an advisory committee to oversee restoration. Supporters channeled money and influ-ence through Friends of the Columbia Gorge.

The 1986 Scenic Area Act committed the state of Oregon to restore, pre-serve, and interpret the Historic Columbia River Highway and authorized

$2.8 million towards the restoration work—a pittance, as it would turn out. The work would require rebuilding stone guardrails and concrete caps, recasting and installing delicate concrete arches, and restoring Vista House, the beloved art deco "comfort station" that crowned Crown Point.

In a 1989 essay, longtime Oregon State Parks Director David Talbot admitted to some ambivalence about the large investment Oregon had made over the years in buying land and developing parks in the gorge. The gorge "is not a Crater Lake," he wrote. "It is not the Grand Canyon. It is where a major river cuts though a mountain range. If you appreciate geologic spectacle, it is a pretty exciting place. It also is a main travel corridor, so the scenery is highly visible." Talbot also bemoaned the fact that construction of the interstate freeway along the Oregon shore had marred the experience of motoring through the gorge. "The system of parks in the Columbia Gorge that Sam Boardman put together was essentially butchered by the freeway," he wrote. "The water grade parks are bits and pieces left over from highway construction in the 1950s for the most part. Some of the highway people anguished over it, but with the railroad and the river on one side and the Cascades on the other, there wasn't a lot of room to move. They had to build out into the river in some places, which would be difficult to do today."

Nonetheless, the Oregon Department of Transportation set an ambitious goal of restoring as much as possible of the original highway. Some would remain part of the designated scenic highway. Some, along sections too narrow to accommodate the passage of modern vehicles, would become trails for hikers and cyclists. Because nearly all of the highway remained on the National Register of Historic Places, no roadway widening would be permitted. The project captured the public's imagination. Road crews set to work on the massive restoration project.

In 1996, the section of the highway between Tanner Creek and Eagle Creek, near Bonneville Dam, was restored and reopened as a hiking trail. Two years later, crews completed restoration of the section between Eagle Creek and Cascade Locks, which required rebuilding a new undercrossing of the new freeway, now Interstate 84.

Restoring the Hood River to Mosier section as a state trail began in 1995. The famous Mosier Twin Tunnels had been filled with rock in the mid 1950s, when the new water-level route was opened, but they had not been destroyed. The Twin Tunnels Visitor Station opened on Memorial Day weekend in 2000. Because a 700-foot-long catchment had to be completed to protect hikers and cyclists from falling rock, the dedication of the trail was delayed until July. The actual tunnels were opened the following year. The cliff-hanging roadway offers a spectacular view of the newer highway and the river below.

An old gravel pit at the west end of the trail, just east of Hood River, was restored with native vegetation and named the Senator Mark O. Hatfield West Trailhead. It's near the site where the Confederated Tribes of Warm Springs once vowed to build a new high-rise casino.

The Moffett Creek to Tanner Creek section was completed in 2001, a project that involved restoring the Moffett Creek Bridge. Accessibility for the disabled was improved later that year when the Starvation Creek to Viento section was upgraded, making it possible for people in wheelchairs to view Starvation Creek Waterfall.

It's a 4.6-mile bicycle ride from Hood River to Mosier, with many opportunities to view the vistas that opened for those first sightseers nearly a century ago. From Mosier east, the Historic Columbia River Highway once again becomes a scenic drive, connecting Mosier to The Dalles along a 15-mile route that remains intact. The route passes Memaloose Overlook, offering a view of burial grounds on Memaloose Island below, then climbs to Rowena Plateau and the viewpoint of summer wildflowers at Rowena Crest. From there, the highway descends in graceful loops to a view of two popular sailboard sites: East Mayer State Park and Doug's Beach.

A major milestone was achieved in August 2006, when crews removed the last boulders and reopened the 125-foot-long Oneonta Tunnel adjacent to Oneonta Falls, which had been plugged for decades.

As of 2012, a total of 62 miles of the original 73-mile road had been opened to travel, either by motor vehicle or by hiking or biking the route. And the work continues.

In 2010, the Oregon Department of Transportation, Oregon Parks and Recreation, the Forest Service and Hood River County completed a plan to reconnect the remaining 11 miles of the old highway and to restore the Mitchell Point Tunnel.

"Upon completion, visitors will have access to many of Oregon's underdeveloped state parks, undiscovered waterfalls and majestic views of the Columbia River," the agencies said in announcing the new restoration plan.

"Completion will create a 'King of Trails,' allowing pedestrians and cyclists to experience the gorge between Troutdale and The Dalles without ever having to share the shoulder of Interstate 84 with cars and trucks."

Like some 73-mile-long Humpty-Dumpty, this masterwork of highway and bridge design is slowly, tediously, and at great expense, being put back together again.

Photo by Darryl Lloyd.

Chapter 21
The Recreation Challenge

In the quarter-century since passage of the National Scenic Area Act, the Forest Service has polished the tarnished gem of the Columbia River Gorge.

Congressional appropriations totaling more than $67 million have enabled the agency to purchase more than 41,000 acres of private land from willing sellers in the gorge—29,249 acres in Washington and 11,775 acres in Oregon. From wetlands on the west end to oak forests in the mid-gorge to canyons and grasslands in the east, much of the land needed restoring. A quarter-century later, visitors can enjoy a dazzling variety of recreation options—wildlife refuges, new hiking and mountain biking trails, windsurfing beaches, paths to misty waterfalls—within a couple of hours' drive from the Portland-Vancouver metro area.

Yet even before Congress established the Scenic Area, the Columbia Gorge was a busy, crowded place. The Forest Service was handed the conflicting tasks of expanding recreation opportunities while keeping the brakes on development to avoid damaging the resources—the trails and waterfalls and vistas—that people came to enjoy.

The Forest Service didn't do it alone. State parks and wildlife agencies, conservation groups and platoons of volunteers all contributed. Their efforts improved safety at windsurfing beaches, built new trails and developed pastoral picnic grounds along the Washington shore. Gravel pits and garbage dumps were closed and restored.

But the money came with difficult decisions about public access, recreational priorities, and tribal treaty rights. It also forced the Forest Service and other agencies to confront an overriding question: What is an appropriate and sustainable level of recreation use in the Columbia River Gorge?

The 1992 management plan called for an ambitious program to develop trails and parks on both sides of the gorge. It identified suitable levels of recreation use for eighty potential sites. Each site would be evaluated to determine what level of use was compatible with protecting scenery, cultural treasures, Indian treaty rights, and sensitive natural areas.

Under the act, some $10 million would be authorized for recreation development, in addition to the $2.8 million earmarked to restore and reconstruct abandoned sections of the Historic Columbia River Highway.

The plan acknowledged that the Forest Service's recreation mandate posed "a number of unique and formidable challenges....Because of construction of federal highway and dam projects and the presence of railroads on both shores of the river, a very limited number of potentially usable areas for recreational river access exist," the plan noted. It also recognized that the once-extensive Columbia River flood plain held countless natural and cultural artifacts that the federal government was obligated to protect. "Given the long history of human settlement in the gorge...the presence of remains of past cultures is to be expected." The explosive growth of wind surfing invited potential conflicts with the treaty tribes. And many existing, heavily used launch sites along highways posed public safety and sanitation concerns.

During a review of the management plan in the early 2000s, the commission and the Forest Service ran out of time and never revisited the original 1992 recreation management plan. Yet the work on the plan progressed. The Forest Service restored hundreds of acres, including numerous rock and gravel pits and unsightly trash dumps. It was a relatively new role for the agency.

On Burdoin Mountain, on the Washington side, Forest Service crews used selective logging of Douglas fir to enhance rare oak woodlands by opening the forest canopy. They removed an airstrip from the Rowena Plateau on the Oregon side. A former historic homestead dotted with apple trees and once overrun with blackberries is now St. Cloud Day Use Area, an oasis of quiet where visitors can picnic and walk along the Washington shore.

A new, safer, and more environmentally sensitive Cape Horn Trail, complete with tunnels under Highway 14, has replaced a maze of informal footpaths and animal trails.

And the Forest Service has built hundreds of miles of new trail, including a 13.5-mile section of a former rail bed that now connects the communities of Lyle and Klickitat along the Klickitat River.

One of the agency's most challenging restoration projects has been the Sandy River Delta, Oregon's western gateway to the Scenic Area. The Forest

Service acquired the delta from Reynolds Aluminum Company in 1991, with funding from the Trust for Public Land. The acquisition was part of the mitigation the federal government required for the construction of Columbia River hydroelectric dams.

The 1,500-acre delta was damaged land. It had been grazed by cattle for decades. The Sandy River's original channel had been dammed in the 1930s and diverted into a manmade "Little Sandy River." The original river channel had subsequently silted in and become a slough. The delta was overrun with invasive reed canary grass and Himalayan blackberries, kept in check, barely, by livestock.

In 1997, the Forest Service unveiled a long-term habitat restoration plan for the delta. In the interim, it terminated grazing. The short-term result was disastrous: blackberries and other invasive species exploded, voles girdled the hardwood trees, deer devoured them. Manual weeding was too costly. Crews tried mowing the reed canary grass with tractors, caging the trees, and finally using herbicides to eliminate all vegetation. They started over with a blank slate.

By 2012, hardwood seedlings were gaining a foothold in some sections of the delta. The next phase of the project will be removal of the small dam at the river's mouth. In the meantime, thousands of Portland-area dog owners converge on the Sandy River Delta on sunny weekends to give their dogs a run in designated off-leash areas.

While managing complex restoration projects, the Forest Service has scrambled to keep up with the demand for recreation in the gorge, from hiking and sailboarding to mountain-biking and rock-climbing. At the same time, it has taken care to protect fragile cultural sites, native plants, and other features from damage. The Scenic Area gets at least two million visitors annually, not counting visitors to state parks, Skamania Lodge in Stevenson, the Gorge Discovery Center in The Dalles, and motorists just passing through.

As the population of the Portland-Vancouver metro area continues to grow, recreation use in the gorge also grows, particularly at a time when many people are short of both time and money. "It's a quick, easy trip from Portland or Vancouver," recreation manager Stan Hinatsu said in 2011, as the Scenic Area marked its twenty-fifth anniversary. "We've found that a lot of barriers to recreation are time and distance. If you've got to travel two hours to go for a hike, you'll be less likely to do that. But the gorge overcomes those barriers."

One challenge the Forest Service is understaffed to deal with is un-authorized trail-building, especially on formerly private lands recently acquired. Most of those lands are unposted and undeveloped. With 41,000 acres of new public land, "we're seeing impacts," Hinatsu said. "Cape Horn is an example of that. It was all private land, then it was public land, then someone built illegal trails."

At Catherine Creek, a former ranch that rises to scenic bluffs in the mid-gorge, the Forest Service has had to figure out how to keep users from damaging the very resources they visit to enjoy, including a maze of infor-mal trails and a fragile arch.

"We are identifying the trails we want to keep and getting rid of the ones that aren't sustainable," Hinatsu said. "There are sensitive resources. There's wildflower viewing. Will horses be allowed? How far should moun-tain bikes go? It's that whole collision of social and natural resources."

Immediately west of Catherine Creek, at the dramatic syncline known as Coyote Wall, the agency faces a similar challenge. Coyote Wall is criss-crossed at a density of four miles of trails per square mile of land. Heavy use by hikers and especially mountain bikers over the rugged terrain has taken a great toll in erosion. No formal trailheads exist and there is no off-road parking. In 2007, the agency proposed to close some trails and limit some to hikers only.

At Multnomah Falls, Oregon's most-visited natural attraction, the For-est Service made a deliberate decision several years ago not to increase parking despite the hordes of visitors who jockey for parking spots on summer weekends.

"We figured 1,500 people at one time was about all that place could handle," Hinatsu said. To protect habitat for anadromous fish, the agency also decided to close access to a pool at the base of the falls.

Solitude can be hard to find at waterfall areas along the Oregon side such as popular Eagle Creek, near Bonneville Dam. Surveys show people who visit those places don't seem to mind. "The waterfall corridor is an attraction in itself, more like a national park," Hinatsu said. "The Wash-ington side tends to be a more traditional national forest experience, more dispersed, but that's where we are seeing most of the impacts on new public lands. We haven't had the resources to post all of our boundaries. We've produced a forest map that shows the most recent land ownership, but people have to be careful that they aren't trespassing on private land."

Catherine Creek, in the Gorge. Photo by Darryl Lloyd

When Dan Harkenrider retired as scenic area manager in 2011, he left to his successor, Forest Service career officer Lynn Burditt, the continuing challenge of defining what is sustainable recreation in the Columbia River Gorge. "We want to understand better what connects people to places, and to help people understand the resources and values that public lands provide," Harkenrider said. Too much access, he said, can destroy the very qualities people travel to the gorge to experience.

Windsurfing has been both a boon and a bone of contention in the gorge. As early as 1987, when the mid-gorge was just beginning to gain an international reputation for its unique combination of stiff wind gusts and rambunctious waves, some Washington boosters strategized to bring more wind surfers to their side of the gorge. They hoped to lure boarders from the windsurfing capital at Hood River, Oregon to beaches in Skamania and western Klickitat counties by developing fancy beaches of their own. "Hood River is maxed out. It can't comfortably deal with any more people," Albert Hamilton, a Klickitat County booster, declared. Without developed launch sites, he said, "we're pushing dollars out of two counties that are extremely economically depressed."

Mountain biker on Coyote Wall. Photo by Darryl Lloyd.

In fact, an estimated 40 percent of windsurfers use Washington beaches to launch. Boarders generally agree that Washington has three-quarters of the best locations based on wave action and wind velocity, though until recently most beaches lacked even the most basic amenities. But at the end of the day, most windsurfers still cross the Hood River Bridge to Oregon to eat, sleep, and play.

The boosters envisioned construction of up to a dozen windsurfing parks stretching from North Bonneville to Roosevelt, east of the Scenic Area. Their theory was that the parks would attract windsurfers, who would attract tourism in the form of motels and restaurants.

But windsurfing, especially in the gorge, is not a traditional tourism industry. Boarders seek out those rare beaches that have the perfect combination of gusty winds and thrilling waves. BNSF Railway owns the tracks along the Washington shore and thereby controls access to the river. And at many sites, Columbia River tribes exercise their treaty rights to fish in their "usual and customary places" without fear that some sailboarder will cut their nets.

In fact, the BNSF Railway tracks present a serious obstacle to river access on the north shore, just as the Union Pacific tracks block access to prime beaches on the Oregon side. Two dozen trains a day travel the gorge on the Washington side at speeds of up to 70 miles per hour.

In 2006, the Columbia River Gorge Commission gave a green light to BNSF Railway to build a siding near Doug's Beach, one of the most popular windsurfing sites in the gorge. The 8,400-foot stretch of track would be constructed parallel to and within the BNSF right of way. Windsurfers protested loudly, saying the new track would eliminate fifty to eighty of the undeveloped park's two hundred twenty parking spaces.

"The loss of parking is a major deal," said Diane Barkheimer, executive director of the influential Columbia Gorge Windsurfing Association, which at the time claimed a worldwide membership of 1,260. Doug's Beach "is one of the sites that can't be duplicated, with the afternoon winds and the sandy beach," she said. "Our members are people who come here to sail and own second homes here. They are hugely disappointed."

But the railroad had its priorities, and they trumped the windsurfers' wishes. BNSF spokesman Gus Melonas said the proposed $10 million project near Lyle represented the first significant expansion of railroad infrastructure in the gorge in recent years. "We're moving record volumes of freight, running forty-five to fifty trains in a twenty-four-hour period," he said. "This project is the first west of Wishram. It will provide efficiency and added reliability."

The Gorge Commission found in favor of the railroad, with some mitigation. Executive Director Martha Bennett pointed out that BNSF had looked at four other sites, but each had more impacts on wetlands than the one at Doug's Beach. "I think we made the best decision we could under the circumstances," she told the *White Salmon Enterprise*. "This has been one of the hardest projects we've wrestled with. I've been here five years, and this one has it all. It's a classic case of competing interests."

Most visitors come to the gorge to hike its trails. The profusion and variety of hiking trails in the gorge is a big selling point for Friends of the Gorge, which organizes hikes from mid-March through mid-July and again from mid-September through October. The hiking season starts in the eastern gorge and follows the wildflower bloom westward. Friends' hikes focus on the natural history and wildlife of the gorge. "We have education themes to our hikes," says Maegan Jossy, outdoor programs manager for Friends. "Our outings are about more than witnessing the beautiful scenery. We're teaching on the trail as well." A 10-mile round-trip hike to the top of Washington's Table Mountain, Jossy said, "offers fantastic views of the

Bonneville slide," a landform that according to geologists tumbled down the mountain in about 1450, blocking the Columbia River and creating a natural bridge at the site of what is now the Bridge of the Gods.

One of Friends' most popular outings brings a bald eagle expert to the Balfour-Klickitat Day Use Area along the lower Klickitat River, the wintering site of the largest concentration of bald eagles within a two hundred-mile radius of the Portland-Vancouver area. Eighty people typically show up over two January weekends to watch the eagles preen.

In honor of the scenic area's twenty-fifth anniversary in 2011, Friends challenged hikers to visit twenty-five gorge trails. About one hundred fifty people made the pledge.

The variety of landscapes now accessible on the Washington side of the gorge comes as a surprise to many hikers, including Jossy, who grew up in the Northwest. "I really thought I knew the gorge, but there's so much to explore," she said. The Klickitat Trail, a former railbed that offers access along the Klickitat River and to remote areas further east, is a new favorite. "We offer at least one or two hikes there every season," she said. "It is a gem."

In fact, Friends of the Gorge is laying plans to step up its trail development role in a big way. At Friends annual membership breakfast in April 2012, Executive Director Kevin Gorman announced the launch of a new project to mark the second quarter-century of the National Scenic Area. Gorge Towns to Trails has two goals, he said: To draw visitors to visit and spend money in gorge communities, and to invite gorge residents to explore the scenic landscapes in their own back yards.

The campaign will focus on three specific projects: Completing the long-envisioned, 34-mile Washougal-to-Stevenson trail, of which 85 percent of the right-of-way is now in public ownership; connecting Mosier to The Dalles across what is now a patchwork of public and privately owned land; and linking the Lyle Cherry Orchard near Lyle, owned by the Friends of the Gorge Land Trust, with a trailhead that will begin at the Lyle High School. "It's a vision for a trail system that would wrap around the Columbia River Gorge and connect with gorge communities." Gorman said. It's loosely modeled on the European system, where trails link urban centers. Friends of the Gorge envisions hikers using gorge communities as hubs for multi-day trekking opportunities.

Hiker in old-growth forest on the Herman Creek Trail. Photo by Darryl Lloyd.

Hidden treasures lie along these undeveloped sections of the gorge, said Renee Tkach, who is overseeing the ambitious land acquisition program: a little-visited waterfall, an elk herd on Hamilton Mountain. She recalled finding a large group from the Mazamas mountain-climbing club parked at the base of an unmarked area owned by the Friends Land Trust. "They had discovered this spot that is not in any trail book," she said. "People are looking for places to get away from other people."

Gorman says Towns to Trails is the first gorge-wide effort by Friends to support both Scenic Area goals—protecting natural resources while boosting economic development. It will clearly be Friends' biggest project ever.

The group needs to raise $15 million, including $3 million in private donations, to acquire the rights-of-way. But affected communities generally support the concept, as do Oregon's two U.S. senators and U.S. Rep. Earl Blumenauer, who have pledged to help finance it. Public dollars could come from the Land and Water Conservation Fund, which generates about $250 million a year.

"This initiative brings trekking from town to town, providing a different economic benefit than the typical wilderness-style hiking experience," said Skamania County Commissioner Paul Pearce in endorsing the project.

The response from the Forest Service has been guarded, as Gorman admitted. "They are short-staffed and have a lot of unmanaged lands. We do have to address the overuse issue while protecting the landscape."

As of spring 2013, the Gorge Commission had taken no formal stand on the project.

The Mosier-to-The Dalles route is perhaps the most ambitious of the three. Hood River and Mosier already are connected by a state historic trail. The new trail would head east from a city park in Mosier through a donated easement and across the Mosier Plateau, a 45-acre property owned by Friends of the Columbia Gorge Land Trust. It would traverse the spectacular Memaloose wildflower area, connecting to the Tom McCall Preserve and continuing along Seven Mile Hill before dropping down to the Discovery Center, where it would connect to the nine-mile Riverfront Trail in The Dalles.

Hikers would be able to walk from downtown to a city park, past a waterfall, and explore 40 acres of flowers and a breath-taking gorge viewpoint. Said Mosier City Councilor Kathy Fitzpatrick, "A hike can end with dinner at the restaurant or a beer at the pub without ever getting back in your car."

Chapter 22
Cape Horn Convergence

Dave Bennick maneuvered his forklift into position at the front of the rambling, low-slung house. Daniel Casati revved up his chain saw and sliced through the posts supporting the roof of the front walkway. Bennick slid the forks under the roof section, deftly lifted it in one piece and set it down away from the house. A deconstruction pro, Bennick had been hired by Friends of the Gorge Land Trust to remove this house perched on the rim of the Columbia Gorge, high above Cape Horn. Most of the materials would be sold to a Portland rebuilding center. Up to 90 percent would be reused or recycled.

Within a year, when the $1 million, 5,500-square-foot house was gone, the asphalt removed and the land recontoured, the Forest Service would buy the four-acre property, using $570,000 from the federal Land and Water Conservation Fund. Eventually, it would build a trail to this site offering panoramic views of forests, meadows, Beacon Rock, and points east. Eventually, Friends of the Gorge would build a simple amphitheater of basalt blocks here in memory of Nancy Russell, the organization's founder and major benefactor.

For Friends of the Gorge, the dismantling of the million-dollar house on the rim of the bluff in July 2008 was the realization of a long-held dream. In the 1980s, before there was a National Scenic Area, a Skamania County developer had platted a sixteen-lot subdivision called Rim View Estates atop this bluff. No zoning was in place to stop the project. So Nancy and Bruce Russell made a $100,000 no-interest loan to the Trust for Public Land, enabling it to buy twelve of the sixteen lots.

Since 1986, the Forest Service had purchased those twelve lots and more than fifty other properties at Cape Horn from land trusts and willing sellers. It had committed to building a new Cape Horn Trail to provide public access to Washington's premier gorge viewpoint. Yet as late as 2008, the Forest Service had not committed to Friends' proposed trail atop Pioneer Point.

The house Friends dismantled, known as the Cleveland property, was the only one ever built at Rim View Estates. Friends had bought it from its elderly owners in 2006, then launched a $4 million fundraising campaign to cover the cost of purchasing and dismantling the structure. Meanwhile, Nancy Russell acquired an option to buy a nearby house on 32 acres, known as the Collins property, with the understanding that its owners would remain there for the rest of their lives if they chose.

Before the Forest Service would buy either property, its rules required that all structures be removed. Now the Cleveland house was disappearing, board by board.

"Million dollar houses usually stay put," said Friends Executive Director Kevin Gorman. "But this is a once-in-a-lifetime opportunity to restore the natural landscape and create a spectacular gorge overlook. "

If Friends Land Trust had its way, the Cleveland property would connect with about 1,000 acres of adjacent public land at Pioneer Point. Friends envisioned an eight-mile Cape Horn loop trail and a family-friendly park. The new trail would replace a makeshift path on the bluff that detoured around both the Cleveland and Collins properties and forced hikers back 1,000 feet from the edge.

Removing the twenty-five-year-old house, attached garage and barn, and tearing up the asphalt would cost about $60,000. Disassembling any house carries surprises; contractors quickly realized that sticky spray-on insulation would make it impossible to recycle some of the lumber. Nonnative ornamental trees and shrubs were dug up and given away. The foundation was dumped into the daylight basement and buried.

After everything was hauled away, the land trust would be required to recontour the land to a more natural grade and remove dirt fill and a retaining wall beneath the existing rim viewpoint. That would require the services of a geotechnical expert, because the viewpoint was a precipitous straight drop down to Highway 14.

The removal of the Cleveland house marked a turning point in Friends' long campaign to dedicate the bluff above Cape Horn for public use. What happened at Cape Horn was a story of partnerships forged, visions realized, and a big dose of serendipity. Chance and timing played important roles.

The Friends of the Gorge Land Trust had been established only recently, with a $4 million bequest from philanthropist Norman Yeon, son of the wealthy lumberman and philanthropist John B. Yeon.

In 2006, Friends used $1.5 million from the recent bequest to buy the Cleveland property, then sold the land to the Forest Service for $570,000. Nancy Russell had secured an option to buy the 32-acre Collins property for $2 million. When she died in 2008, she left that option to Friends in her will. The organization had to scramble to take advantage of the gift. "We had to get a bridge loan to buy it," Gorman said.

The Washington Department of Transportation played a key role. Highway engineers had long wanted to straighten a mile-long stretch of Highway 14 just west of the narrow Cape Horn pullout. It was one of the most dangerous stretches of the highway, and not only for motorists. Hikers using a makeshift trail that looped below the highway to steep cliffs below took their lives in their hands crossing the busy road.

After years of delay, in the summer of 2011, crews began straightening the perilous highway curve. They also added a new left-turn lane at a dangerous intersection, the site of a busy park-and-ride lot. And, with a $2 million federal grant, they dug two pedestrian tunnels under the highway, about a mile apart, to give hikers safe passage on the new, rerouted Cape Horn Trail.

As workers dug the tunnels, masons far above on the bluff were putting the finishing touches on a simple, elegant overlook where the house had once stood.

Nancy Russell cherished the view from Cape Horn, a panorama that took in the fields and forests below, the Oregon shore, and the Columbia River east to Beacon Rock and beyond. Not only had she made it possible for the Forest Service to acquire the undeveloped land atop the bluff, she had also secured the original options to buy the two houses already there.

Meanwhile, a group of dedicated trail advocates called the Cape Horn Conservancy, led by real estate agent Dan Huntington, had been working with the Forest Service for years to design an improved Cape Horn Trail. The conservancy's longer-term goal was to see the completion of a continuous trail following the wooded bluffs above Highway 14 from Washougal to Stevenson, with a loop trail down to the steep palisades of the cape and up to Pioneer Point.

The existing Cape Horn trail, made mainly by hikers, had many safety and environmental problems. It crossed wet areas, steep talus slopes, and busy Highway 14. It skirted a nesting area for peregrine falcons along the cliffs south of the highway.

The Forest Service finally settled on a plan to build a new Cape Horn loop trail that would begin and end at the new park-and-ride. But for years, planning for the future trail by trail advocates and the Forest Service proceeded on separate tracks.

The Forest Service kept its distance from Friends of the Gorge. "The Cleveland property up at the top is gorgeous," Scenic Area deputy manager Greg Cox said in 2009. "It's icing on the cake. Could we have had a trail without it? Yes."

Attitudes changed, Gorman said, when Friends removed the house. "When the house came down, that was the trigger. Locals got together and embraced it. Once you had all those players, it became much easier for the Forest Service to endorse it, and once they did, they jumped in with both feet."

Over the years, Skamania County had often crossed swords with Friends of the Gorge and Nancy Russell. But when the county decided to build the park-and-ride lot at Salmon Falls, Russell agreed to sell the land to the county at a bargain price, on condition the lot would serve as a trailhead and interpretive site for the Cape Horn Trail.

Russell "was very generous in her negotiations," recalled Skamania County Commissioner Paul Pearce. He said he hoped Cape Horn would someday become a section of a Washougal-to-Stevenson trail. In fact, Pearce said, the county was actively considering "naming the trailhead, or perhaps the park-and-ride, for Nancy Russell."

August 13, 2011, began with rain and thick clouds that obscured the view from the new scenic overlook atop Pioneer Point. Wrapped in rain parkas, people walked through wet grass, followed along a section of the Cape Horn Trail still under construction, and took their places at the new overlook, a simple amphitheater with curved benches carved from Columbia Gorge basalt.

The small audience of about two hundred included several members of Congress. Senator Mark Hatfield, the public official most responsible for establishment of the National Scenic Area, had died the previous Sunday, at eighty-nine. Several speakers gave him credit for muscling the law through Congress in the face of stubborn opposition from President Reagan.

On a drizzly summer morning in 2011, a small crowd assembled for the dedication of the new Cape Horn Overlook, built atop a premier viewpoint, the site of a demolished million-dollar house, to honor Nancy Russell, founder of watchdog group Friends of the Columbia Gorge. Photo by Steven Lane of *The Columbian*.

"When we sent this legislation to the White House, it was with certainty that it would be vetoed," recalled former U.S. Rep. Don Bonker, now a member of the Gorge Commission. "Hatfield made it clear to the White House that should the Scenic Area Act be vetoed, some of the President's programs would be in jeopardy, including funding for Star Wars," Bonker recalled. "A week later, the National Scenic Area Act was signed into law." The story might be apocryphal, but after twenty-five years it had attained the status of legend.

Scenic Area Manager Dan Harkenrider, who was about to retire from the Forest Service, recalled Nancy Russell's "doggedness and her refusal to take no for an answer."

"She interrogated me about what my land ethic was," he said. They didn't always agree. "But over the years I felt fortunate to hear her describe what could be the possibilities."

Aubrey Russell, son of Nancy Russell, said his mother "didn't love memorials, but she would have gotten a great deal of satisfaction to see this overlook." She would have appreciated that its design was in harmony with the ethic of Samuel Lancaster, the designer of the Historic Columbia Gorge Highway, whose overriding goal, simple yet profound, was "to not mar what God has put here."

Sternwheeler in the Columbia Gorge. Photo by Darryl Lloyd.

Chapter 23
A River Unleashed

On a cool morning in late October 2011, dozens of people gathered near the east bank of the White Salmon River to witness a historic event—the breaching of a ninety-eight-year-old dam. Thousands more from all over the world tuned in to a live-streaming video feed to watch the dam crumble.

At 12:07 p.m., a five-minute warning sounded. One minute later, there was a second warning. Then, the explosion. Crews detonated 700 pounds of dynamite planted in the concrete base of Condit Dam, breaching the 125-foot-high structure and releasing an estimated 2.7 million cubic yards of sediment and debris downstream. The leading edge of the torrent reached the Columbia River, three miles away, in just over an hour, far exceeding the predictions of demolition engineers.

The breaching of Condit Dam, located north of the Columbia River Gorge National Scenic Area boundary, marked the end of a dozen years of planning and legal wrangling that resonated across the Pacific Northwest and beyond. For the first time in a century, fall Chinook salmon which had migrated to the upper reaches of the White Salmon from time immemorial, would be able to reach their spawning grounds. Fish biologists who had kept the run alive through propagation at a nearby federal fish hatchery hoped that native steelhead also would return to their ancestral waters.

In the weeks before the dam's breaching, Rod Engle of the U.S. Fish and Wildlife Service led a team of fish biologists who deployed boats, net, weirs, and truck-mounted tanks to move the husky spawners from below the dam to a stretch of river above the reservoir, known as Northwestern Lake. There, the fish slid down a chute into the clear blue-green waters, fed by glaciers on Mount Adams, and, with a sweep of their muscular tails, swam away. Two years of trial runs had convinced Engle and his colleagues that these fish would gravitate to the places where their distant ancestors had spawned before the dam was built.

The Endangered Species Act required the dam's owner, Portland-based energy giant PacifiCorp, to restore fish passage for threatened and endangered salmon and steelhead runs and, as a condition of renewing the dam's federal license, to protect other listed species likely to be affected by the dam's removal.

Because the fall Chinook in the White Salmon River were listed as threatened, PacifiCorp was required to protect them. However, many other aquatic species in the lower river, including other fish runs, lacked federal protection and would be wiped out by the sediment surge.

Engle's goal was to keep the runs alive through natural propagation. Would they spawn in the upper river, and if so, would the smolts be able to find their way downstream to the Columbia through all that sediment the following year?

Members of the Yakama Tribe meanwhile celebrated the return of a free-flowing White Salmon River. For millennia their ancestors had inhabited this gentle valley, a mosaic of conifer forests, apple orchards, and waterfront homes in the shadow of Mount Adams. There's a Native American graveyard in the town of Husum, and a tribal fishing site at the mouth of the White Salmon. The breaching brought tears to the eyes of Yakama Indian Davis Washines. He had wondered whether he would live to see this day. The torrent, he said, reminded him of wild horses running free. "The water just took off," he said. "It was anxious to get going."

White-water rafters partied and watched the breaching via live video from a big tent in the back yard of a Husum whitewater rafting company. They relished the chance to run the untamed river all the way down to the Columbia, perhaps within a year's time.

Some local environmentalists, Dennis White among them, had waited two decades for this moment. White and others had organized Friends of the White Salmon in the 1980s to block a plan by a local public utility to build eight dams and water containment structures on the river to generate power. Not only had they killed the plan; they had also managed to get a portion of the White Salmon River included in the federal Wild and Scenic Rivers system.

Not everyone was glad to see this day come. Owners of rustic cabins along Northwestern Lake mourned the imminent loss of a quiet retreat. "It's kind of a hard thing to get used to," said Jerry Bryan. On the morning of the breaching, the fifty-nine-year-old took a walk to the reservoir to

Jeff Jolley, left, and Joe Skalicky of the U.S. Fish and Wildlife Service pull a tule fall Chinook salmon from a seine in the lower White Salmon River in September 2011. The threatened salmon run had been kept alive through hatchery breeding for nearly a century. The wild salmon were released above Condit Dam, which was breached the following month in a historic plan to restore a wild, free-flowing tributary of the Columbia River. Photo by Steven Lane of *The Columbian*.

look out on a body of water he had known and loved all his life. In a way, he said, the White Salmon flowed through his veins. "I was born and raised right here and spent all my youth up here fishing with my brother."

As for PacifiCorp officials, they breathed a sigh of relief when the breaching went off without a hitch. For the investor-owned utility, taking out Condit Dam was, in the end, all about saving money.

Breaching Condit Dam without dredging the reservoir behind it would cost the utility an estimated $32 million, about double its 1999 estimate. But even that inflated price tag represented a huge savings for PacifiCorp. It was about one-third the cost the company would have incurred if it had built fish passage structures allowing fall Chinook salmon and steelhead to reach their historic spawning grounds above the dam. Condit produced only a tiny fraction of the utility's hydroelectric capacity. It was a dam the company could afford to lose.

And the method it chose—blasting a hole in the dam and unleashing the accrued sediment of one hundred years with only minimal dredging— also saved the company millions.

Over a decade, the breaching even brought together former political foes. Skamania and Klickitat counties had opposed the dam's removal, in part because they would lose a popular recreation site, in part because they coveted the power Condit generated. In an effort subsidized by Klickitat County's lucrative regional landfill, they had hired lawyers and signed on as formal interveners in the arduous process required to remove a federally licensed dam. In the end, the counties received a modest settlement from PacifiCorp.

More than any of these local considerations, the breaching of Condit Dam on October 26, 2011, marked a significant turning point in the era of dam-building that had reshaped the Columbia River over a century. Rather than build new dams, utilities were taking dams out. Rather than destroy fish habitat, they were restoring it.

PacifiCorp had some experience in navigating these new political and environmental waters. By the time it breached Condit Dam, the utility had removed two smaller dams, Hemlock Dam on the Sandy River and Power-dale Dam in the Hood River watershed. To the north, the utility had faced major challenges in getting its three dams on Washington's Lewis River relicensed. In that case, it had worked with federal regulators for years to win approval of a plan that would improve fish passage. The Lewis River dams remained.

Condit Dam, perched in the narrowest part of a steep canyon, presented PacifiCorp with an equally complicated project. The utility began negotia-tions with state agencies, conservation groups and the tribes in the late 1990s in preparation for the expiration of Condit's federal license.

In 1999, it announced a settlement with more than twenty parties, including several national and local environmental groups, state agencies, and the Yakama Tribe. Under the terms of the agreement, the utility would remove the dam, but it would do so without dredging the millions of cubic yards of sediment that had built up behind it.

In exchange, parties to the settlement would agree not to file suit chal-lenging that method, which was dubbed "blow and go," or other aspects of the breaching. Neither Skamania County nor Klickitat County was invited to be a party to the settlement.

The original timeline called for breaching the dam in 2006. Five ad-ditional years were needed to satisfy all federal and state requirements. A big stumbling block was obtaining a state water quality permit that would allow the release of massive amounts of sediment into a major waterway of the state—a legally sticky issue for the Washington Department of Ecology, which was a party to the settlement.

Supporters of the breaching boasted that Condit Dam would be the highest dam ever breached in the United States. It was a close call. Work on removal of the 108-foot-high Elwha Dam on the Olympic Peninsula's Elwha River began in September 2011, a month before Condit's breaching. By late spring of 2012 the Elwha Dam was gone and salmon were returning to their ancestral spawning grounds. All five salmon species had spawned in abundance in the Elwha before the river was dammed.

Some conservationists dreamed of a day when the four dams on the Lower Snake River, built in the 1960s and 1970s, would be gone. The dams were built primarily to allow barges loaded with wheat to travel from Lewiston, Idaho, to the Pacific Ocean. They presented major obstacles for salmon that spawned in the Snake and its tributaries, hundreds of miles from the ocean. Those fish now had to surmount as many as eight dams to reach their spawning grounds. Due to their imperiled state, in the early 1990s, several Snake River salmon runs were listed as threatened or endangered.

Breaching of the Snake River dams was opposed by virtually every elected official in the Pacific Northwest. But it was more than a pipe dream; in a long-running federal lawsuit, U.S. District Judge James Redden consistently admonished the federal government that it must do more to save the endangered runs, holding out the prospect of dam removal if all other efforts failed.

Meanwhile, Columbia River treaty tribes imagined a day when The Dalles Dam would be gone and the great falls at Celilo would return. A sonar survey of the riverbed by the U.S. Army Corps of Engineers in 2008 revealed that Celilo Falls had not been blown up during construction of the dam, as some tribal members suspected. The distinctive horseshoe-shaped falls remained, in the reservoir behind the dam. Spectacular underwater images broadcast by Oregon Public Broadcasting's *Oregon Field Guide* offered hope that on some distant day in the future, salmon might leap the falls again.

The White Salmon River wasted no time in revealing its power as it carved its way down through layers of sediment, draining Northwestern Lake and shifting its course slightly to the east.

The unleashed river took its toll. As it found its new course, it undermined some cabins along its banks. The silt that accumulated at the mouth of the river forced the closure of an Indian fishing site. Meanwhile, fish biologists waited to find out whether the smolts would survive the next year's migration to the sea.

In the fall of 2013, they got their answer: Tule fall Chinook were spawning both above the former dam site and in habitat below the dam that was rejuvenated when one hundred years' worth of trapped gravel was released from Northwestern Lake.

Meanwhile, PacifiCorp completed the work of dismantling the concrete dam and other structures. By fall, no trace of the dam itself remained. In November, the rambunctious river was opened to boating for the first time.

The breaching of Condit Dam ushered in a new era of river restoration. It gave new life to a hardy salmon run and reshaped a watershed. And it revealed to a fascinated public the regenerative power of a free-flowing river.

Chapter 24
A Quarter Century

The Columbia River Gorge National Scenic Area marked its twenty-fifth anniversary in late summer of 2011. But the mood was far from celebratory. The Gorge Commission was struggling to carry on its work in the face of steep budget cuts and lagging political support. Some questioned its relevance. Observance of the anniversary was funded entirely with private donations. A commemorative coffee table book of gorge photos was published. Oregon Public Broadcasting produced an ambitious two-hour documentary on the history of the gorge and the Scenic Area Act.

On August 13, a date with no particular historical significance, organizers held a reception at Skamania Lodge, attended by a mix of local officials, Portland politicians, conservationists, and longtime gorge residents. A few miles away, the Nancy Russell Overlook had been dedicated that morning in a separate quiet, reflective ceremony. As attendees sipped wine from the grapes of local vineyards, it fell to Skamania County Commissioner Paul Pearce to acknowledge the 800-pound elephant in the hall: Budget cuts recently enacted by both state legislatures threatened the Gorge Commission's ability to enforce the Scenic Area Act.

"There is an assault on the Gorge Commission coming from both states," Pearce said from the lectern. "I have had to go to the legislature the past two sessions and warn that funding for the Gorge Commission is critical. Without the commission, we won't see plan amendments, economic development, or new recreation activities."

Shortly after the ceremony, Gorge Commission Executive Director Jill Arens, who had worked tirelessly but without success to secure adequate state funding for high-priority programs, announced that she would leave the job at the end of January. Arens, a native of Hood River, had returned to the gorge with high hopes. She had reached out to gorge communities to encourage more partnerships and more ownership of the gorge region by its residents. She made a concerted effort to connect with the treaty tribes, the governors, and state legislators, as well as gorge county officials, business leaders, and gorge residents. Under her leadership, the commission had shifted direction, embarking on a mission to take stock of where it had been and to foresee where it might be headed.

The effort began in 2007, when Arens organized a Futures Forum at the Columbia Gorge Discovery Center in The Dalles. It was a brain-storming session, and an attempt to enlist gorge "stakeholders" in developing strategies for measuring how well the Gorge Commission and the Forest Service were achieving their goals under the National Scenic Area Act.

With the information the process yielded, Arens and the commission launched the Vital Signs Indicators Project, an ambitious effort to evaluate through scientific measures where the Scenic Area stood after a quarter-century. Arens made the project a top priority. She hired a staffer to work fulltime on it, using GIS programs and data bases to measure such things as changes in the forest cover, views from key viewpoints and the acreage covered by houses and pavement.

But this effort coincided with the onset of the Great Recession of 2008. And as the Washington and Oregon legislatures set about cutting their budgets to deal with declining revenue, the Scenic Area budget, which supported the equivalent of 10.5 full-time employees, did not escape the ax.

In 2009 and 2010, the commission suffered cuts in line with those of state agencies. In 2011, the Washington Legislature passed a budget that eliminated funding for the Gorge Commission altogether in the 2012-13 fiscal year.

The commission now faced a true crisis. Longtime staff members were laid off or saw their hours reduced. The commission office closed on Fridays, and commissioners agreed to meet only every third month, instead of monthly, to save travel costs.

Arens enlisted influential Gorge Commissioners, including former Oregon Gov. Barbara Roberts and former Washington Congressman Don Bonker, to try to get congressional funding to keep the Vital Signs project going.

When that didn't succeed, she applied for a grant from the Bullitt Foundation. The Seattle foundation said it couldn't fund Vital Signs directly, but it did offer to facilitate a meeting bringing together Gorge Commissioners,

Forest Service Regional Forester Mary Wagner, and representatives from the offices of Washington Gov. Chris Gregoire and Oregon Gov. John Kitzhaber. "It was the first time those stakeholder groups got together in one room," Arens said. But the result was not what she had hoped for. The message, she said, was, "We don't want any surprises."

In an interview in August 2011, a few months before she announced her resignation, Arens didn't hide her frustration over how the Gorge Commission had been treated in recent legislative sessions. "It would be nice if the governors were openly committed to a strong Gorge Commission," she said. "But the governors had already made commitments in their budgets. The Oregon Legislature was willing to match Gregoire's budget if the Washington Legislature was willing to pass it, but that didn't happen. Then the budget on the Washington side was cut deliberately."

Arens learned that a Washington state senator had proposed saving $300,000 by eliminating that amount from the Gorge Commission's budget and consolidating commission operations with those of state environmental agencies. The consolidation never happened, but the senate cut the money anyway. "Our funding died in the last minute of the session and no one knows what happened," Arens said. Rumor had it that the senate had traded away funding for the Gorge Commission in exchange for Sen. Jim Honeyford's vote on the senate budget. Honeyford, a conservative Republican whose district included the east gorge, had often expressed the opinion that the Gorge Commission had outlived its usefulness.

In late summer of 2011, Arens informed the commission that there was no money to continue Vital Signs and no money to hire a lead planner, a position essential to the upcoming task of revising the Scenic Area Management Plan. "The position is strategic, a link to the commissioners on larger policy issues," she said in an interview. "The principal planner helps the commission understand what are the most important things to focus on. We need to focus."

Beyond updating the management plan, Arens saw several unresolved issues looming. The Dalles was considering expanding its urban boundary, a move that would likely require action by Congress and might open the door for other boundary expansion petitions. The commission needed to find a better way to protect agricultural land for people who actually made their living farming, not only wealthy hobby farmers. Towns and local port districts complained that the existing urban area boundaries made it difficult for them to expand along their riverfronts. And the commission needed a strategy to attract private recreation development, which was allowed but severely limited under the existing plan.

Arens wasn't the only gorge official who was leaving. Longtime Forest Service Scenic Area Manager Dan Harkenrider was retiring; his successor would decide how to accommodate exploding recreation use in the gorge

At the quarter-century mark, the National Scenic Area Act remained a work in progress. The commission had taken a political hit in exercising its responsibility to enforce limits on development. In the end, it was at the mercy of the legislatures, which had much bigger issues to deal with as state revenue declined in the wake of the Great Recession.

But if the twenty-fifth anniversary marked a low point in political support for the Gorge Commission, positive change was happening in many gorge communities. There was steady movement toward a new and powerful regional identity. It was time for new blood, new visions, new energy. Economic change was transforming some communities. Some local officials were ready to set aside old grievances and work together to solve local problems, such as providing public safety and emergency medical services to residents of struggling communities.

The National Scenic Area, driven by growth in technology, green energy, recreation, tourism, and a housing trend known as "amenity migration," which draws well-heeled home buyers to areas of natural beauty, was reinventing its economy. The Mid-Columbia Economic Development Council, which covers five gorge counties in the two states, had targeted five business sectors for development: Technology, renewable energy, wine-growing, arts and culture, and health care information. The new economic blueprint represented a dramatic shift from the timber, aluminum, agriculture and gravel mining that sustained the rural gorge for a century.

Since the early 1990s, it had become obvious that the gorge economy could not survive on natural resource extraction alone. By 2011, more than 60 percent of Skamania County's workforce was commuting to jobs outside the county.

The arrival of a Google server farm in The Dalles in 2006 pumped new energy and about one hundred jobs into the town, which at the time was still struggling to recover from the 2000 closure of an aluminum smelter, the town's longtime anchor industry. During its boom years, the smelter ran twenty-four hours a day, seven days a week, providing good-paying jobs for five hundred workers. The loss of the industry flattened The Dalles.

"We had 19 percent unemployment," recalled Dan Durow, the city's development director, in a 2012 interview. "Our property values dropped by 50 percent. We lost population. There was a home for sale on every block." But The Dalles did not give up, Durow said. "During that time the community came together. They passed a $5 million bond issue to upgrade the port. They voted for $8.5 million to get a community college located here. We built a middle school, and the county built a veterans' home."

Google, drawn by reliable power, fiber connectivity, and available "shovel-ready" land, further boosted job opportunities, though it did not turn out to be the savior city leaders had hoped for. Its confidentiality policy—city and port officials were sworn to secrecy during negotiations over its purchase of the site—and the $1.2 billion in tax breaks the company received for an initial investment of $10 million left a sour taste among some city and county officials.

"We did expect to see some ancillary companies local close by," Durow said. "That didn't happen. But it's still been a great opportunity. Google has been very generous to the community. It paid for a Wi-Fi system for the entire city."

Insitu, a pioneering manufacturer of unmanned drones, was launched in 1994 in founder Ted McGeer's Underwood house with just three employees. Its first prototypes were deployed to conduct ocean research. By 2004, Insitu was preparing to move into a new 24,000-square foot building at the Port of Klickitat in Bingen, where it would employ nearly fifty highly skilled engineers, designers and technicians to manufacture the ScanEagle unmanned aircraft in partnership with Boeing Co. In 2010, Insitu, now owned by Boeing, moved its engineering staff from Bingen to Hood River.

The company's impact on the gorge economy has been significant and continues to grow; of its eight hundred employees at manufacturing sites scattered throughout the National Scenic Area, five hundred live in the gorge.

Skamania County, historically the most timber-dependent gorge county, still has two operating mills, but timber no longer dominates its economy. The county once pinned its hopes on acquiring a former Forest Service tree nursery near Carson and turning it into an economic engine. That effort failed, in part due to the property's remote location and lack of a reliable water supply. Stevenson, the county seat, is a bedroom community with growing tourist appeal. Skamania Lodge attracts visitors from across the region. Shops and restaurants and landscaping have spruced up downtown.

Bingen and White Salmon, 20 miles to the east, have gentrified as well, with new brewpubs and pizza restaurants that buzz with business not only from local residents but from hikers and white-water rafters exploring the gorge.

Even Cascade Locks, which for a decade pinned its hopes on a tribal casino, was moving on. In 2011, the port broke ground on a 10,000-square-foot industrial building, which it planned to market as an incubator for small businesses at a bargain rate.

Hood River remains a magnet for windsurfers and outdoor sports enthusiasts of all kinds. The town had an unemployment rate of 6.9 percent in May 2012, the second-lowest rate of any Oregon county.

Retired Forest Service landscape architect Jurgen Hess arrived in 1986, at about the same time the first wave of windsurfers descended on the town from all over the world. In an interview, he recalled Hood River's rapid evolution from an agricultural center to a world-class recreation destination—and what came after. "Windsurfing hit this town in 1987 or 1988," Hess said. "It was increasing logarithmically. People were coming in and buying four or five houses at a time. Then people started coming here to see the windsurfers. Hood River was on the map."

"Then windsurfing leveled off, but people kept coming. A lot of businesses transitioned. A hardware store became Doug's Sports. The clothing stores and fresh fruit places and shops went more and more toward tourism. For a town of 6,000 people, we had a lot of restaurants. They kept changing hands."

Over time, the town's economy found a new balance, Hess said. "The windsurfers started getting involved in the community, running for city council and county commission. As windsurfing tapered off, the tourists kept coming. It became a shopping town. People saw the town and liked it. You've got two mountains, the river....Then mountain biking took off, then kiteboarding." Like any boomtown, Hood River has matured, Hess said. "Before the recession hit, people were coming up here from all over the world. That has stopped."

Hood River County's economic base today, as historically, lies in its apple and pear orchards. As for the town, Hess said, "Its economy has stabilized around recreation and tourism. People who have nothing to do with windsurfing come here."

There's a not-so-subtle competition between Hood River and The Dalles, 20 miles to the east. In Hess's view, The Dalles has made some unfortunate choices.

"We fought a super WalMart, but The Dalles hurt itself by allowing all these big-box stores that killed retail in the downtown area," he said. "Now the thrift stores have migrated downtown. The downtown is a 1950s downtown."

Durow disagrees. He's proud of the town's decision to preserve its historic downtown and to stay true to its roots. "Our economy is a real economy," he said. "It's not based on speculation, not dependent on tourism or recreation. It's a more balanced economy."

In fact, local, state and federal government operations, including The Dalles Dam, provide a significant part of the town's economy, and its largest private employer is the health care industry, which employs about eight hundred people. It's also a regional shopping center for all of the mid-gorge area.

Tiny Mosier, five miles east of Hood River, has its own unique political and conservation ethic. A former cherry-packing center, in 2000 the city won a $500,000 federal grant to pay for improvements to its waterfront, including better and safer access to the Columbia River for windsurfers. The project transformed the town, giving it its own windsurfing beach, and its own quirky identity.

In the fall of 2011, as activists took over two parks in downtown Portland to demonstrate their support for the Occupy Wall Street movement, Mosier launched its own Occupy Mosier movement. Activists went door to door to engage their neighbors in serious discussion about how they had been affected by the economic meltdown of 2008 and the Great Recession.

Meanwhile, Klickitat County continues to follow its own path, relying on lucrative landfill revenues and wind power. But even there, wineries and bed and breakfasts are slowly transforming its natural resource-based economy as tourists discover the Mount Adams Country, a portal to natural wonders that lie to the north.

The Columbia River near Hood River. Photo by Darryl Lloyd.

Chapter 25
The Fight for the Gorge Continues

The Columbia River Gorge regularly turns up in travel magazines as a hip, photogenic destination for active, environmentally aware and culturally sophisticated tourists. The appeal of the gorge shows no sign of waning as Northwest city dwellers—and tourists from around the world—look for opportunities to hike and commune with nature within commuting distance of a major metropolitan area.

Summer and fall weekends in the gorge are packed with farmers' markets, winery tours, and art exhibits. Skamania County offers a summer bluegrass festival. The historic Columbia Gorge Hotel near Hood River, with its lavish, well-tended gardens, offers a taste of an earlier, grander era of tourism. Art galleries and upscale shops selling recreation gear and garb have popped up in downtown Hood River, the cultural hub of the gorge.

There's year-round hiking on mostly gentle trails to Oregon waterfalls and more rigorous climbing on Washington's Dog Mountain and Table Mountain. There's mountain biking at Coyote Wall and white-water rafting on the Klickitat and White Salmon rivers. In winter, there's snowshoeing and cross-country skiing in the wide-open country of rural Klickitat County. Within a few years, a network of trails and roadways may reconnect Troutdale with The Dalles along the route of the Historic Columbia River Highway.

The gorge may be the Pacific Northwest's version of Shangri-La. But it also remains a vital western transportation corridor, and thus its future is always up for grabs. The second quarter-century of the National Scenic Area began with the very real prospect that the gorge could become a conduit for trains and barges carrying vast amounts of coal from the Rocky Mountains to West Coast ports—coal ultimately destined for China and other Asian markets. Plans surfaced in the fall of 2011 for development of as many as six ports in Washington and Oregon exporting as much as 150 tons annually from the Powder River Basin of Montana and Wyoming to Asian shores.

The pushback was immediate. Gorge communities found common ground in opposing a major increase in coal traffic through the gorge. The Sierra Club, which had run a successful "Beyond Coal" campaign in the Pacific Northwest, sounded the first alarm. "Locally, coal exports could bring 26 mile-long coal trains through the gorge every day, spewing toxic coal dust into the air and water, contributing to asthma and respiratory diseases, choking our railroads, and degrading our property values," the club warned. The issue was a top priority for the club, which had played a key role in getting utilities in both Washington and Oregon to end the burning of coal by 2025.

Brett VandenHeuvel, director of the environmental group Columbia Riverkeeper, predicted that as communities learned about the public health, safety, and economic impacts of coal export, opposition would swell.

Coal companies, which would reap their profits far from the Northwest, tried to make the case that expanding markets in Asia would save American jobs in coal country and generate new jobs on the West Coast. The coal industry also warned that if the United States did not move quickly to capture the new markets, some other nation would.

In April 2012, the Hood River City Council joined other gorge communities—Dallesport, Mosier, Washougal, and Camas—in voting to oppose the export of coal through the gorge. "Our council sees the proposal to ship huge quantities of coal through our city by rail and barge as a major threat to our quality of life," declared Mayor Arthur Babitz. "Our job is to protect the health and safety of our citizens. Turning the gorge into a coal chute is not a future we want to see." The council predicted local impacts would include air pollution from diesel emissions and coal dust, constant train noise, long delays at train crossings, reduced property values and expansion of railroad tracks into environmentally sensitive areas.

Neither the Gorge Commission nor the Forest Service had direct authority to block the transport of coal through the gorge. Decisions on whether to allow the shipments would lie with the railroads, the barge companies, the ports, and state and federal regulatory agencies, starting with the U.S. Army Corps of Engineers.

A proposal by Australia-based Ambre Energy North America was the furthest along. The company bought a 50 percent share in a mine just north of the Montana border in 2011 and, soon after, signed a deal with two South Korean companies to supply them with up to four million tons of coal annually.

Ambre Energy proposed to transport the coal by train from Montana and Wyoming to the Port of Morrow in northeast Oregon, load it onto covered barges for transport through the gorge, then transfer it to ocean-going vessels near the Port of St. Helens. Both barges and loading facility would be enclosed to minimize coal dust.

The company's first regulatory hurdle was winning a permit from the Corps of Engineers, required by the Federal Rivers and Harbors Act. The unanswered question was how the Corps would define its scope of environmental review under the National Environmental Policy Act.

"Our position is that it should be mine to smokestack, including climate change," said Michael Lang of Friends of the Gorge.

In May 2012, several hundred activists gathered in downtown Portland's Pioneer Courthouse Square to rally against coal exports from Northwest ports. Robert F. Kennedy Jr., a vocal opponent of the coal industry, predicted that allowing a major expansion of coal transport in the Northwest would corrupt politicians, damage public health and the environment, and "turn government agencies into the sock puppets of the industries they're supposed to regulate."

Kennedy had fought big coal in the nation's courtrooms. He argued that federal law required the coal companies to prepare an extensive environmental impact statement. "The minute they release a true and proper EIS, their proposals will be laughed out of town," he said. But it remained unclear whether the Corps of Engineers would conduct a full environmental review or prepare a less rigorous environmental assessment.

More than four hundred people turned out for a listening session held by U.S. Sen. Ron Wyden of Oregon in August 2012, including a large contingent from Friends of the Gorge. "No coal trains" quickly became the rallying point for environmentalists, who faced a potent adversary in Big Coal.

In early 2012, as the coal train issue picked up steam, a new executive director with new ideas took the reins at the Gorge Commission. Darren Nichols was no stranger to the gorge and its issues. For five years, he had worked closely with Jill Arens, his predecessor, and local gorge officials as a regional administrator with the Oregon Department of Land Conservation and Development, advising them on the thorny issue of expanding urban boundaries in Oregon.

Oregon's land use law requires cities and towns to have twenty years' worth of buildable land available—residential, commercial and industrial—under their land use plans. The landmark law technically conflicts with the Scenic Area Act, which allows the Gorge Commission to approve "minor" boundary changes for urban areas but requires an act of Congress to make major changes. The federal law does not define "minor."

The issue of boundary expansions was ripe in The Dalles. Dan Durow, who had served as director of planning for both Wasco County and the city of The Dalles over his long career, argued, in effect, that Oregon's land use law should trump the Scenic Area Act. The city, he said, was rapidly running out of available commercial and residential property.

The Dalles, seven miles long and one mile wide, wraps around the south shore of The Columbia River. Six thousand acres of irrigated cherry orchards lie to the south. Only a few small parcels of vacant land within the town's urban area boundary were still available for residential development in 2011. Durow said the city needed to expand by a square mile.

"We have enough industrial land for 20 years, including the 100 acres where Northwest Aluminum was," Durow said. "But for commercial and residential, we are short of a 20-year supply. What we need is 640 buildable acres, one square mile, to accommodate population growth and job growth."

He acknowledged that the Gorge Commission was short-staffed to deal with the issue, but said that was not the city's problem. "We're not in compliance with our 20-year plan. The citizens of The Dalles have a right to develop as a community."

Durow had argued his case for a boundary adjustment with Arens and Nichols as early as 2010. Nichols was sympathetic, and also saw a bigger issue. The Gorge Commission should do more to help gorge communities grow and prosper, he believed—including being open to expanding urban area boundaries into places where development was currently off-limits.

"My worst fear is that The Dalles can't get what it wants through the existing process and goes to Congress to get a boundary change," Nichols said in an April 2012 interview. "Our management plan in the National Scenic Area is fraught with vague language. I think to approach this issue as if it were just about a number or acres is unrealistic. To say this is about containing urban sprawl is dumb."

Nichols' approach was a shot across the bow to Friends of the Columbia Gorge, which was wary of any effort to expand urban area boundaries. At his first meeting with the Gorge Commission, on April 10, Nichols made an attention-grabbing announcement. "I took this job knowing that there was a possibility I might not have a job," he said.

Funding for staffing the commission had dropped to its lowest level ever. The commission now had the equivalent of just five-and-a-half full-time employees. It had lost half its staff in two years.

Nichols had a skeleton crew—one fulltime and one half-time planner, one part-time staff attorney—to review all development proposals in the Scenic Area, to prepare for review of the Scenic Area management plan in 2014, to develop a strategy for dealing with urban boundary expansions, to implement a court-ordered analysis of the cumulative impacts of development in the Scenic Area, and to continue work on Arens' Vital Signs Indicators Project.

Already, the commission had given itself permission to miss deadlines for responding to applications for development because of its critical staff shortage.

At this first Gorge Commission meeting, Nichols vowed to stand up to bullies in the state legislatures and demand adequate funding so the commission could do the job Congress had assigned it to do. He outlined a plan for scaling down the Vital Signs project by reducing the number of "indicators" from fifty-one to about a dozen. The project would focus on information already gathered by the Forest Service and state agencies on such issues as the ecological health of the gorge, agricultural activity, housing starts, and commercial and economic development. Nichols made it clear he had other priorities in mind. The Gorge Commission was responsible for protecting a wide range of resources, he said, including scenery, flora and fauna, cultural resources, recreation, agriculture, geology, renewable energy, and air quality.

"The Area Act has two purposes," he said. "For the first twenty-five years, we've done a phenomenal job of protecting those resources. In the second twenty-five years we want to support the economy of the gorge region. This is a place that is rich in interests. We want to harness those interests."

To Friends and some of its supporters on the commission, this was a form of heresy. They believed that Congress, in writing the Scenic Area Act, had already struck the balance between protection and development. But Nichols said he was a believer in consensus-building. He wanted to see gorge communities working closely together to deliver services and build their economies. And coincidentally, he had some unexpected revenue that would allow him to look further into that approach.

The state of Washington had disbursed about $60,000 to the commission, money erroneously withheld from its 2012-13 budget. The funds must be spent by July 2012.

He proposed hiring two consulting groups to interview up to eighty stakeholders on the subject of whether the Gorge Commission should adopt a consensus approach to problem-solving. The Gorge Commission could then use that approach, he said, to build an urban area management policy. "It could be a national model for how to develop strong, vibrant communities in a sensitive national environment."

Commissioner Jim Middaugh of Portland, who was closely allied with Friends of the Gorge, pushed back. The commission's most vital role, he said, was to serve as a watchdog. "There is not today a consensus on this commission that we need an overall policy on urban boundary changes," he said. 'Our resource protection plan is the most important thing we do. I'm highly skeptical of consensus-based processes. We are not just a stakeholder. It is our job to protect the resources."

In the end, the commissioners gave Nichols permission to spend the $60,000 windfall on stakeholder interviews as a first step toward deciding whether it should wade into the murky waters of consensus-building.

The verdict, released in a September 2012 report by the William D. Ruckelshaus Center and the Oregon Consensus National Policy Center, was skeptical at best. Their interviews revealed that there was "widely held dissatisfaction with the status quo." Most of those interviewed agreed that current regulatory, adversarial, and political approaches to solving problems in the Scenic Area were not working, that progress was "slow and overly influenced by a number of interests," and that funding gaps contributed to the frustrating status quo. Many expressed general approval for collaborative problem-solving, but said they doubted the commission's ability and willingness to successfully engage in such processes.

Congress had deliberately designed the composition of the Gorge Commission to encourage consensus. For example, prevailing on any issue on the twelve-member board required attracting not only a majority of votes but votes from both states. Sometimes it worked; other times, it was a recipe for paralysis.

There was a larger issue as well: Had the Gorge Commission lost its compass, its mission, its sense of history? Where was the passion? Nichols had that, at least. But whether he could sell his vision of revitalized, growing gorge communities to commissioners and advocacy groups was an open question.

Nichols' tenure got off to a rocky start on many fronts. Not only did he have to deliver a strong message to the two legislatures regarding the commission's level of funding. Not only did he have to assign new projects to a hard-working but diminished staff that was barely holding things together. Not only did he have to bring a batch of newly appointed commissioners up to speed. Nichols also had a new and highly visible clearcut in the heart of the gorge to explain.

The shocking 110-acre clearcut appeared in April on the steep face of the Gorge between Hood River and Mosier. Nichols could see it from his office window in White Salmon. Michael Lang of Friends of the Gorge discovered it on a drive through the Gorge. He was outraged.

Nearly twenty years earlier, in its 1992 management plan, Gorge Commissioners had designated the slope as one of the most sensitive landscapes in the Scenic Area and one of the most deserving of protection. The private land logged—32 acres— was in an area zoned as Open Space in the General Management Area. Under the management plan, it was off-limits to logging. The remaining 80 acres logged were in a tribal allotment that was exempt from Scenic Area land use rules, but the Bureau of Indian Affairs was still required to conduct an environmental review of logging proposals on those lands. No review had occurred.

Lang launched an investigation into how this had happened. He learned that the Yakama Tribe owned the tribal allotment and wanted to log it, but its only access to the land was across commercial timberland owned by SDS Lumber Co. The company agreed to provide access, and decided to log some of its own property at the same time.

SDS submitted a forest practices application to the Oregon Department of Forestry and Hood River County. In February 2012, a state forest practices employee contacted Nichols to find out the status of the SDS land. Nichols, brand new to the job, consulted with staff attorney Jeff Litwak and staff planner Angie Brewer. Then, without notice to the public or the Gorge Commission, he gave the green light for logging to proceed.

Though at first he denied that he had been contacted by the Oregon Department of Forestry, Lang followed the paper trail, gathering emails from both ODF and Hood River County. They showed that Nichols had in fact been contacted by both agencies in February, and after talking to his staff, had made a unilateral decision that the logging could go ahead.

His rationale: The Scenic Area Act required only that timber companies follow state forest practices rules when they logged in the General Management Area. The law, he decided, trumped the management plan.

The Gorge Commission had been sensitive to the issue in the early 1990s, when it was writing the management plan and had sought opinions from the attorneys general of both states on whether it had the legal authority to limit logging in General Management Areas zoned as Open Space. The Oregon attorney general had given the green light; the Washington attorney general had not.

In March 1991, the Gorge Commission had instructed its staff to "use the Open Space designation only to protect the most significant and sensitive resources, and only when alternate techniques will not provide the level of protection required." Because of its scenic and environmental value, the Hood River to Mosier bluff area was ranked the most sensitive such site in the Scenic Area. For twenty-one years, it had enjoyed protection as Open Space in the GMA.

Armed with this information, Lang accused the ODF, Nichols, and the Gorge Commission staff of acting in bad faith in letting the logging go ahead. He notified the press. In June, he made a presentation before the Gorge Commission.

Nichols was furious, but the record spoke for itself. In late summer, he finally issued a statement taking responsibility for the decision and acknowledging that the logging violated the management plan. But that acknowledgment came only grudgingly. Nichols added that it was time for the Gorge Commission to reconsider protecting land zoned as Open Space, and said he would seek legal opinions from the state attorneys general.

The raw clearcut bordered a state park and a section of the recently restored Hood River-to-Mosier trail. It was clearly visible from key viewing areas in the mid-gorge. It would take many decades for the slope to heal. And Nichols, who had been less than forthright in describing his role in the fiasco, now had a credibility problem.

As the National Scenic Area entered its second quarter-century, Friends of the Gorge was clearly its most effective watchdog. The nonprofit had a staff twice as large as the Gorge Commission's, including a fulltime staff attorney. Its membership was growing, after declines in 2009 and 2010, and now stood at 5,400. Under the leadership of executive director Kevin Gorman, Friends was attracting more members who lived in the gorge. Its land trust had won support from Congress for an ambitious gorge-wide trails project.

Between 2008 and 2011, Friends' assets had grown from $7.4 million to $11.9 million, of which $5.4 million was in the value of lands held by its land trust. Most of its assets were from bequests; Friends was not heavily dependent on foundation support, which gave its board of directors and staff the freedom to chart their course independently. Friends was involved in protecting the gorge on many fronts, from filing lawsuits to monitoring development reviews to organizing hikes and public events. The organization had recently negotiated a $1.78 million agreement with the Bonneville Power Administration to reduce the visual impact of new 200-foot-high power transmission lines in the east gorge by putting some of them underground.

Friends had a prickly relationship with the Gorge Commission and did not hesitate to sue when it disagreed with its decisions. Nearly every executive director of the commission had crossed swords with Friends at some point. And the rocky relationship between Nichols and Friends of the Gorge continued.

Lang was particularly skeptical of the new director's ability to embrace consensus-building. "Friends believes that there is a need for more collaboration," he said. "The commission is perfectly placed to do that." But instead, he said, Nichols had taken an assertive, even aggressive approach with the state legislatures and various agencies involved in the Scenic Area.

Even before he took office, Nichols warned Washington Gov. Chris Gregoire in a stern letter of the toll budget cuts had taken on the commission.

"I'm not going to put up with that garbage anymore," he said in an interview. "We've lost 50 percent of our staff. You're gambling with the National Scenic Area. If you don't have the Gorge Commission, you have no other avenue of appeal except the courts."

Nichols proposed a 55 percent increase in the Gorge Commission's budget for 2013-15. "There is no support for that," Lang said. He noted that the Gorge Commission had not even held a hearing on the budget proposal, though its own bylaws required it to do so.

It remained to be seen whether the new executive director's approach would win the Gorge Commission new friends or create new enemies.

Whatever the political future of the Gorge Commission, the gorge itself was on a positive trajectory—environmentally and economically—as the Scenic Area Act entered its second quarter-century. It had many powerful protectors and advocates, including regional and national environmental groups, influential members of Congress, state and federal agencies that had a stake in its future, and the general public.

There would always be threats to confront. Would coal trains and barges come to dominate commerce through the gorge? Would its residents become pawns in a massive power play by some of the world's largest energy companies? Though the coal industry was a powerful adversary, the prospect seemed unlikely.

One thing was certain: The Columbia River Gorge National Scenic Area would continue to be a vortex of controversy and competing visions, protected by an unlikely, imperfect piece of legislation that had managed to become law back in a time when such things were still possible in Congress—and by the enduring support of ordinary citizens who loved the gorge.

Sources

The author conducted extensive interviews with the following men and women in researching this book:

Bradley Andersen, Skamania County prosecuting attorney, 1994-2002
Jill Arens, executive director, Columbia River Gorge Commission, 2006-January 2012
Richard Benner, executive director, Columbia River Gorge Commission, 1987-1991
Martha Bennett, executive director, Columbia River Gorge Commission, 2001-2006
Bowen Blair, executive director, Friends of the Columbia Gorge, 1982-88
Jeff Breckel, director, Washington and Oregon state Gorge Commissions, 1978-87
Wilson Cady, founder, Columbia Gorge Refuge Stewards
Ed Callahan, Skamania County Commissioner, 1979-94
Art Carroll, director, Columbia River Gorge National Scenic Area, U.S. Forest Service, 1991-2000
Don Clark, Columbia River Gorge Commissioner, 1987-91
Jonathan Doherty, executive director, Columbia River Gorge Commission, 1992-1999
Dan Durow, director of development, The Dalles, Oregon, and former director of planning, Wasco County
Kevin Gorman, executive director, Friends of the Columbia Gorge, 2000 to present
Jurgen Hess, landscape architect, Columbia River Gorge National Scenic Area, U.S. Forest Service, 1986-2002. Acting manager, National Scenic Area, 2000
Stan Hinatsu, recreation director, Columbia River Gorge National Scenic Area Office, U.S. Forest Service
Michael Lang, conservation director, Friends of the Columbia Gorge, 1998-present
Bob Leick, Skamania County prosecuting attorney, 1967-94
Steve McCarthy, Columbia River Gorge Commissioner, 1996-98

Sid Morrison, Republican, U.S. Representative, Washington, 1981-93

Sally Newell, Columbia River Gorge Commissioner, 1994-97

Darren Nichols, executive director, Gorge Commission, 2012-present

Bob Packwood, Republican, U.S. Senator, Oregon, 1969-95

Claire Puchy, executive director, Columbia River Gorge Commission, 1999-2001

Bud Quinn, Columbia River Gorge Commissioner, 1996-2000

Chuck Williams, founder, Columbia Gorge Coalition, 1979

Sources by Chapter

Chapter 1: Hardly Wilderness

Background on the first humans to settle in the Columbia River Gorge was drawn from the author's interview and tour of archaeological sites at Horsethief Lake State Park with Forest Service Archaeologist James D. Keyser and from Keyser's book *Indian Rock Art of the Columbia Plateau*, University of Washington Press, 1992. Background on early exploration and development of the Columbia Basin is from *The Columbia*, by Stewart Holbrook, Comstock Editions, 1956. Information on early photographers in the gorge is from a 2008 review in the *Oregonian* of *Wild Beauty: Photography of the Columbia River Gorge, 1867-1957*, by Terry Toedtmeier and John Laursen, Oregon State University Press, 2008 and from Oregon Public Broadcasting's *Oregon Experience*, "The River They Saw."

Historical background on the drowning of traditional Indian fishing sites and artifacts behind Bonneville Dam and the tribes' sixty-year struggle to win treaty rights to those fishing sites is from Roberta Ulrich's book *Empty Nets: Indians, Dams, and the Columbia River*, Oregon State University Press, 1999.

Chapter 2: The Watchdogs

Background on the development of the Columbia River Highway is from Holbrook's *The Columbia*. The early history of the Oregon State Parks system is from *Oregon's Highway Park System, 1921-1989, An Administrative History*, by Lawrence Merriam, Oregon Parks and Recreation Department, 1992. The story of how Beacon Rock became a Washington state park is from Chuck Williams' book, *Bridge of the Gods, Mountains of Fire*, Friends of the Earth and Elephant Mountain Arts, 1980. In recounting the early campaign for federal protection of the gorge, the author relied on news accounts from the Associated Press, the *Oregonian* and the *Columbian*, and extensive interviews with Williams, Jeff Breckel, and Don Clark, among others. An anecdote describing John Yeon's effort to woo Nancy Russell to the gorge campaign is from "The Long View" by Randy Gragg from *Portland Monthly* magazine June 2012.

Chapter 3: Saving Steigerwald

Wilson Cady, founder of the volunteer group Columbia Gorge Refuge Stewards, described in an interview the history of his long campaign to save Steigerwald Lake from industrial development. Background on management and development of the waterfowl haven at the west end of the gorge is from interviews and tours with Steigerwald Lake National Wildlife Refuge Manager Jim Clapp of the U.S. Fish and Wildlife Service.

Chapter 4: Balancing Act

This author is indebted to Bowen Blair, the first executive director of Friends of the Columbia Gorge, for his permission to adapt a 100-page law review article for use in this chapter, "The Columbia River Gorge National Scenic Area: The Act, Its Genesis and Legislative History."

Blair spent most of four years, 1982-86, in Washington, D.C., following every twist and turn in the legislative campaign to win federal protection for the gorge. Because the tactics of opponents forced the bill's sponsors to rush the bill through the committee process at the eleventh hour, not a single congressional committee report was ever adopted. Thus, a piece of historic legislation profoundly affecting the Pacific Northwest has no formal legislative history.

To remedy that lack, Blair spent a year writing his own detailed, carefully footnoted account of the bill's history. Blair's account was published in the Lewis and Clark Law School journal *Environmental Law* in 1987.

The author also drew background on the congressional fight from news accounts in the *Oregonian* and the *Columbian* and from the Associated Press and States News Service. She gained insights from interviews with former U.S. Sen. Bob Packwood, former U.S. Rep. Sid Morrison, former Gorge Commissioner Sally Newell, former Skamania County Prosecuting Attorney Bob Leick, former Skamania County Commissioner Ed Callahan, environmental advocate Chuck Williams, and Jeff Breckel, former director of the two state gorge commissions.

The *National Journal* provided background on the era of political moderation in Congress in the early 1980s that made it possible for the Scenic Area Act to become law.

Chapter 5: Writing the Rules

This account of the early implementation of the National Scenic Area Act is drawn from news accounts in the *Oregonian* and the *Columbian* and from extensive interviews with Dick Benner, the first executive director of the Gorge Commission; Bowen Blair, the first executive director of Friends of the Gorge, and Jurgen Hess and Art Carroll of the Forest Service's National Scenic Area Office. A discussion of the debate over the Forest Service's interim guidelines for development in the gorge is from *Planning a New West: The Columbia*

River Gorge National Scenic Area, by Carl Abbott, Sy Adler, and Margery Post Abbott, Oregon State University Press, 1997.

Chapter 6: Early Friction

Background on the early years of implementation of the Scenic Area Act is drawn in part from an extensive e-mail interview with Jonathan Doherty, executive director of the Columbia Gorge Commission, 1992-99. Other sources include an interview with former Skamania County Prosecuting Attorney Leick; *Columbian* staff reporter Bruce Westfall's accounts, published 1987-89, detailing frictions between local property owners and the Gorge Commission over proposed developments in the Scenic Area; and the author's interviews with Gorge Commissioners Bud Quinn and Steve McCarthy for an article published in 1997 in the regional newspaper *Cascadia Times*. Senator Mark Hatfield's comments on the ten-year anniversary of the National Scenic Area are excerpted from the *Congressional Record*.

Chapter 7: The Too-Tall House

The Bea house controversy was covered extensively in the *Oregonian* and the *Columbian* and by Portland-area broadcast media and national media. Background for this chapter was gathered from those sources and from interviews with Hess of the Forest Service; former Skamania County Prosecuting Attorney Andersen; and former Gorge Commission Executive Director Jonathan Doherty, among others. Stephanie Thomson, a staff writer for the *Columbian*, reported on the previously untold story of the Bea family's efforts to develop their property in a story published February 24, 1999. The author broke the news of the Beas' out-of-court settlement with Skamania County and the Gorge Commission in the May 20, 2003 *Columbian*.

The saga of Gail Castle's battle to replace her dilapidated house was first reported by the author in the September 12, 2000, *Columbian*, and in a series of stories concluding December 28, 2000, after Castle won her victory before the Columbia River Gorge Commission.

Chapter 8: Fear and Loathing

Klickitat County's hostility toward the Columbia River Gorge Commission, state environmental agencies, and local environmental activists was reported by the author in a series of stories entitled "Fear & Loathing in Klickitat County," published in the *Columbian* June 24-26, 2001.

Chapter 9: Land Rush

The author reported on challenges facing the Forest Service's gorge land purchase program in the National Scenic Area and efforts by Congress to resolve those challenges in a series of stories in the Columbian in the summer of 1999. Background on Nancy Russell's early purchases of scenic and ecologically significant lands in the gorge was drawn in part from a profile of Russell written by Katy Muldoon, reporter for the *Oregonian*, published Sept. 19, 2008.

Chapter 10: Oregon Pushback

The author attended and reported for the *Columbian* on the first Oregon legislative field hearing regarding the performance of the Columbia River Gorge Commission, held in The Dalles, Oregon, in March 2002.

Chapter 11: A Pile of Rocks

This account of archaeological preservation hurdles faced by a couple attempting to build a house in the National Scenic Area is adapted from an account by the author published in the *Columbian* May 20, 2002.

Chapter 12: Time to Amend

The author's coverage of the lengthy process of amending the National Scenic Area Management Plan was published in the *Columbian* in a series of stories in 2003 and 2004.

Chapter 13: Showdown at Lyle Point

Background on the dispute over Lyle Point is from news accounts, from Roberta Ulrich's book *Empty Nets*, which told the story of the protest against development of Lyle Point as a subdivision, and from the author's interviews with Klickitat County officials, the Trust for Public Land, and Bowen Blair, the attorney who represented tribal interests in their efforts to acquire the land. Sale of Lyle Point to the Yakama Tribe was first reported in the *Yakima Herald Republic* in May 2007.

Chapter 14: A Destination Resort

Background on Broughton Lumber Co. was gathered from historical accounts of Broughton and SDS Lumber Co. operations in Skamania and Klickitat counties. The author's reporting for the *Columbian* detailed the process developers followed to win a plan amendment from the Gorge Commission that would allow a large destination resort in a rural area of the gorge.

Chapter 15: Rails to Trails

The author first hiked the Klickitat Trail with trail advocates in November 2002 for a story published in the *Columbian*. Other background on the campaign to convert an abandoned rail bed to a national trail along the Klickitat River came from the Forest Service, the Washington State Parks Commission, members of the Rails-to-Trails Conservancy, and the Klickitat Trail Conservancy, and trail opponents.

Chapter 16: The Haze Curtain

Background is from the author's coverage of Gorge Commission hearings and from scientific studies documenting the sources and extent of Gorge haze reported in both the *Oregonian* and the *Columbian*. Accounts of environmentalists' litigation against the Oregon Department of Environmental Quality for failure to enforce the Clean Air Act against Portland General Electric's Boardman coal plant were first published in the Oregonian. Linda Geiser, a Forest Service lichenologist, provided information and a tour illustrating the role of lichens in measuring air quality trends in the gorge.

Chapter 17: Logging Loopholes

Material came from the author's reporting for the *Columbian*, including a story about Roy Ostroski's attempt to log his land through a conversion loophole in the Scenic Area Management Plan, published November 22, 2003.

Chapter 18: The Casino Deal

Efforts by the Confederated Tribes of the Warm Springs to site a new casino in the gorge were widely covered over more than a decade by the *Oregonian*, the *Columbian* and the *Hood River News*, among other media. The author also interviewed tribal representatives, Forest Service officials, opponents of a gorge casino, and officials of Cascade Locks, and studied changing policies on off-reservation casinos during the George W. Bush administration, the Obama administration, and the administrations of Oregon Governors Ted Kulongoski and John Kitzhaber.

Chapter 19: Whistling Ridge

Material for this chapter is drawn from the author's reporting for the *Columbian*, including a tour of the proposed wind farm just north of the Scenic Area with project proponent Jason Spadaro, president of SDS Lumber Co. and Broughton Lumber Co. Other sources include officials of the Forest Service and the Washington Department of Natural Resources; residents of the Underwood and White Salmon communities; and staff of the Washington Energy Facility Site Evaluation Council. Eric Florip of the *Columbian* reported on Gov. Chris Gregoire's decision in late 2012 to permit a scaled-down wind project at Whistling Ridge.

Chapter 20: Rebuilding a Historic Highway

Background on the extraordinary effort to restore trail, bicycle, or auto access to the full length of the Historic Columbia River Highway is from the Oregon Parks and Recreation Department, the Forest Service's Columbia River Gorge National Scenic Area Office, and news accounts in the *Oregonian* and other publications.

Chapter 21: The Recreation Challenge

For background on the Forest Service's original recreation goals for the National Scenic Area, the author relied on the 1992 Columbia River Gorge National Scenic Area Management Plan. Present and former Forest Service officials, including Dan Harkenrider, Jurgen Hess, and Stan Hinatsu, described the challenges the agency faced and continues to face in providing public access while protecting sensitive areas of the gorge. The challenge of restoring the Sandy River Delta is detailed in a Forest Service environmental impact statement. The author learned of the Friends of the Gorge "Towns to Trails" project at a Friends' membership breakfast held April 15, 2012, at Skamania Lodge.

Chapter 22: Cape Horn Convergence

A story by the author reporting the events that led to the protection of a promontory atop Cape Horn that was once slated to become a subdivision and is now an overlook dedicated to Friends co-founder Nancy Russell was published in the *Columbian* on June 30, 2011.

Chapter 23: A River Unleashed

The author followed the story of the breaching of Condit Dam on the White Salmon River for a dozen years. Her reporting on the historic dam removal project included interviews with PacifiCorp officials, fish biologists, environmental activists, dam removal contractors, and local officials who opposed the dam's removal. The account describing the actual breaching of the dam on October 26, 2011, was written by Kathie Durbin and Eric Florip and published in the *Columbian*, October 27, 2011.

Chapter 24: A Quarter-Century

An assessment of the Columbia River Gorge National Scenic Area Act at the twenty-five-year mark drew on interviews with numerous gorge officials, including Jill Arens, then executive director of the Gorge Commission, and on events held August 13, 2011, to mark the anniversary. For a discussion of the economic health of the gorge at twenty-five years, the author relied on data from the Mid-Columbia Economic Development Council, interviews with local development officials, and published accounts of the arrival of a Google server farm in The Dalles and the expansion of Insitu, a manufacturer of unmanned aircraft that is now a major employer in the gorge.

Chapter 25: The Fight Continues

Regarding proposals to transport coal through the Columbia Gorge to Pacific ports for shipping to Asia, the author relied on news accounts, including coverage by Scott Learn of the *Oregonian*, and on posts and backgrounders from Sightline, a Seattle-based sustainable growth organization.

On the issue of boundary adjustments for urban areas in the gorge, the author interviewed Darren Nichols, executive director of the Columbia River Gorge Commission, and Dan Durow, development director for The Dalles, Oregon.

For coverage of the controversial Mosier clearcut, the author interviewed Nichols and Michael Lang of Friends of the Columbia Gorge and reviewed email correspondence between Nichols and officials at the Oregon Department of Forestry and Hood River County. She also drew background from a June 26, 2012 story published in the *Portland Daily Journal of Commerce*, and from a history of the Gorge Commission's decision to protect the Mosier bluff from logging in its 1992 management plan by designating the bluff as open space.

Index